EXTRAORDINARY

PSYCHIC

DEBRA LYNNE KATZ is the author of the groundbreaking work *You Are Psychic: The Art of Clairvoyant Reading & Healing* and *Freeing the Genie Within*. An internationally acclaimed clairvoyant reader, healer, teacher, and spiritual counselor, Debra is the founder of the International School of Clairvoyance. She holds a bachelor's degree in psychology and a master's degree in social work and is a former federal probation officer. Debra has studied at the top psychic training schools in the United States and with a variety of faith healers in the Philippines. She was the host of *The Psychic Explorer*, a popular television show in Sedona, Arizona. An aspiring director and screenwriter, Debra currently lives in Moorpark, California. Please visit Debra's website at http://www.debrakatz.com, where you will also find her contact information.

Proven Techniques to Master Your Natural Psychic Abilities

EXTRAORDINARY
PSYCHIC

DEBRA LYNNE KATZ

Llewellyn Publications
Woodbury, Minnesota

First Edition
Second Printing, 2009

Book design by Donna Burch
Cover design by Ellen Dahl
Cover illustration © 2008 David Julian
Editing by Brett Fechheimer

Library of Congress Cataloging-in Publication Data
Katz, Debra Lynne, 1968–
  Extraordinary psychic : proven techniques to master your natural
psychic abilities / Debra Lynne Katz. — 1st ed.
      p.   cm.
  Includes bibliographical references.
  ISBN 978-0-7387-1333-5
  1. Psychic ability. I. Title.
  BF1031.K236 2008
  133.8—dc22
                                     2008017780

Llewellyn Worldwide does not participate in, endorse, or have any authority or responsibility concerning private business transactions between our authors and the public.
  All mail addressed to the author is forwarded but the publisher cannot, unless specifically instructed by the author, give out an address or phone number.
  Any Internet references contained in this work are current at publication time, but the publisher cannot guarantee that a specific location will continue to be maintained. Please refer to the publisher's website for links to authors' websites and other sources.

Llewellyn Publications
A Division of Llewellyn Worldwide, Ltd.
2143 Wooddale Drive, Dept. 978-0-7387-1333-5
Woodbury, MN 55125-2989, U.S.A.
www.llewellyn.com

Printed in the United States of America

To the memory of two of America's most extraordinary visionaries, Lewis Bostwick and Ingo Swann, and to my son, Manny Felipe Katz

Contents

Acknowledgments

In everyone's life, at some time, our inner fire goes out. It is then burst into flame by an encounter with another human being. We should all be thankful for those people who rekindle the inner spirit.
—ALBERT SCHWEITZER

I'd like to acknowledge the following people:

My psychic twin sister, Amy Beth Katz; my beloved son, Manny Felipe Katz; and my sweetie pie and knight in not-so-shiny armor, Danny Kohler. Thank you also to my dearest clairvoyant friends and co-teachers, Francine Marie-Sheppard, Kazandrah Martin, and Rachel Mai. Thank you also to Carrie Obry, Brett Fechheimer, and the entire staff at Llewellyn Worldwide, as well as to the staff at American Hapkido Mixed Martial Arts in Moorpark for taking such good care of Manny while I completed this book. Thank you to my brother, Brad Katz; sister-in-law, Rachel Katz; my parents, Nedra and Robert Katz; and to one of my favorite people on this planet, Tony Carito. Thank you to Masaru Kato, Deborah Sharif, Kevin Pittman, David Kearby, Krishanti Wahla, Jessica Cooney, and to all my awesome students and readers everywhere—I love you dearly. Thank you to my early clairvoyant teachers still in the body (including but not limited to David

Pearce, John Fulton, Denise Bisbiglia, Chris Murphy, the Skillmans, and Raphaelle and Michael Tamura), and to all those beings in spirit form whose teaching, guidance, and love made this book, and my life as it is now, possible. Last but not least, thank you God!

*Those who say it can't be done
should not interrupt the person doing it.*
—ANCIENT CHINESE PROVERB

Prologue

The gift is not being psychic. It's knowing you are.
—DEBRA LYNNE KATZ

Many people ask me what was most challenging about writing my first book, *You Are Psychic*. They expect me to say finding a publisher (which was actually quite easy) or finding the time as a single working mom to write a book. (Sleep? What's that?)

What most people don't expect is the truth: that the most difficult thing for me was getting over the ideas that were stuck in my head that clairvoyance can't or shouldn't be taught in a book available to a general audience. Along with such thoughts, I also had some pretty intense feelings of fear—fear that I was revealing secrets that some people would not be happy to have revealed. Which people? The list includes some of my former teachers, and those who ran the psychic schools that only shared such information with students who agreed to sign up and pay for in-person, twelve-to-twenty-four-month training programs. I'd also include some of the untrained professional psychics who didn't want to admit even to themselves that millions of other people could be doing exactly what they were doing—and perhaps even doing it better.

There have, of course, been other books on the market for over a century that have taught ways to enhance psychic abilities, but there wasn't anything else that provided step-by-step instructions for instant access of information through clairvoyance—a very specific psychic ability that allows people to "see" visions, images, and pictures about anything and anyone at any point in time. Furthermore, most books on psychic development do not explain how utilizing psychic abilities can enhance one's life or lead to a quickening of personal transformation and development, nor do they offer the tools for such utilization.

The main reason for the lack of available written resources was that those running the clairvoyant training schools had themselves come from a tradition in which training only occurred in person, under close supervision, and over a long period of time. These techniques are so powerful that they bring about fast—if not instantaneous—change in people, which can be emotionally tumultuous for some students. Those who ran these schools knew how effective their programs were for training psychics within a supportive environment, and they couldn't imagine doing things differently. So some, perhaps most, of their reluctance to share this information was due to genuine concern. Some of their reluctance resulted from a lack of flexibility and imagination; some of it was a product of economic interest and fear.

Fortunately, over the past five or six years just about all of the larger schools (mostly those in California) have begun adjusting themselves to the changing needs and lifestyles of overworked and underpaid Americans. Many of these schools are now offering modified programs that can be taken over one weekend per month or even online. The result is that people all over the country have greater access to clairvoyant training.

The thirteen months I spent as a clairvoyant student was certainly one of the best times of my life, and it helped form who I am today. I thought the program I went through was perfect, except for one area within the curriculum that I felt was severely lacking and that still seems to be deficient in some of the schools today: there was little to no training to help students deal with being psychic, particularly with being professional psychics, outside the security of the schools that train them. In fact, we were taught that it's cold and lonely out there in a world filled with atheists, skeptics, untrained psychics, and the ungrounded mainstream masses.

Leaving the school as a lone psychic for the big, scary world was terrifying, but it didn't take me long to discover there were lots and lots of wonderful, supportive people out there with similar interests, even if they didn't have the same kind or level of training as I did. This is why I made sure to include chapters in *You Are Psychic* such as "The Business of Spirituality," "Psychic Ethics," and "Dealing with the Mainstream" (retitled as "The Psychic Minority"), as well as to discuss other topics of concern to people seeking to incorporate their psychic skills into their work or who really wanted to live life honestly—as the psychics they truly are.

While writing *You Are Psychic*, I knew with certainty that the techniques worked when taught in class and workshop settings. However, there was no way I could know for sure how effective teaching the techniques in a *book* would be. Now, with the book having been out for three years, I have no doubt. Hundreds of readers of *You Are Psychic* have come to my workshops, called me, e-mailed me, even given *me* readings, and they never cease to amaze me with their level of clairvoyant skill. These psychics swear up and down that before reading *You Are Psychic* they had never seen a clairvoyant vision in their life nor had the slightest idea how to do a reading or healing.

All of this is not to say that such people don't still have questions, or areas in which they feel they need clarification or further guidance. In fact, that is why I decided to write *Extraordinary Psychic* and to give it the subtitle *Proven Techniques to Master Your Natural Psychic Abilities*. I felt it was time to offer additional techniques for psychic reading and healing that would help those already practicing to fine-tune their skills and overcome certain challenges that many clairvoyant students and even professional psychics struggle with. Furthermore, as I have gained more experience training psychics in various formats—from very short demonstrations to psychic "bootcamps" to a long-distance telephone training program—I've learned how to present the techniques more concisely, which appeals to certain types of personalities and learning styles.

In my personal practice as a psychic and as a teacher, I have been fine-tuning my other psychic abilities of clairaudience, telepathy, and remote viewing, and I've discovered how to help my students incorporate these abilities into their clairvoyant practice as well. In *You Are Psychic*

I introduced concepts and clairvoyant techniques that can increase your ability to manifest your goals and help you to let go of that which is no longer serving you. Now, in *Extraordinary Psychic*, I offer guidance into why these concepts don't always work for everyone, or why they don't always work quickly enough and what you can do about this (besides being patient, which is the hardest thing of all and the last thing you want to hear!). In *You Are Psychic* I introduced basic energy healing and touched upon the spirit world. Here, in this book, I go into much greater detail about the beings you are most likely to encounter when removing "the veil" and how to communicate with some while eradicating others. In this book I also offer advice about how to protect yourself as a psychic and as a healer, and how to create and enforce boundaries.

I know that many of you are reading this book about exploring your psychic abilities because there are few other topics that excite you as much. Others of you are still quite undecided as to whether you want to have anything to do with being psychic, but instead are desperately seeking answers to questions about unusual and sometimes even disturbing phenomena that have been happening to you, either recently or for as long as you can remember. Still others have started to practice the techniques in *You Are Psychic* and now have some questions, or are hungry for more practical instruction.

I have written *Extraordinary Psychic* both as a sequel to *You Are Psychic* and as a training guide that can stand on its own. Whether you see yourself as ordinary or less than ordinary, I can assure you of two things: One is that by the fact of your mere existence, you are already extraordinary. Two is that as a human being you cannot help being psychic to some degree, any more than you can help breathing. Whether you know it or not, your psychic abilities are influencing you—and your thoughts and feelings and creations—at every moment of your life. If you attempt the techniques in *Extraordinary Psychic* even once or twice, you are going to see results. If you continue to practice them, you are going to realize that *you are an extraordinary psychic* after all, even if you have lived many decades thinking otherwise. This is because the gift is not *being* psychic—it's *knowing* you are.

PART I

Clairvoyant Techniques

CHAPTER I

Introduction

What happens when you take a million ordinary citizens and turn them into extraordinary psychics? Evolution!
—DEBRA LYNNE KATZ

Many people would love to experience clairvoyant visions that contain useful information for themselves and others, but they haven't got the foggiest idea how to initiate or control this process. Some believe the only way to do so is to put themselves through extreme circumstances, such as fasting for long periods, banishing themselves into harsh wilderness conditions, taking hallucinogenic drugs, or paying thousands of dollars for remote viewing or lengthy and costly clairvoyant or remote-viewing training programs.

While long-term, in-depth, and in-person training is a path I fully endorse and is the path that led to the writing of this book, countless readers of my first book, *You Are Psychic*, have demonstrated that such training is not necessary to access and utilize one's clairvoyance. In fact, during a recent expo in Los Angeles at which I conducted a clairvoyant training demonstration, I taught a group of sixty-five people how to perform a clairvoyant reading in less than forty-five minutes, something even I was not sure would be possible in such a short period of time.

Out of the twelve or so volunteers I called up to the front of the room, four were "seeing" almost the exact same images within minutes. Even though the woman they were practicing on stated nothing more than her name, they each saw her standing before a microphone singing passionately. A few others saw her with suitcases and sipping drinks on a beach in what appeared to be or felt like a resort in Mexico. The woman confirmed she was leaving that night to go perform at a resort in Cancun.

The mood changed drastically as another volunteer offered herself up to be "read." Even before I finished leading them through the opening exercise, four or five of the readers had tears in their eyes, while one actually burst out in sobs. At this point they had no idea why they were having this kind of emotional reaction. However, soon a few more novice readers began receiving images and clairaudient messages indicating that this woman was grieving the death of someone close to her. She later confirmed that several of her family members had died very recently, including a parent. I wasn't surprised to discover that the reader who had the strongest initial emotional reaction had recently lost a parent herself. This is an example of clairsentience, the psychic ability of feeling others' emotions and physical sensations. This ability naturally emerges when utilizing one's clairvoyance.

What Exactly Is Clairvoyant Reading?

Clairvoyant reading is a very intensive form of meditation in which you focus on some simple visualizations, pose questions to these visualizations, and then wait patiently for the information to arrive. This information can be about anyone or anything. The only way it can work is through complete inward focus and concentration. But wait, don't let that scare you! When you know the right techniques to use, which you will soon, this intense concentration will be effortless. Why? Because when you are doing clairvoyant readings, you are not *trying* to quiet and empty a mind that by nature is addicted to being busy and noisy. Instead, your mind is so active with the techniques that the end result is you are focusing without *trying* to focus. This is particularly true when you are doing a reading on someone else, which is a lot easier than reading yourself.

When you see visions or use your clairvoyance, and you take the time to communicate the information to someone else, this is called a *reading*. When we "read" other people we can see into any aspect of their lives. The information comes from a variety of sources. Some of it comes from what I'd call a universal source of all knowingness. Very little is known about this source except that it's there to tap into it whenever we like. This source is the same one that I believe Carl Jung was referring to when he coined the term *collective unconscious*. The information contained within this source is largely or perhaps entirely of a visual nature. Because the information exists in the form of pictures and archetypal images, it can be accessed by people of every nation, regardless of their verbal language or ability to use verbal language at all. We all interact with this source every night through our dreams. It's possible even animals can tap into this source, although I don't know that for sure.

MEI Pictures/Filters/Programs

When we access information from this universal source, we cannot help but view it through own filters of perception. These filters are our own personal pictures made up of thoughtforms and feelings upon which our personalities and egos are based, and which very much determine how we approach life and all relationships, including those with others and with ourselves. In *You Are Psychic* I refer to these pictures or filters as Mental/Emotional Image pictures (MEI pictures). These filters are like minute programs running through our psyches. They are connected into particular parts of our bodies and energy fields and can even result in disease or physical pain. Sometimes they consist entirely of pain. They are like secret scripts that echo past traumatic experiences. Quite frequently these programs or scripts are written and passed on by those who raised us, or by our own selves to make sense of our past disappointments. We often carry these pictures or programs with us from other incarnations into our present one. They then act as shackles that keep us from expressing our true essence and experiencing greater freedom to be who we are or who we truly want to be in present time.

When we read other people who have something in common with us, who are strong mirrors for us, not only do we become more aware of these pictures or filters, but energetically they actually begin to shift and fall away, regardless of whether we can identify them at the time. In this way, performing a clairvoyant reading or healing on another person can be a powerful method of self-transformation because it allows us to deprogram ourselves so we are freer to be our own true selves in the present moment. This is really what all transpersonal and psychological modalities attempt to do, but clairvoyant reading can do it much faster. As a clairvoyant reader aware of this process, we can be our own therapist. Our clients are our mirrors and the impetus for change within ourselves. It's important to understand that this process occurs whether or not you think you have something in common with the person you are reading and really has nothing to do with your cognitive awareness, although the more readings you do, the more impressed you will be with the fact that you tend to read people who are in fact dealing with issues similar to those you are also dealing with in the present moment.

Other Sources of Information

Apart from the universal source of knowingness, during a clairvoyant reading other sources of psychic information can be accessed to obtain information. These include telepathic communication from other living people, as well as deceased individuals and beings we call *spirit guides*, which behave as if their job is to help out with such matters. (As I will discuss in chapter 13, I've never had an entity actually hand me a business card that identifies him literally as a "spirit guide," but this term does correctly embody the intentions of a variety of beings available to assist us.) Sometimes as the clairvoyant, it will be you who is the source of the information as your spirit travels to a particular location to observe a lost object or incident that has occurred or that will occur at a specific point in time.

Readings can be done by letting the information come to you or by you going to the information, and you will be learning both these methods in the next few chapters. Much of the time when you seek information about a person, particularly one who has solicited your assistance and is sitting beside you or is talking to you on the telephone, you will discover the bulk of the information about that person's life resides in their aura, which is another word for the energy field that surrounds every living thing. An aura is a map of the body and a history book of the soul that accompanies that body. The first chapter of this historical epic begins long before the soul was thrust into this current lifetime; indeed, our auras contain information about all our incarnations—past, present, and to some extent future (see chapter 7). Often, when a person asks a question about their health or a goal, a clairvoyant's attention will be drawn to a specific location within the aura. This is particularly true with health and relationship questions.

Many times a readee will want to know why they are suffering from a particular ailment or what can be done about it. Often, in addition to receiving an answer about the readee's physical anatomy, an image will come up that indicates the person had a weakness in that area related to emotional trauma or neglect prior to the manifestation of the illness or problem. Carolyn Myss, in her book *Anatomy of the Spirit* and her excellent audiotape series *Why People Don't Heal* and *Three Levels of Power*, does a great job of explaining various ailments with their corresponding energy dynamics. My own readings with thousands of clients have led me to come up with similar connections. After practicing the techniques in the following chapters, you will likely begin to make similar observations.

Foreign Energies

Our auras also contain a plethora of foreign energies that profoundly influence our physical, mental, and emotional health. These energies are derived from sources apart from ourselves, but they merge with us when they enter our field or when we enter the fields of others. Some of these foreign sources include family members, lovers, bosses, ancestors, spirits, and an assorted cast of other characters, with or without bodies. The type and amount of these energies that dwell within our auras and body at any given time largely determine how we feel and experience ourselves (self-esteem), and the ways in which we manifest on a creative level.

These energies influence our level of personal freedom and power, which obviously has an impact on our everyday life experiences such as finances, relationships, work, and on our overall development. Many clairvoyants have observed that these foreign energies travel back and forth through things that look like cords of electricity. These cords also sometimes show up in photographs. (I am currently working on a new book, which includes a collection of such photos taken by a close friend of mine, Kazandrah Martin, who is a healer and clairvoyant in Sedona, Arizona.) Sometimes, two people's energy fields are so merged together that they look like Siamese twins. This corresponds with the degree of codependency between the two. Most often I see this with an emotionally dependent parent and a child who has allowed that parent to feed off their energy system with the hope that someday the parent will change and give them what they were missing as children.

A common image I encounter in my readings is that of my client standing in front of a mirror. Sometimes the client is smiling, sometimes frowning; there are often other faces and bodies standing around my client in the mirror. I've discovered through corresponding symbols and intuitive information that this usually indicates the client is experiencing himself or herself through another's eyes and emotions. Now this might be terrific if the other person is a happy, encouraging, self-loving person who loves the client. But what if the "other" is picky and depressed, or filled with anxiety and self-loathing? Most of the time when I describe what I am seeing, the readee knows exactly who I am talking about, and verifies that their self-esteem and feelings of self-worth have been less than positive since being involved with this other person, or since this person began having problems in their own life.

I have personally encountered dramatic shifts in my own self-perception and self-esteem—particularly my satisfaction with my body and even my ability to lose weight—after performing some self-healing techniques during which I released from my aura the foreign energy of someone I was dating. Some of these techniques are presented in chapter 3 and chapters 15 through 17. It doesn't matter how much you love your partner or your children or your clients. Their thoughts, feelings, and pain often do not serve you when they are in your body. It is like running the wrong fuel through your engine. It will clog things up, slow you down, burn you out, and even cause your immune system to break down.

If you feel as if you are living a life that is not your own or if your job and the people around you don't make you feel good, most likely you are running other people's programs and energy through your body, which has caused you to make the choices that have led you to your current situation. As soon as you clear these out and get back in touch with your own life force, vibration, energy, path, whatever you want to call it, your life will begin to reshape itself to fit who you really are right now, in the present moment. This is what giving and receiving clairvoyant readings and healings can do for you.

Seeing Is Not Just Seeing

After twelve years of experience as a clairvoyant reader and healer, I am thrilled to be discovering the extent of quality research that confirms many of my own personal observations and experiences. Some of the books that do a fantastic job describing this research are *Mind-Reach* by Russell Targ and Harold E. Puthoff; Dean Radin's *The Conscious Universe* and *Entangled Minds;* and Lynne McTaggart's *The Field* and *The Intention Experiment.* All these authors note that quantum physicists, in their early research, discovered that particles—the building blocks of atoms, made up of electric charges, magnetic charges, and light—changed as they were being observed, even when researchers were doing nothing more than looking at them. Long before I ever heard about the above-mentioned research, I would often be looking at someone's aura or some kind of energy, and I would notice that it immediately began shifting, even before I communicated what I was seeing to the readee. After alerting the readee to the energy I was seeing, I would many times see an even greater shift in that energy.

In *The Intention Experiment*, McTaggart makes a distinction between *attention* and *intention*. Attention is focusing on something without intent; intention is focus with a desired outcome. Likewise, *clairvoyant reading* is putting your attention on the target or object, while *clairvoyant healing* is reading with the intention to initiate a change. This intention can be general—as when you approach a reading with the attitude that you are going to do your best to see and offer the most accurate information in order to help your readee achieve maximum health and happiness. Or your intention may be specific, in that it might address a particular issue—for example, your readee suffers from headaches or depression, and your intention is to free them of these ailments. For myself and most psychics I know personally, we naturally bring this general goal to our work with every client, so we can't say that we are ever just merely observing without any intent behind it. But there are definitely different degrees of intent and, as McTaggart explains, intention is not just desire; it's a definitive commitment to achieve results. From my own observations, there seems to be a proportional connection between the strength of the desire and the impact of the healing, particularly when the one being healed has the same commitment to their own healing as the one doing the healing. (You'd be surprised how often the healer is more invested in the outcome than the person being healed!)

For example, I might do a clairvoyant reading for a client and discover that she currently has cancer. As I look at the cancer cells, their location, and the underlying energy and issues that seem to be related to the cancer, I will often begin to see a shift happen in the energy field. For some reason I tend to see cancer as white, and there are times when I am just merely looking at the white color that it begins to move and dissipate. Sometimes when the movement occurs, the readee actually begins to experience a sensation. Yet it is when I actually decide to actively heal the person of their cancer, by imagining and willing or demanding that the white release out of the affected area and go down a grounding cord, that I observe the greatest changes and the client experiences the most profound physical shifts or has the greatest emotional release. This release occurs whether or not the client had any idea that I was actually performing a healing.

Quite often when reading a person, an image will spontaneously come to me that I can then work with when I am ready to perform a clairvoyant healing on them. For example, I might see a black streak cutting across my client's heart, so I will use my imagination and visualize that black color releasing from the heart. Or I might see an image of the client's heart as if it were feeble and gasping for breath. In this case I would ask the heart to show me the color of whatever has been causing the weakness in it. The color doesn't really mean anything to me other than giving me something to hold on to—to work with or manipulate. If the color seems to represent something that is not healthy, I can visualize it releasing. If it is something pleasant, such as a vibration of joy or creativity or passion, I may choose to visualize it washing away any other colors as if it were clean water swirling inside a washing machine. I may also choose to visualize this color as if it were completely filling up the client's body and aura, or a particular area in need of this energy. I may share this color with the client or ask them to describe their favorite color or one that makes them happy, in order to see if it corresponds with the one I am seeing. Then I will give the client an assignment to work with this color in their own meditation space as a self-healing empowerment exercise.

This is how a basic clairvoyant healing is done. We set the intention to make a strong difference and utilize visualizations to achieve this purpose. In a pure clairvoyant *reading*, we are just observing—with kindness, but we are not intentionally changing what we are seeing, even though such a change may in fact be the end result. Remember: it's as simple as shining a light exactly on the area that needs illumination, and the readee's spirit will see the spot that they could not quite reach before on their own, and a shift will take place.

Sometimes this spiritual communication in the form of a clairvoyant reading is all the person needs; other times the reading is just one thing in a cumulative series of events. At other times, intentional healing is necessary, and even then it may not have immediate and complete results but rather move the client one small step on their journey to health. If the client is not at all open to growth or change due to fear or a compulsive need to control something that they cannot control (which is almost always due to fear anyway), then the reading and healing may have no effect other than to really piss the client off!

I once received a letter from a woman who stated that her boyfriend was very abusive, was currently serving a prison term for attempted murder, and was addicted to methamphetamine. This man told the woman who wrote me that he never wanted to see her again. She asked me what I could do to help him (translation: change him) so that she could get back together with him. I told her, "Absolutely nothing," but I added that I might be able to figure out why she was settling for someone like him and to help her emotionally let go of this very destructive attachment in her life. I wasn't surprised when I never heard back from her. *Her problem wasn't with him. It was with herself.*

Healer, Heal Thyself

One of the most important things to understand about clairvoyant reading is that it's not just the readee who is being influenced by the clairvoyant's attention and intentions. The clairvoyant is very much affected as well. This is where we may have to part ways with the quantum physicists—not because they aren't being influenced by the particles they are observing, but because most of them would never even think to consider this as a possibility, and I can't imagine that the particles themselves would have enough strength to elicit the same effect that one person's energy field can have on another. This is why we need more of these very smart physicists to study larger particles—i.e., people!

During a clairvoyant reading, the readers will also be experiencing their own clairsentience—the ability to feel others' emotions and physical sensations as one's own, including pain, exhaustion, and sexual arousal. As I mentioned, during a reading the clairvoyant will be encountering and working through their own issues and matching pictures with the client, which will be stimulated and brought to the surface for the purpose of healing. When psychics are unaware of these matching pictures, it's easy to get stuck and fall into resistance of them, which usually translates into resisting the person they are reading, or feeling fear about doing the reading at all. If psychics are aware of how the process works, there are techniques they can utilize to allow them to use this process to their advantage. In this respect, clairvoyant reading can be a tool for paradigm shifts, emotional release, and over-all rapid and significant growth. However, with rapid growth comes change—and as you know, change can sometimes be more than a bit distressing.

In clairvoyant circles this process is called a *growth period*. In other spiritual disciplines it's called a *dark night of the soul*. This is because the soul suddenly becomes aware that it was operating from false premises, such as fantasies or fears, or other people's ideas, dreams, and limitations. These premises may have been exactly the ones the spirit needed in order to learn certain lessons or achieve certain goals in life up until this point, but they no longer serve the spirit. When this occurs, sometimes our previous belief structure—in which our identity was enmeshed and into which we grounded in order to be secure—collapses. The only way we can really feel better is to adopt a new belief system that fits us better in the present time.

Sometimes, however, there is a gap in time before we can form that new belief system or ground into it. While there is much to learn and experience in that gap, our ego may actually feel as if it is dying or has died and has nothing to hang on to; this can be downright terrifying. Actually, it isn't being in that gap that's a problem, but instead it's the lack of understanding that unnerves us and tricks us into wondering if we are going nuts. This is because during such a growth period we really are losing touch with "reality." Yet that can be a good thing, if the "reality" we were previously in touch with was not really real.

When we are in this limbo, in this gap of not knowing any longer what to believe, and when we can recognize this state for what it is, and actually celebrate it, we will be in an extremely powerful place because the possibilities for what we can create and where we can go will be astounding. Unfortunately, most people don't really get this until after they've come out on the other end and can look back at the experience from a safe distance and not only say, "Wow, that was intense. I don't want to go through that again!" but also appreciate it as a defining point in their personal and/or spiritual development. This period is often followed up with extreme changes in a person's life, which can include ending relationships and giving up jobs, material items, and ways of behaving that were no longer productive in order to make way for a whole new bundle of opportunities often associated with greater creativity and peace.

It is my most sincere hope that this book will help you use clairvoyant reading to initiate this growth process in yourself, and that you will remember to congratulate yourself for the changes you are making if and when life as you know it begins to feel a bit topsy-turvy. I promise that such a feeling won't last long—although I guess *long* is a subjective word!

The process of psychic development and reading (which is also a form of remote viewing—see chapters 10 and 11) that I will focus on in this book can be merely a set of mental exercises you can utilize to call upon any kind of information through extrasensory perception, or it can be a spiritual discipline and practice that yield deep and lasting results for self-development. If you practice the techniques just a few times, you will most likely discover that they yield immediate results. The longer and deeper you practice, the greater fruits they will bear—as is true in the other spiritual disciplines, whether yoga, martial arts, or even any of the creative arts such as painting, music, writing, dance, and so on. With all of these, it takes courage, faith, determination, focus, and patience to get past both the inner resistance and outer resistance that are in operation every moment, even right this moment as you decide whether to read one more word of this book or abandon it and turn on the TV instead. One of the reasons I have written this book is to help people get past this resistance. *Resistance* here is defined as

anything that would keep you separate—physically, mentally, or emotionally—from your abilities, your own inner voice, or your affinity for
yourself. The root of resistance is fear (see also chapter 20).

The tricky thing about resistance is sometimes, even often, people
confuse it with a "gut feeling." The expression "Listen to your gut"
always makes me cringe because most of the information connected
with our guts (which correspond to the third chakra) has to do with
issues of power and control, and sometimes plain old-fashioned gas or
menstrual cramps! Control is a mechanism that attempts to avoid and
protect us from fear. But when we realize we cannot control what we
fear, this part of our body will send signals that scream out "Danger!
Danger!" and secrete all kinds of toxins and acids that cause indigestion, ulcers, or even cancers.

I am in no way disputing the power of intuition; rather, I am suggesting that intuition doesn't really come from your "gut." Instead, it
stimulates the fear sensation or reaction in your gut, which is probably
why people think it's their gut that is the voice of intuition. *Intuition*
is a term used to describe a wide variety of psychic abilities and sensations, and I believe intuition originates more in the upper chakras or
energy centers of the body than in the lower ones.

Fortunately, we have our clairvoyance, the ability to see information in the form of pictures and images. When we know how to work
with our clairvoyance, which you will after reading this book, we have
a way to obtain more detailed, accurate, and objective information so
that we can make better decisions, such as whether or not we really
shouldn't get on that plane, or if we just need to ground ourselves, take
a nap, a yoga class, or an Alka-Seltzer.

If you don't know for certain that you are psychic, if you have
never had a clairvoyant vision as far as you recall, if you have had one
but don't know how to control it, or if you know beyond all doubt
you are clairvoyant but are not using your clairvoyance in the ways or
to the degree you suspect you could, *there is a reason for that!* You are
"stuck" in a reality that says these things are not real, possible, or safe,
at least not for you. However, I can guarantee you that this "reality" is
anything but real! It is an illusion. Up until now there was something

else at play—a force within you, or outside yourself in the form of a person, people, the entire society perhaps—blocking your awareness, preventing you from having the knowledge and access to the knowledge. I can be as certain of that as I am certain that *you are psychic. You are clairvoyant. You are clairsentient. You are clairaudient. You are a medium!*

Overcoming years of unconscious resistance to your own psychic abilities can be more than just challenging, particularly when you are surrounded by others who continue to be stuck in this very same resistance. Developing your abilities within a structured and supportive group setting is the easiest way to achieve your goal. However, it may not be practical for you right now in terms of time and family commitments, your other goals, your location, or your finances. Therefore, it is my sincerest desire and intent to give you everything you might possibly need that is in my power to give you, in order to help you help yourself as you move up, down, along, in circles, sometimes backward, but mostly forward along the never-ending path of your clairvoyant development.

I am going to give you the tools and pass along the lessons you need to pull yourself out of any potholes, to create bridges from one signpost to the next, and to slay any trolls, demons, or hollow-eyed aliens that are threatening to huff and puff and blow your house down. It will of course be up to you to make good use of these tools.

CHAPTER 2

What Is an Extraordinary Psychic?

God doesn't look at how much we do, but with how much love we do it.
—MOTHER TERESA

Most of society thinks that an extraordinary psychic is someone with special psychic powers. What people don't understand is that it's not about *having* the powers as much as it is about what we do with them. There are many people with tremendous psychic abilities who don't have the courage, self-esteem, focus, sincerity, perseverance, or communication skills to utilize their abilities consciously and effectively.

Courage, Perseverance, and Self-Discipline

The best psychics and healers are the most courageous ones. They don't let anyone or anything, particularly their own emotions, get in the way of them seeing and speaking the truth, even when this truth is the last thing they think anyone wants to hear. Usually, that which we are most afraid of seeing and reporting is the very thing our client needs to and longs to hear the most, because it is reflective of the truth of their current experience, regardless of whether we as the messengers judge it to be pleasant or unpleasant, desirable or undesirable.

Courage does not mean lack of fear. It means facing the fear, working through it, not letting it get in your way. Those who don't have enough courage give up as soon as they see an image they don't understand, or they give up before the image comes—which means they give up within five minutes since something almost always comes within five minutes of reading someone else when using the techniques taught in this book! You will learn how to recognize these images so that when you stumble you can forge head at full speed or get back on track as quickly as possible. By utilizing the basic preparatory techniques offered in chapter 4, you will be able to gain control over your emotions, both by recognizing when you are allowing them to impact you and by learning how to work with them.

Control vs. Receptivity—Balance

Using your clairvoyance involves a balance of intention (control) and receptivity (passivity). The toughest part is being passive, which requires you to let go of your will, ego, and need to control. It can be very scary to be in a position in which you are waiting for the information to come—not knowing if it will ever arrive, what form it's going to show up in, whether you will be accurate, or if the person you are reading is going to like you, agree with you, or criticize you. Many people just don't want to put themselves through this uncertainty. That's why they will never know how psychic they really are.

Practice

The only way to build your muscles, whether your biceps or your clairvoyant "muscles," is by exercising them. The more you practice, the faster and easier the information will flow. One reason for this is that after a while, you will begin to build up a library of symbols and experiences you will be able to interpret right away. Clairvoyant reading is a lot like learning a new language or musical instrument, only much easier than both. One of the purposes of this book is to encourage you to continue to practice and to help you with whatever challenges may arise in the course of your practice. Just like real life, every time you take a step or reach a goal, a whole new set of challenges you may never have faced emerges. If you have some idea what to look out for before you encounter them, you will be better able to face these challenges, and to conquer them and persevere.

I have recently been corresponding with a reader of my book *You Are Psychic* who has just completed her hundredth clairvoyant session on her own. She's been reading everyone from her neighbors to strangers she meets in online chat rooms. Yes, she gets a lot of positive feedback from these volunteers. Most of them tell her how accurate and helpful she is. But that doesn't really impress me. "Why?" you may ask, surprised. Because I expect that. I know if people utilize these techniques, they will soon receive the same kind of feedback that she gets. What *does* awe the hell out of me is her self-initiative, ingenuity (it's not that easy to find that many volunteers), and raw courage.

I've been working with several other students in my long-distance training program who also take it upon themselves to find lots of people to practice on in between our sessions. Sometimes these people are quite challenging in terms of their personalities and issues. Yet even when they've had a trying experience, these students jump right back in with both feet to the next reading to regain their confidence. These are examples of extraordinary psychics!

Holding Nothing Back

As a teacher, I have come to realize over the last several years that there is nothing more exhilarating than taking a student who has never had a clairvoyant image in their life, or no idea how to control such an image, and within one or two days or sessions seeing that student be blown away by the detail and information I've just coaxed from their not-so-confident lips. This is why I can teach the same material over and over again: once I have helped students to jump-start their clairvoyance with a few simple techniques (as I will do with you), there are a billion possibilities for what will happen next. It is like watching a thriller over and over that starts fairly similarly but has a drastically different middle and end each time. So in this book, as in *You Are Psychic*, I will hold nothing back. I don't want you to be merely as good a clairvoyant

as I am; I want you to be much better. Since my own opinion of myself
as a psychic is pretty darn high, that means you are going to be nearing
Mt. Everest in no time!

I absolutely refuse to believe in the idea of scarcity when it comes to
clients, students, or any opportunities, so if your newfound skills lead
you to work with the same clients I do, then all the more power to you!
We need more psychics, not fewer. In fact, as the veil is lifting; as our
entire population seems to be evolving into something quite different
from where we were technologically, spiritually, and psychologically
even a decade ago; and as we face greater economic and global challenges than ever before, we are going to need more and more trained
clairvoyants to help everyone deal with these changes and their emerging, out-of-control psychic abilities. I hope this message gets out there
to those psychics who are at home sulking about their lack of clientele,
something that has far more to do with resentful attitudes, self-esteem,
and depleted energy levels.

The Extraordinary Psychic Creed

As extraordinary psychics we do not fear words, particularly not the
word *psychic*. We neither run from it nor try to cover it up; rather, we
reclaim it! We serve as shining examples of who psychics really are and
what we can really do. Furthermore, we do not waste our time or energy on the hapless army of self-proclaimed "professional," anything-
but-scientific skeptics who will not even accept the now-definitive and
significant findings of thousands of well-designed and repeated studies
that have utilized stringent protocols to prove the existence of ESP,
psychic energy, and the power of healing through intention. (Most of
the standard psi research far exceeds that for any other kind of research, including studies performed on pharmaceuticals approved by
the FDA.) Furthermore, as *extra*ordinary psychics we do not resist or
resent others' versions of reality (even those of the skeptics). Instead,
we seek to understand them, and expand them through a commitment
to understanding and expanding our own beliefs.

As extraordinary psychics we seek to demolish stereotypes that psychics are supposed to look or behave in some ridiculous way. There is no

reason psychics have to wear crystal-studded purple muumuus, change our names to those of rocks or other celestial objects, or wander around like wide-eyed flower children on LSD—any more than computer programmers need to be geeky-looking guys with glasses and pocket protectors. These stereotypes have really made it much harder for those who wish to maintain a professional image to allow themselves their own abilities and to respect their psychic brothers and sisters.

We Can Be Happy and Abundant as Psychics!

Many psychics (as well as other spiritually-oriented people) end up being doormats or denying themselves the necessities or joys of life because they think that is what they are supposed to do.

A book containing Mother Teresa's most intimate letters, entitled *Come Be My Light*, was recently published. From this book it was clear Mother Teresa suffered from intense emotional pain throughout her more-than-extraordinary career. Upon the book's release there was a frenzy of attention in the mainstream American media, even suggestions of a "scandal" because Mother Teresa, while maintaining a public image of faith, had questioned whether or not God had abandoned her.

What some people don't understand is that faith moves up and down an ever-changing continuum ranging from serious doubt to conviction, and back to doubt as new challenges are encountered along the path. Faith is about trusting when you don't yet have all the evidence, and constantly reexamining your beliefs as new experiences are had and new information discovered. What I find most incredulous in the insinuation of "scandal" is why for an instant anyone in their right mind would or did suppose that Mother Teresa was a joyous and carefree person. Sure, she put on a brave smile for those who needed to see it, but how could anyone, while honoring their vows of poverty and chastity, and while encountering thousands of desperate, suffering people falling apart from leprosy and the worst diseases imaginable in the bowels of hell, not get depressed from time to time? Perhaps we wanted to believe she was happy so we wouldn't feel guilty about leaving the dirty work to her.

Still, I have to wonder: was it God denying her every human pleasure, even the most basic of comforts, or was it her own belief system about God, and the pictures she held about how best to honor her relationship with her creator, that made her life so difficult and led her into periods of despair? Was this self-denial truly necessary in order to carry out her accomplishments of establishing hundreds of much-needed hospitals and schools around the world? If she had treated herself better, would these never have been created? Or might she have had even more energy to do more good deeds?

These are the same questions we need to ask ourselves as psychics and healers. Why is there a perception that people in every other profession can make a living, even grow prosperous from their work, but not us? Why? Because of the idea of "the gift." God has given us this gift and we must now take advantage of it, right? Well, what about the gift of an awesome voice? Why are singers making millions? And what about smart people like doctors? Aren't they gifted with intelligence and the ability to sit through long, boring classes without falling asleep? Why should they make so much money? Oh well, they go through years of training, whereas psychic abilities just happen to us and don't require any sacrifice, right? *Wrong!*

As extraordinary psychics we need to be able to fess up to the fact that our very desire to be spiritual or even to deny ourselves pleasure or comfort could be as ego-based as a desire to rule the world for our own gluttonous advancement. We need to be real! Any attempts at appearing spiritual are symptoms of the ego. Now, if you want to light candles or incense to get you in the mood, to remind you of your spirit or God, or to honor a spirit that has passed on, that is spiritual. If you want to light candles because psychics are supposed to have candles and other smelly things lying around that impress clients, that is your choice. Just call it what it is: a marketing tactic rather than an act of spirituality.

Eyes Wide Open

As extraordinary psychics we are also not going to deny the existence of things we wish were not there, such as evil, but instead we will learn how to excise these things from our personal lives. If you hadn't noticed, we live in a world where people are not always nice to each other. Sometimes they are downright cruel. Violence is everywhere. Evil exists, no matter how many of us wish it didn't. Because these harsher forces are out there, there are times we need to be able to stand up to them, when being all nice and loving is not the correct response.

As I learned the hard way, spirituality does not occur in a vacuum of *Leave It to Beaver*ish "everything's love and light" (see chapters 12 through 14). Perhaps most important, we are not going to allow ourselves to become trapped in our own definitions, stereotypes, or fantasies of ourselves as psychics and spiritual seekers. There are some very amazing, well-intentioned healers, psychics, and spiritual leaders out there who are very screwed-up people. These same healers may be instrumental in transforming your life and may later help you to mess it up in a big way. At the same time you might encounter some very evil, selfish people who could not care less about healing, but who serve as the catalyst for you to get in touch with yourself on a very profound level. Being spiritual means paying attention to spirit. Nothing more, nothing less.

Rewards of Clairvoyant Reading

- You can see just about anything at any time.
- You can learn about yourself and anyone else.
- You can know a truth from a lie.
- You can see a situation for how it is rather than how you wish it to be.
- You can use clairvoyance to help others.
- You can use clairvoyance in conjunction with just about any other therapeutic practice.
- You can use clairvoyance to heal yourself or anyone else of pain and illness.
- You can use clairvoyance for dreams and inspiration.
- You can use clairvoyance for manifesting goals and creating abundance.

- You can use clairvoyance to help you communicate with the deceased and with spirit guides.
- Your communication with your heart, your Higher Self, God, and your guides will increase.
- You can speed up your natural transformation process.
- You can be a psychic spy.
- You can save a lot of time by diagnosing any problem, from another's health-related concern to an issue with your car.
- You will work through your fears and resistance to your own abilities.
- You will understand how you are already being psychic all the time.
- You will have more freedom in your life in general.
- You will become a more conscious, more enlightened person.
- You will learn new coping skills for dealing with troublesome entities, psychic parasites, and other troublesome beings both in bodies and out.
- You will learn how to attract and heal relationships and get over a broken heart easier.
- You will gain a better understanding of the relationship between you and the organizations you are associated with.
- You will learn how to be in the now.
- You will become better equipped to make the best choices for yourself, including whether to accept a certain job, rent or buy a particular house, or date or marry a particular person.
- You will prepare yourself for a smoother transition in death.
- You will be able to see information about past incarnations and integrate this information to help you in the present.
- You will increase your overall self-confidence.
- You will never have a reason to be bored again, since you will have round-the-clock entertainment, even when you are alone.

CHAPTER 3

Preparing Yourself to Do Readings and Healings

We are what we repeatedly do.
—ARISTOTLE

Preparation Techniques—Psychic Tools Revisited

The following visualizations can be used to prepare yourself for your clairvoyant readings. They are powerful, transformative meditation tools in themselves that can be done ten minutes before a clairvoyant reading or performed at a completely different time, for any length of time. The longer you do them, the more you will feel their effects and the more you will benefit from them, so I highly encourage you to try utilizing them so you can experience their effects, even if only once a month for at least an hour each time. Don't let lack of time or discipline keep you from practicing them even for short periods of time.

Please keep in mind that once you are adept at using these visualizations on yourself, you can then begin applying them to other people seeking your help, as these visualizations are very powerful tools for healing. Also know that it doesn't matter if these are brand-new to you or if you have done them, or variations of them, one million times.

They have a cumulative effect, so every time you do them they will assist you with maximizing your energy flow, centering yourself, reconnecting with your body and the earth, and they will help you release any energies you've taken on from other people or your environment. When you first begin practicing them, it may seem as if all you are doing is fooling around in the playground of your imagination, but what you will soon discover if you "play" consistently and diligently is that your imagination is the control panel for directing, creating, and releasing energy of all kinds that affect your thoughts, emotions, health, relationships, and your ability to manifest your goals. Energy is as real as your physical body.

Optimal Environment

It is best when you are starting to practice that you find a quiet place where you won't be disturbed. Turn off all music, your television set, your computer, and your phone. It's best to not even have a TV on in another room since you may pick up images from it when first getting started, but don't sweat it if that's the only thing that's going to keep the family busy while you are stealing a few precious moments for yourself!

If you hear noises around you, notice the distance between where you are and where the noises are, and tell your subconscious mind that the noise will bring you deeper into yourself and into a state of relaxation. Believe me: you can do any of these exercises anywhere, any time. However, the quieter it is, the easier it will be for you to focus, relax, and have fun.

Close Your Eyes

When you close your eyes, you are turning inward to a place of connection with yourself. It is pretty amazing how little time we spend inside ourselves when we are not sleeping or consciously meditating. When I was filming the DVD presentation of *You Are Psychic* with the help of my brother Brad, who was producing the DVD, he found himself following along with the instructions for grounding and running energy. He had never once meditated in his thirty-four years of existence. Afterward he could barely contain his excitement, but also he was dismayed that he could have lived his entire life without even considering that there is a whole playground right inside his very own head in which he can do tons of fun things he had never even considered. If you think about it, other than sleeping, when is it even socially acceptable to close your eyes and go within? Try closing your eyes at work or when you're with friends, and they will accuse you of sleeping or being rude, or they'll think you're nuts! I wonder what this says about our society as a whole, since closing your eyes forces you to concentrate and connect with yourself. This apparently is not the American way.

We are going to change that here. You can see visions with your eyes open, but then you have to strain and work a lot harder to ignore all the outside stimuli. Some people don't like to close their eyes because it makes them nervous. They are afraid they will miss something, or that they won't be able to control or be prepared for something with their eyes closed. Every once in a while I get students in a class who are so resistant to keeping their eyes closed at first that they almost have to experience a panic attack before they can let themselves relax.

Other people are just so used to looking at someone when they talk that they go through lots of guilt-related inner turmoil before they start to realize that they can really be of more service when they close their eyes, since doing so allows them to "see" more clearly without the distracting visual cues from their client. When we can witness every glimmer of hope, disdain, fear, sadness, or glee in the eyes or face of our client, we begin to filter out any information that might elicit an unhappy reaction, which affects how honestly we can communicate and ultimately doesn't serve anyone.

Optimal Reading/Meditation Position

Although you can use your clairvoyance or meditate in any position, sitting in an upright position in a chair or on a sofa that fully supports your back, with your legs bent at the knees and your feet touching the floor, maximizes the energy flow and release. I don't know why, but the energy flow and release is much stronger in this position than when sitting in the crossed-leg lotus position, which seems to inhibit the flow through the legs when done for a period of time. Energy can flow well when you are lying down, but in this position it's too easy to drift off to sleep. I suspect the energy flow is also maximized when standing up straight; however, most people cannot perform a reading in that position without losing their balance or getting tired.

Grounding

Grounding provides a vehicle through which your body can focus and release its excess electrical energy. Grounding works best with your feet touching the ground outside, but you can most certainly do this exercise inside any structure as well. There are a variety of ways to ground. Grounding yourself from the first chakra strengthens your natural connection with the earth, and makes it feel safer for your spirit to be inside your body. However, by strengthening this grounding you may become the most grounded thing in the room.

Electricity always seeks grounding to complete its circuit; it seeks the shortest possible route to the source with the least amount of resistance. In order to protect our homes and ourselves from being electrocuted by lightning, every electrical box has a ground stake about six feet long that has been hammered into the earth. The stake is made out of steel and is coated with copper. It channels any extraneous electricity, such as lightning, into the earth rather than into your electrical outlets, where it would seek you as the source to ground through.

When we visualize ourselves with a grounding cord, we are essentially creating a grounding stake so that extraneous foreign energies will go into our cords instead of into the rest of our body. When we extend that visualization to include the building we are in, then the various foreign energies that are already in that space will have someplace to go besides into us or our newly created grounding cords. Since gravity works with our grounding cords to form a vacuum effect, by grounding the building we are essentially giving it its own vacuum hose, thereby lessening the possibility of our own getting congested or clogged.

Grounding the Room

Sit in a comfortable position with your feet touching the floor, palms resting on your thighs and turned upward toward the ceiling. Ground the room by imagining a huge metallic beam running from the center of the ceiling deep into the core of the planet, which you can visualize as containing various metals such as iron, copper, silver, and gold. The beam can be half the width of the entire room or match its entire diameter. You can also see beams running from each individual corner of the room downward into the earth. You can also visualize these beams surrounding the outside of the house. If you feel the space really needs a healing, you can call forth the cosmic energies, which you can visualize as an intense colored light pouring down through the beams into the earth. Imagine they are washing away whatever needs to be released, such as emotional energy from yourself or other people who have occupied the room.

Grounding Yourself

Visualize any strong object that will connect your body at the base of your spine to the core of the earth to form a grounding cord. Some of my favorite objects are a redwood tree trunk, a cruise ship anchor, a heavy column made from pure gold, a crystal, or a stone that looks similar to those that form Stonehenge. It is best to see this object being at least as wide your hips. Some people just have a heck of a time seeing their grounding as anything stronger than a thread or a wobbly vine. This is because they are ungrounded or thinly anchored into their bodies. Don't worry if this describes you, because with time your grounding, and therefore the visualization of your cord, will grow stronger.

Next imagine that your grounding cord has a hollow, slippery center, and then give your grounding cord two directives. First tell it that it is going to absorb anything that comes your way that you wouldn't really want to stick to you, and then tell it that it is going to operate as the vehicle by which you will spontaneously release any pain, emotions, or thoughts that no longer serve you. Let your attention run between the points at which the cord meets the base of your spine, at the first chakra and the ground.

You can also imagine that the gravitational pull is increasing to draw out any toxins from your body. Visualize a gravity gauge and see the number rising up. You might also imagine that your grounding cord is like a straw, and the earth is like a mouth that is sucking out the energies you are now expelling. If you are sitting in a lotus or cross-legged position on the floor or sofa, you can maximize your grounding and energy release by imagining that you are drawing a line from your first chakra to one knee, to the next knee and then back to the first chakra, to form a triangle shape. Then visualize your grounding cord as if it were a triangular tube running deep into the earth.

Grounding Your Aura

Our auras hold on to the energy of pain. Many times I will feel pain in a person's aura before they report experiencing it in their body. (By running my hands through it, I can feel the pain in my hands.) Conversely, I will feel pain in a certain part of a readee's aura that corresponds to a part of their body where they felt pain a few days before but are no longer experiencing it.

Our auras or energy fields are stretchy. They expand or contract as easily as we can extend our arms to hug another or bring another close to us in a gesture of protection. During readings and healings, it helps to know where your energy field ends and begins so that you can have control over the reading experience. If your aura is encompassing your readee, or theirs is encompassing you, you both are going to experience each other's emotions. Now you might think, "Cool, then I will know how they are feeling." While this may be true, you may get very confused about which are their emotions and which are your own, and then become the effect of these before you can consciously realize what is happening. By bringing your aura closer to you and setting boundaries between yourself and the other person, you will be in a better position to observe and remain calm and composed during a reading.

This is an excellent technique to do while having a difficult or heated conversation with someone.

You can ground your aura first by visualizing that you are drawing it in around you about two or three feet (for some of you who are feeling ill or are naturally introverted, this might require you to imagine you are expanding it outward from its natural position). Next, imagine that you are tucking the bottom part of your aura into your grounding cord at the point where it runs below your feet right into the ground. Then demand that your aura release anything that is no longer serving you right into and down your grounding cord. If it doesn't feel like your aura wants to be grounded, I suggest giving yourself a larger grounding cord, giving your aura its own grounding cord, or pretending that you are sewing, nailing, stapling, gluing, or tacking your aura into the cord. Then see a turbocharged level on the side and imagine you are pressing down. As you press down, you will release whatever energy in your aura that didn't want it to ground.

Create a Separation Object

A *separation object* is that which creates an energetic boundary between you and everyone else. It is helpful to use one when encountering a highly emotional person and when performing a reading or healing. First, visualize an object that can rotate around the outermost edge of your grounding cord. You can see this as any object, but make it strong so you know it's absorbent. You can then give it its own grounding cord to strengthen it. I like to use images of smiley faces or bright cartoon flowers—really anything that is lighthearted or that makes me happy. I do this to dispel any resistance to whatever it might be that my separation object is helping to separate me from.

You can program your separation object with the command that any foreign energies directed into your field or body will instead go right into it. You can also remind yourself that everything on the side of the object facing you is you and belongs to you, and everything on the outside is something or someone else. It's a great idea to check in with this every once in a while when doing readings. Afterward, you can visualize it on your screen and look for the colors and read the ensuing energies that entered your separation object so you can get an idea of what was happening around you. You can then destroy this used one and create a new, fresh separation object.

Running Energy

When our bodies are in an optimal state of health, we have the right amount of life force energy moving through each body part and system. When we are in pain or feeling depleted and depressed, there is a problem with the flow, either due to a blockage or to an inadequate distribution of energy in a part of our body or energy field. Fortunately, we can often remove blockages, increase the flow, or bring in a type of energy that will return us or someone we are working with to an optimal state of health.

There are many ways to work with energy. Energy can most easily be visualized as a colored, active, moving substance. You can see it as colored light, water, fire—anything fluid and moving. You can decide what you wish to achieve, what type of energy or vibration you'd like to have more of in your body, and then assign it a color. Once you know the clairvoyant technique, you can use this to find the appropriate color. Until then you can just choose colors that feel good to you. Stay away from those that don't feel comfortable. You may naturally associate certain colors with vibrations based on past experiences or books you have read that assign a particular meaning to a color that stuck with you. The important thing is that you like the colors you work with, and they feel more like you than anyone else you know.

Running energy is like giving ourselves a shower. It also allows us to replenish ourselves, much like filling up a gas tank. Below are some simple but very effective ways to run energy.

Cosmic Energy

Simplest: imagine that the cosmos, or heavens, or the hands of God are opening up, and see torrents of colored light or water pouring down onto your head. Imagine the top of your head (your crown chakra) is opening up like a lotus, rose, or tulip to welcome in this flow. Inhale this breath down to your toes and even let some of it run down your grounding cord. You can imagine that this energy is as neutral as water, or you can assign it a quality you want to have in your life, such as more joy, peace, passion, creativity, and so on.

Cosmic Energy and Energizing the Chakras

The chakras are energy centers within our body and aura that correspond with a certain part of the body. They have a variety of functions that impact our level of power, consciousness, and our overall mental, emotional, and physical health. Again, imagine that the cosmos, heavens, or the hands of God are opening up, and see torrents of colored light or water pouring down onto your head. Imagine the top of your head (your crown chakra) is opening up like a lotus or rose or tulip to welcome in this flow of colored sparkling light. See it circulating in your crown chakra, take a breath, and draw it down into your sixth chakra, where your third eye is located, which also corresponds to the center of your forehead.

As you take a few breaths, see this color swirling through the energy center that you can visualize as a swirling disk. As you do this you may get a clear image of the chakra, and by all means use that image instead if you prefer it. Next inhale and draw the colored light or water down into your fifth chakra, your throat chakra. See it swirling in there like colored soap suds coursing through a washing machine. Continue drawing the color downward and have it swirl around in the heart chakra, then the solar plexus, third chakra, then the second chakra, which corresponds to the reproductive and sexual centers, and then the first chakra at the base of the spine. Once you have reached the first chakra, you can focus more on your breath. As you inhale, imagine you are capturing and pulling down more of the cosmic energy into your head and continue directing it downward every time you inhale. Imagine that as you exhale, you are blowing on your chakras like a pinwheel and making them spin even more.

Earth Energy

Our feet are the exit and entry points for a tremendous amount of energy. As I will be describing in the chapter on healing, one of my favorite healers in the Philippines used to do exorcisms during which he would hold on to someone's toe and extract the pain and negative forces through the feet. If someone is electrocuted, since the energy seeks grounding it exists through the feet. When we are psychically attacked, many times it starts with our feet. Some people who have suddenly come down with a strange illness that could not be properly diagnosed reported feeling strange sensations through the feet right before their health declined.

Earth energy can help us increase our connection to the earth. When we walk, run, or do physical activities outside in nature, we spontaneously increase the flow up through our feet. We can increase this flow easily through visualization.

How to Run Earth Energy

We have little energy centers in our feet. Imagine you are opening these centers by seeing them as spinning disks getting bigger and bigger. Practice imagining them growing large to the point that it would seem uncomfortable and then closing them until they are almost completely shut. See them opening and closing, opening and closing, until it feels as if you are really doing this. It is kind of similar to the feeling of opening your eyes or your mouth really wide and then closing it. We can easily exercise our energy muscles through visualization. Finally, have your feet chakras remain fixed at a comfortable degree of openness that will enable the optimal amount of energy to flow through your feet.

Next, imagine that earth energy is rising from a very deep and clean place, deep within the earth. See this energy as an earthy color that enters your feet. Watch as it swirls around through the little chakras in your feet and flows through every toe, each heel, and up your ankles. See it flow up your calves and legs, let it swish around in your knees, then raise it up through your thighs, really let it wash out every part of your thighs, including the muscles and fat (if you have either one!) From your thighs, direct the nurturing, vibrant earth energy into your first chakra at the base of your spine and then let it circulate in there and flush back down your grounding cord. Visualize this for at least five minutes. Ask yourself if this color feels good to you. If not, choose another one originating from a different spot deep within the ground. Choose a color that feels good to you. After a few minutes you might try to imagine the flow increasing in volume and strength.

Combining Earth and Cosmic Energies

Draw the cosmic energy downward from a clean spot in the heavens into your crown chakra, down your spine where it can circulate in your first chakra. At the same time, see the earth energy rise up from the earth into your feet and up through your legs. It will also be spinning through your first chakra before it falls back down your grounding cord. Imagine the cosmic and earth energies are meeting in that first chakra to form a combined color. Let this combined color be 80 percent cosmic energy and 20 percent earth. Then see it rising back up through the core and front part of your body as if it were a powerful geyser, shooting straight out through the top of your head, spinning the chakras with its force.

Once it exits through your head, you can imagine it shooting higher and higher in the air, and then falling back down around the entire circumference of your body and back down through your aura, cleaning that out. If your aura is grounded, the energy will then wash right back down your grounding cord. Continue to visualize this for several minutes. If you do this for thirty minutes or an hour every day, you will completely transform your entire energy field and begin to feel very different.

Adding Breath Work to Your Cosmic Energy

As you inhale, draw the breath down to your first chakra. As you exhale, let your breath carry the light upward and release out of your head, with a little of it flowing down your arms and out your hands, creating pools of light from your head.

Clearing Out Your Head and
Sixth Chakra with Light and Breath

This next exercise has most recently been a favorite exercise for myself and many of my students, and it has an immediate relaxation and centering effect.

Just sit back in your seat and relax. Close your eyes and go inward. Become aware of your natural breathing; there's no need to change it. Become aware of the point at which the air meets your nostrils. As you inhale through your nose, notice if you can actually feel the air entering that very specific part of your nose. Keep your attention here for a minute or two. Next, imagine that the air is a colored light of health of whatever vibration you'd like. As you inhale, see this color going right up your nose and circulating through your sinuses. Imagine with each inhale that you are drawing it upward and as you exhale, the breath is making the air circulate through your head, spinning your sixth and seventh chakras.

Do this for a few minutes until your entire head is filled with dancing, breath-filled light. After you do this for a minute or two you can add the exhalation breath. Imagine that as you exhale you are drawing the colored light downward from your head, down through the throat and into the lungs where it can circulate and fill up and clean out the lungs and the nearby heart. Then continue to draw it down through the core of the body, down through the lower chakras and right down through the grounding cord into the earth. Let the light and breath also wash down your arms, with some of it releasing out of your hand chakras.

After a few more minutes, you can see this all happen in single breaths; as you inhale it comes in through your nose and up to the top of your head, and as you exhale the air in the form of the colored light goes straight down through you into the center of the earth. However, as your exhales bring the air and light downward, practice remaining centered in your head, so it's as if the air and breath and light are being sent below you.

Calling Back Your Own Energy

Often we travel out of our bodies to retrieve information. While the bulk of our energy remains in our bodies, much of it is sent to other people and projects and places. Some parts of ourselves are stuck in the past while other parts are out searching for answers and security in the future. Some parts are being held hostage by others, but this usually can only happen if we think we need them or we owe them something out of guilt or past agreements. Much of our illness, our exhaustion, our hunger, and our cravings related to addictions are due to us being low on our own spiritual energy. Fortunately, we can retrieve our energy with the aid of the following visualizations.

Simple method: Imagine you are putting out a call to all parts of yourself, any of your energy that is currently part of yourself. Ask yourself what color or colors these parts of yourself are. Watch as they come back to you. Let this color pour into you and fill you up where you are most deficient. As these parts come back, you can visualize your grounding cord and ask that if any foreign or pain energy was keeping your own energy out, or you were holding this foreign energy inside because you didn't have enough energy of your own, that it will release.

Classic Golden Sun Method

Imagine a large golden sun above your head. Imagine that you are writing your name across it, which gives the signal to yourself and anyone else that this is your very own sun. Imagine there is a very large magnet at its core, the strongest magnet in the universe. This magnet is designed to attract only your energy that is outside of your body at the moment.

Start to call back all your energy from anyone, any place, anything it could possibly be engaged with. You will probably intuitively know where some of it is, but you might spontaneously get some thoughts or images of people that you are surprised about. When I have done this exercise or had my students do it, we have been shocked to see faces of people we hadn't thought about in twenty years. Just because a relationship ended decades ago doesn't mean it's not still continuing on some nonphysical level. Sometimes we need to consciously end that connection so we are free to create new and rewarding relationships in the present moment on the physical level.

Just keep calling back your energy into your golden sun until the sun swells up from being so full. Once it is as full as it will or can get, imagine the sun bursts open and all that energy pours right down into the crown of your head, all the way down to your feet, and then back up, like orange juice pouring into a glass and spilling over. Let it spurt out the top of your head and go like a fountain out and down your aura, eventually running back down your grounding cord.

You can also see the energy flowing down your shoulders and arms, with a little bit of it splashing out of your palms in little fountains of light that also seep into your now-glowing aura. You can see the cells of your body expanding with the swirling light. Your cells and entire being will get so full of this light that the light will shine through every pore of your body, forming a million pinpoints of light emanating outward, engulfing your entire energy field in one huge glimmering disco-like ball. Then see this ball of light growing even brighter and bigger, stretching upward and out in all directions like a frenzied fire.

Remember to breathe as you do this, and say prayers of gratitude for your brilliant life and the healthy body that you've been gifted with. (Say these prayers anyway, even if you don't really believe you are that healthy—because you will be soon enough!)

CHAPTER 4

Basic Training: The Clairvoyant Techniques

Dignity consists not in possessing honors, but in the consciousness that we deserve them.

—ARISTOTLE

Before practicing the techniques in this chapter, I strongly recommend at least running through the preparatory techniques in the preceding chapter. They will help to clear your mind and your energy field so as to optimize your viewing pleasure! They also serve as powerful self-healing and meditation tools.

In this chapter we will mainly focus on your clairvoyant ability. However, please be aware that your other abilities of telepathy, clairaudience, and clairsentience will also be activated, and will provide you with information through your inner senses of hearing and feeling as well. We will address your clairaudient abilities in greater detail in chapter 6. In this chapter you will learn how to perform a clairvoyant reading on yourself and others through the use of three alternatives for working with your viewing receptacle, which is the most essential component of your clairvoyant technique.

The first option involves starting off with an image of a single viewing receptacle. The second technique is almost identical to the first, except we will use two viewing receptacles and watch the relationship between the two. This is an excellent technique to utilize when you are seeking information about a relationship or desiring to heal one. The third technique is also similar to the first, but involves using a symbol and dropping it into the receptacle.

The techniques summarized in this chapter are ideal for picking up extrasensory information about a person and every aspect of that person's life, including their relationships. (Some of these techniques were first presented in *You Are Psychic*, which provides more detailed explanations of their benefits.) This chapter focuses primarily on "reading" people. To learn how to access information about remote objects, locations, and unknown targets utilizing these techniques and others, please see chapters 10 and 11.

The following three techniques are intended primarily for doing readings from inside your body, centered in the area of your sixth chakra. Much of the information you will be drawing from will be coming from either a universal source of information accessed directly by your own clairvoyance, or will be projected and communicated on telepathic levels to you by the person you are reading. Occasionally some information will come from other spirits, either ones connected to you or to the person you are reading.

Usually, spirit communication comes in the form of telepathic thoughts of clairaudient hearing. Sometimes a spirit can toss you a picture (this usually has an almost intrusive quality to it), but this is far less common. In chapters 12 through 17, I discuss working with spirits and the various situations and challenges that can arise. For now you don't need to be concerned about the source of your images; it won't have that much bearing on your learning process.

The following three techniques work well for reading people. They also can be used to see into and obtain information about past or future events. There are times when you might have an easier time accessing certain kinds of information by having a part of your spirit or attention travel outside of your body to a particular location, such as when you are searching for a missing object or person or to view a very specific event (see chapter 11). However, many people do successfully access this type of information from the techniques presented below, which I recommend becoming familiar with first.

Basic Reading Technique

This technique is for in-your-body readings of yourself or other people.

Center Yourself

Since your clairvoyance is centered at the point of your sixth chakra that also corresponds to your pineal gland, this is where you will center yourself. It's also where you can observe the emotions you are feelings without being a slave to them or controlled by them. This is very important!

As spirits we can be centered or focused in any part of our body. When we are centered up behind our sixth chakra, we are less emotional. Our clairvoyance becomes activated and we are literally above our emotions. This doesn't mean we won't feel any emotions at all. To the contrary, our emotions will often reflect what the readee is feeling or experiencing; however, when we are centered in this part of ourselves, we will not have to become a victim to our emotions. We can have our emotions and know we are having them. It's the difference between being a spectator to a tornado—merely feeling some of the wind and turbulence—and getting swept away in the tornado. When we read, we are sometimes looking at other people's tornadoes. We can only help our readees if we remain neutral and a bit removed.

Familiarize Yourself with This Place

Come up or down or from wherever you are into the center of your head. You can actually place your fingers on your forehead, slightly above and in between your two eyes, to remind you of where this is. Close your eyes and imagine you are centered smack-dab in the center of your head, so that if there were a window or eye right there you'd be looking out at your fingertip. Once you have a concept of this, you can relax your hand back down to your lap.

Create a Seat

Create a comfortable chair, which will be like a director's seat or driver's seat. Have fun designing it. Imagine you are sitting in the chair. Then see yourself standing up and running circles around it. Then run in circles in the other direction. As you run, imagine you are taking your hands and running them alongside the inside of your head. Jump on top of the chair. Use it like a springboard or trampoline and do flips forward and backward off of it. Fly around the center of your head if you like, and then come back and sit in the chair. Imagine you are sitting in the driver's seat of a car, at the controls of an airplane, or at the helm of a ship on the sea or in outer space. Know that you are in charge. See yourself wearing the appropriate cap or uniform if you'd like. Have fun with this!

Open Your Third Eye

Next, while imagining that you are sitting inside your head and really centered there, also imagine that you are looking out of your forehead. Imagine that you press on the control panel in front of you and focus all your attention on the inside of your forehead. Imagine there is actually a third eye painted on your forehead and now, under your command, this eye is opening up so you can see beyond it. One of my favorite visualizations is of the viewing deck in *Star Trek*. On that TV series, on the other side of the viewing screen there was either a lovely view of outer space or the image of some planetary leader telling the crew they were about to face imminent attack if they didn't turn around immediately.

So watch as either an eye or a window opens up on your forehead, and imagine that you are now looking out of your forehead. I like to start off with a gesture of opening these parts, because that sends the symbolic and hypnotic suggestion that we are now creating a change in ourselves, opening up something not previously open. Even if you think your abilities are wide open already, by doing this visualization immediately before a reading you are sending the signal to yourself that you are now, at this specific time, allowing yourself to be more clairvoyant than you normally are in your everyday life.

Reading Screen

From the center of your head, you are now looking out the eye or window of your forehead. Focus about six to eight inches out in front of this point and visualize a reading screen. Take notice of the screen's appearance and attributes. You can see this as any shape or size. I invite you to try different images every time you do this in order to see what is most comfortable. Some popular images used by students are that of a television screen, a computer monitor, an IMAX theater screen, a black or white board, parchment paper, and the like.

Where Are You in Relation to Your Screen?

From the inside of your head, imagine that you are taking a tape measure and measuring the distance between where you are in your head and where the screen is. Just get a feel for how many inches or feet away your screen is. For the purposes of this exercise, we are reading from within our bodies; if your screen is too far away, this likely indicates your spirit or a part of you is very far from your body. If you feel as if the screen is miles away, then destroy that screen, recheck yourself to see if you are in fact centered in your head, and then create a screen closer to you.

Turn On Your Screen

Imagine there is a lamp or lights attached to the top of the screen. Imagine you are flipping the switch to these lights. Notice how nicely the lights illuminate the screen. Let this be another symbol or hypnotic suggestion to yourself that your clairvoyance is turning on strong to illuminate whatever is about to appear on your screen.

Ground Your Screen

Next go ahead and give your reading screen its own grounding cord, running from the base of the screen deep into the earth. Notice if anything happens to the screen or if it changes in any way. It may or may not.

Optional: Practice your preparatory techniques on your screen.

There are two ways you can perform these visualizations. The first way is to imagine them as if they were really happening to your actual body. The second is to visualize them on the reading screen you will be creating in a little while. There is value to both. Most people spontaneously visualize these techniques happening directly to their bodies. Even after students have grown adept at creating and utilizing a screen during readings with others, they still tend to spontaneously ground themselves or run energy by visualizing it happening directly to their body. Doing so is easier and it tends to make it all feel more real. However, I do encourage you to practice these techniques both ways once you have taken the time to visualize your screen and see what that is like. It's great to go back and forth.

The value of seeing your body and your aura with your grounding cord or energy running through your body on the screen is that you can sometimes be more precise with having a sense of the colors and energies you are bringing in or releasing. Reading yourself and particularly others really requires you to use the screen constantly and consistently, and therefore using it to work with the preparatory techniques and/or in your meditation sessions is great practice. If you haven't yet started practicing any of the techniques, don't worry if you don't quite understand the difference; you will know what I am talking about soon enough. Usually, right before a reading, regardless of whether or not I have meditated first (which I highly recommend), I will, by seeing them on my screen first, run through the above-mentioned meditation tools of grounding, running one of my energies, tuning in to my aura, and establishing a separation object. It's a great warm-up routine.

Clairvoyant Technique #1: Creating a Single Viewing Receptacle

Once you have created your reading screen, create a clear, transparent image of an object that has the ability to hold something else. This is what I refer to as a *viewing receptacle*. This receptacle can be in the shape of a rose, a tulip, a crystal ball, a chalice—really any object that could possibly contain other objects.

I like using a rose the best because roses have so many layers and attributes that will change and take on various forms during a reading.

A rose is harder to visualize than a ball, but ultimately the complexity can provide a richer tool to work with. Once you visualize this on your screen in as much detail as possible, go ahead and destroy it until it no longer exists. You can blow it up, set it on fire, shoot it, erase it, see it getting smaller and smaller until it dissipates, or you can fling it off your screen and watch it fly off somewhere and evaporate.

Sometimes it helps to first roll the rose up into a little ball. Sometimes after you destroy it, you will have a sense that there are still pieces remaining. You can take these and roll them up into a ball and repeat the process until all the pieces have disappeared. This is a step you should never skip because these contain energy that can impact you if you just leave them there. If you feel like you don't want to get rid of them because it took you a while to create them, or it seems too rude or hostile to destroy them, or whatever resistance to this comes up, know that this same resistance could very well be affecting you in your own personal life when it comes to letting go of things.

Invite the Information into Your Reading Receptacle

After creating and destroying a few roses, which will help exercise your clairvoyant muscles and move any energy off your screen, create a brand-new receptacle. Now you are reading to invite in the energy of the person you are going to read.

Read Yourself

Take a really good look at the clear, transparent receptacle or rose you have put up on your screen. Notice its size and shape. If you are interested in learning something about yourself, you can pose a question to it and then just observe it. If you want to know something about someone else in your life who is not present, you can say their name a few times to the receptacle, even write their name underneath it with an imaginary pen and then watch the rose.

The first thing to look for is a color or colors. Just sit back, be very patient, and ask the rose to show you a color that represents the person or information you are seeking. You can watch to see if the rose changes in the slightest way from when you first began to visualize it, or if it demonstrates some sort of movement or does something you did not expect. While you are doing this, an image or picture might arise as well. Whether you can barely notice a minute glimpse of a color or whether you see something in such bold Technicolor that it makes you jump in your seat, be assured that you are on the right track.

Please be aware that if you are reading yourself or someone who is not present, it is going to be a lot harder for you to stay focused. One thing that will really help in this case is to utilize some kind of voice recording device that you can speak into as you do the reading. This will keep you on task. If you find it hard to read yourself first, try practicing on someone else.

Observe Your Viewing Receptacle

The key here is to relax, observe, and have no expectations. Never underestimate the importance of anything that comes up for you, and please do not disregard something just because it looks or sounds ridiculous and you have absolutely no idea what it means. Doing that is the biggest mistake people make. The critical and analytical part of you is going to want to judge everything you see as good/bad, right/wrong, important/insignificant, impressive/dumb, normal/weird—and this is the part of yourself you have to completely ignore. Everything you notice is happening for a reason. You are a detective, an explorer, a researcher. You should not leave any stone unturned—that stone may just turn out to be the most precious of gems. All we need is the first clue, and then we have something to work with, to sink our psychic teeth into. Again, that clue can be a simple color or a very clear image.

If you are not noticing a single thing after a minute or two, I suggest destroying your viewing receptacle and checking to see if you are still centered behind your third eye. Then destroy your current reading screen and create a new one; put up a brand-new receptacle and repeat the above process by stating the name of the person you are interested in learning about, or the question you are desiring information about. You may want to ask your question in a different way. (Please see chapter 5 for a description of questions that will elicit the most helpful information.)

Once You Have Your Clue, Pose a Question or Command

Once you have the first clue—such as a color, a change in your re-ceptacle, or an image—then you have a couple of options. One is to pose a question to that attribute, such as "What do you represent?" or "What do you want to show me?" The other is to give it a command, "Hi there, show me a clue to understand you better" or "You will now reveal more information I can understand." Then all you have to do is sit back and watch the attribute of the receptacle again as a whole, and wait and see what happens next.

Another option is to destroy that receptacle, create a new one, and ask it to show you the meaning or a clue about what you just viewed in the first receptacle. I recommend doing this when you don't feel that anything else is happening from looking at the same one. Remember that when you create and destroy any image, you are moving and re-leasing energy and stimulating your clairvoyance, so don't be afraid or lazy when it comes to recreating your viewing receptacle over and over. At the same time, you must be patient. Sometimes it takes several minutes before you start to notice anything.

From the above description you will start to see that once you have noticed anything, regardless of whether or not it makes sense, you are 90 percent of the way home because you now have something to focus your attention on that is related to the subject of your inquiry.

Reading Another Person Who Is Present

When you are doing a reading for another person who is present, you will use the same techniques as discussed above. The only difference will be in establishing the initial connection and then disconnecting at the end.

Preparing to Read Someone Else

Start off by asking the person you are reading (whom I will refer to as your *readee*) to sit across you at a comfortable distance, usually a few feet away. You can inform the readee that you will have your eyes closed for most if not all of the reading, but that they should keep their eyes open and remain as alert as possible. If the readee matches you in a meditative state, they may be more prone to leave their body and then it will be harder to read them.

Make sure you give yourself time to run through the preparatory visualizations before you begin the reading. This will help keep you secure, energized, and focused, and will also give your clairvoyance a warm-up and jump-start. Some people need more prep time than others, particularly when starting out and particularly if the analytical part of their mind tends to be in overdrive. So it's best to spend time meditating, ideally about thirty minutes before you invite the readee to sit down in front of you. If you don't meditate, you will still be able to do the reading, but just be aware that the information may not flow as easily, it may take you longer to be able to focus, or you may struggle with more self-doubt.

The more readings you do, the more your brain waves will naturally switch over at the beginning of the reading and the less premeditation time you will need. I am at the point after twelve years of consistent reading that the moment I dial the phone to call my client, or I close my eyes as someone sits down before me, I can feel my brain pass into a deeper state, and it becomes difficult for me to just have a normal conversation. Instead, I pretty much need to go right into the reading.

Create a Reading Bubble or Circle

Once you are ready, you can say a prayer if you'd like. You can then visualize a bubble of energy in any color you like surrounding yourself and your readee. You can give the command that any spirits or energies not needed right at that moment, or not serving either one of you, will have to wait outside the circle. Notice if you get a sense of any other colors in your bubble. You can imagine these floating outside the bubble or that you are blowing them away with your exhalations.

Greet the Readee's Spirit

During a clairvoyant reading, we are getting in touch with the essence of a person. We are reading their spirit along with their personality and body. When you put your attention on your readee's spirit, your readee will spontaneously become more in touch with that part of themselves. You can do this simply by imagining that you are sending them a note that says "Hello, spirit" or a present in the form of a bouquet of flowers. You can even ask yourself, "What would this person really like to have?" and then see what comes to you, and send over a symbol that represents that. Then watch to see where this gift you are sending to them goes and whether or not it seems they are receiving it. Wherever it goes is where they are centered. It may therefore go to a certain location within their body or somewhere outside their body. If it seems as if they aren't receiving this gift, then repeat the process. If they still don't appear to receive it, this may be an indication that they will have a hard time receiving the rest of your communication or that it may just take a while for them to get comfortable with the process. Regardless, continue on with the reading for as long as the readee has verbally asked you for one. This process of greeting the readee's spirit is a good one to repeat during the reading if you feel that you need to establish a stronger connection in order to stimulate the flow of images coming to you.

Establish a Connection

There are a couple techniques you can use to establish a stronger connection with your readee, so you can ensure you are reading your readee and not someone or something else.

Option 1—Traditional Color Method: First, you imagine a clear, transparent receptacle such as a lotus flower, to represent the crown chakra. You can see this either on your reading screen or you can imagine it is floating directly above your readee's head. Have the readee state their current name and date of birth a few times, and invite the main color their spirit is vibrating at to come into the flower.

Sit back and wait until you get a sense of a color. If you see many colors, you can give this flower a grounding cord by using the image of its stem to go into the earth. Ask that all extraneous energies and their corresponding colors release, leaving the one energy that represents them right now in present time. If you are not satisfied with this process, you can destroy the lotus flower and create a brand-new one, repeating the process of having the readee say their name.

When your readee says their name, listen to their voice and postulate that the tone and quality of the voice will come into your receptacle and translate itself into visual information such as a color. Once you notice a color, you can match your crown chakra to it by simply visualizing your crown chakra vibrating at this same color, but a notch or two brighter. When you are finished with the reading, you will want to make sure you remove this color from your crown chakra. You can do so by seeing it return to a neutral gold color and then either looking at it to see what color it wants to turn to, or assigning it a color that matches a vibration that seems to represent you or that makes you feel good.

Option 2—Musical Bridge Connection: I developed this method as an alternative to the first, since I was sometimes seeing too many colors and finding it very confusing to decide which one to use.

Visualize a bridge forming between your crown chakra and that of the readee. Imagine that the readee's crown chakra is vibrating at a certain musical note or tone. Then imagine this tone is running down the bridge to your crown chakra, and you are going to tune it to theirs just as if you'd match a note on one string of a guitar to the same note on another string.

When they are in harmony, the two crown chakras and the bridge should be seen as one united color, or you can see a rainbow-type stream and imagine these are vibrating at a faster and faster frequency. Make sure when the reading is over that you call back your energy from this bridge, release any of the readee's energy that might have come through it, let your own crown chakra go back to its original tone, and then completely destroy the bridge in your imagination.

Wrapping Up Your Reading

The best way to end your reading is to create a new receptacle and ask it to show you a next step or action the readee can take that will help them achieve a goal. This is not about you giving advice, but really asking for the answer to come clairvoyantly. Providing the readee with actions that they can take will empower them and remind them that *they* are in charge of their destiny, not you.

A Final Message from Their Guides

You can also ask for the readee's guides to provide a message about the next step to take. Put out an image of a rose, and imagine you are pointing at it. Ask the readee's most helpful guide to put their message inside the rose. You can then watch the rose and imagine you are listening to it as well. Many times, particularly when there is an established time frame during which you are going to complete the reading, you will find that the information about the readee's next step just spontaneously arrives.

Clairvoyant Technique #2

In Clairvoyant Technique #1, we performed the reading using one viewing receptacle, as I've discussed so far throughout this chapter. Clairvoyant Technique #2 is virtually the same, but we will utilize two receptacles, or roses, and look at the relationships between the two. Whether you use roses or another object for your viewing receptacle, it's important to begin using the same image for both receptacles so you can compare the changes within these as the energy/information enters and then transforms them into more complex symbols and images.

I really enjoy working with two roses because it gives me even more to look at. I can focus my attention on one at a time, or step back and watch to see how the two interact with each other. I can also look at what might stand in between them by putting out a third rose in the middle and labeling it as a communication receptacle. This is the best technique for reading relationships of any kind.

Label Your Receptacles

It is important for you to know which receptacle represents which person or thing. So visualize the first one and consciously decide if it should go to the right or left of your reading screen. Then, in your imagination, write the name of the person or thing underneath it or above it. You can say the name of the person as well to that particular receptacle, or if you are reading someone you can ask them to say the corresponding name a few times and you can invite the person's energy whose name it is to show itself in that receptacle.

Then visualize the next receptacle and put that on the opposite side of the screen and repeat the process with either you or your readee stating the second person's name. If you are reading a couple and both people are present with you, you can have one person say their name, and observe the receptacle until you see a color. Then create the second receptacle, invite the second person to say their name, and look for a color.

If both people are not present, have the one person who *is* present say both people's names, one at a time. Tell your receptacle that it is going to show you the nature of the absent person, not as the one saying the names thinks of them, but as the absent person actually is.

As is usually the case whenever one person talks about someone else who is not there, we need to understand that we are going to tend to be more sympathetic to the person who is present, at least at that moment. It helps to keep this in the back of your mind because if all is not perfect in paradise, it's going to be natural to assume that it's the absent person's fault, when in actuality our complaining readee may be the real problem. This fact will usually emerge during the reading, but it helps to go into the reading being conscious of your natural biases, which will favor the person you are speaking to—and who might be paying you for the reading!

Clairvoyant Technique #3

This technique works with reading relationships between people, or between a person and anything they are wondering about. This could include their own clairvoyant or healing ability, their finances, their future, a particular person, any creative project, and so forth.

Instructions

Once you are looking out at your reading screen and have created your connection with whomever you are reading, create a clear, transparent, neutral 3-D receptacle or viewing object such as a rose. Take a good look at this so you have a starting point to work with. Let this rose represent yourself or the person you are reading.

Next, above the rose, create a symbol of something that represents the person's goal again, whether that be more money (perhaps a dollar sign or gold bar), a relationship (you can visualize a wedding ring), a child (visualize a baby), stronger clairvoyant abilities (visualize a third eye), and so on.

Then simply drop the symbol into the rose and notice what happens to the rose once it is filled up with the symbol. You'll be amazed at what comes up!

This is analogous to giving a pill to the client to see how the client responds. In fact, you can do this exercise around medication or a course of treatment if a person is sick and wondering how best to proceed. We can also ask, "Is this food / exercise / therapy / man / job / project good for me (or the client)?"—and then drop it into the viewing receptacle and watch what happens.

I really enjoy this exercise because it's always interesting to see what comes up. Does the rose accept it or spit it out? How does the rose change? Does it look better or worse? If you would like information about the future, then visualize a calendar. Rip out a page with a particular month on it and drop it into the receptacle. You can also do this with a map of a place you are considering moving to, and see what happens.

Examples of How to Work with the Three Techniques

Below I present some common questions asked by readees as well as examples of how to work with the receptacle. I use the words *rose* and *viewing receptacle* interchangeably.

Question: "How is my job going?"

1. Look at one rose that represents the readee's job.
2. Look at one rose for the readee, one rose for their job. Instruct the two roses to show you the nature of their relationship.

3. Look at one rose for the readee, and above this visualize a symbol representing their job. Drop the symbol into the rose and notice what happens to the rose.

Question: "What is wrong with my marriage?"

1. Look at one rose for the marriage.

2. Visualize a rose for each person in the relationship. How do the roses interact?

3. Visualize a rose for each person in the relationship. In the middle put up a third rose to represent the communication.

Question: "Have I hired the right attorney for my lawsuit?"

1. Look at one rose for the readee, one rose for the attorney.

2. Look at one rose for the attorney, one rose for the lawsuit.

Question: "I am considering investing in a few business ventures. Which is the best?"
Or, "I am dating a few guys. Which one is the best?"
Or, "I have a few job offers. Which one is the best?"
Or, "I have a few places in mind to move to. Which place is the best?"

Option 1: Look at a single rose for each venture. Do one at a time; after you are done with one, destroy it and then look at a rose for the next.

Option 2: Put up one rose for the readee and one rose for the venture (or guy, job offer, or location). Watch what happens between the two roses. Once you are satisfied with what you get, destroy all these images and start over with the next person or thing the readee is considering.

Option 3: See three viewing receptacles. Label each one with the thing it represents. Ask for the strongest possibility to stand out among the rest, and look at all three and see what happens.

Question: "I would like to know if I am on my spiritual path."

1. Look at one rose for the readee, one rose for their spiritual path. How do they interact?

2. Look at one rose for the readee. Put up a symbol representing their spiritual path. Watch how the two interact.

3. Look at one rose for the readee. Put up a symbol representing their spiritual path. Drop the symbol into the rose and notice what happens with the rose.

4. Put up a rose that represents the readee's spirituality. See what comes up.

5. Put up one rose for the readee's spirit, one rose for their body.

6. Put up one rose for the part of the readee that is asking the question, one rose for the part of themselves with which they desire to be in touch.

Viewing Receptacles Are Just a Tool to Get You Started

In order to be able to effectively do clairvoyant readings in any situation, we need to understand how to navigate our way and guide ourselves through the reading. As you have seen, we are not just waiting for inspiration to drop from the heavens and hit us over the head, any more than we'd consider sitting down on a sofa and hoping the TV will turn on by itself.

Our reading screen is like a TV that we position at a comfortable distance in front of us. When we visualize a transparent 3-D rose or another object on our screen, and invite the information we are seeking to come into it by saying the name of the readee, it is similar to consciously selecting a TV channel or a specific radio station. We still won't know exactly what program is going to come on, or what the story line or the identity of the characters will be, but we do know we can expect something to appear with as much certainty as if we were to press the on button of a TV.

Asking specific questions is like tuning in to a particular television show. We may understand we are about to view a show that has to do with detectives or romance or animals, and we may even know who some of the characters are and what they are like because we watched it last week, but we still don't know the story line or how the characters might surprise us, nor do we know how the show will ultimately turn out until the images show up on our screen.

Reading screens and viewing receptacles are tools you can always use to access your clairvoyance and that you can return to when you get stuck, when the information stops flowing, or when you aren't sure how to proceed. Once you get started and the information *is* flowing, you will find that you don't need to be focusing on the receptacle/roses on your screen. Some of you may not even want to use a screen, but just the receptacle or vice versa. Often the images will flow freely, mixed in with a knowledge of what the images mean, and you may realize that for several minutes you haven't needed to use your screen or a rose or receptacle, or even consciously pose a question.

Many psychics use tarot cards, tea leaves, or crystal balls in the same manner as the screen and viewing receptacle. Even remote viewers use a technique called an *anagram* to get started. In fact, it can be quite fun to use any of the above as the visualization for your viewing receptacle. You can play around by starting off with the image of a blank tarot card or a tea leaf, crystal ball, or geometric pattern, and see how those work for you.

The advantage to the techniques taught in this book is that they allow you to be self-reliant. You don't need anything other than yourself. If you lose any part of yourself, you will always know how to bring it back!

CHAPTER 5

Navigational Techniques: Asking the Right Questions

He who asks is a fool for five minutes, but he who does not ask remains a fool forever.
—CHINESE PROVERB

One of my strengths as a clairvoyant teacher is helping beginning students learn how to navigate their way through a reading by giving them questions to pose to their reading screens and reading receptacles. Eventually, students begin to ask these same questions without my prompting, and that is when I know they are ready to begin reading on their own or with less supervision. Some people are naturally talented at framing questions or guiding themselves during a reading. Such students often are already experienced counselors, therapists, or interviewers who tend to be more psychologically oriented.

Not every question is created equally and not every question will elicit the response you would like. If you are not "getting anything," if you don't feel as if you are getting clear enough answers, or if you just aren't sure how else to proceed, then you need to create a new, clear viewing receptacle or rose, and pose a new question to it.

From the list below you will notice that two types of questions are generally missing. The first category includes yes or no questions. Yes or no questions usually lead to a dead end. They are overly simplistic and devoid of insight. When a psychic merely reports "yes" or "no," what are you supposed to do with that? It gives you almost no insight into the dynamics of the situation. You are left with a feeling like "Okay, now what?" Also, it's far too easy for our own minds or the plethora of spirits around us to play tricks on us.

The other types of questions to avoid are those that include the word *should*. "Shoulds" are judgments, human constructs of the mind. There really is no such thing as "should" in the realm of spirit. Instead, it's much more fruitful to ask questions that help determine the best course of action that will elicit the most desirable effect.

Below you will find an assortment of questions to ask in a variety of situations. Remember, I am not talking about posing these questions out loud to your client; rather, these questions are to be posed to the viewing receptacle you have created on your reading screen. Sometimes you won't need to pose a question at all. Instead, just put out a receptacle, invite the client's energy into it, and begin to talk about whatever comes. You may find after studying and practicing these questions and possibly referring back to them from time to time that they will become ingrained in your mind so you will never for an instant be stuck asking, "Okay, what next?" In fact, the more you use them, the more the answers will arrive when they are needed—even without you having to consciously voice or pose these questions.

Remember that it's always helpful to frame the question within a particular time frame. Past, present, and future are fine, but when it comes to the future you could be more specific, such as posing questions like "How do things look in three, six, nine, or twelve months, or year to year?"

Questions about Relationships When Someone Has a Particular Person in Mind

- What is the nature of the relationship in the present?
- What are the dynamics of the relationship in the present?
- Can you give me a symbol of the relationship?
- Can you give me a symbol of X to know I am looking at the right person?
- Why is X behaving as he/she is right now?
- Let me see the communication and what might be influencing it.
- How does X feel about Y or Y feel about X?
- Is X going to do what Y wants or vice versa?
- What is in my client's best interest or the best interest of both people at the present time?
- What is the spiritual agreement between X and Y?
- Why have X and Y come together?
- Have X and Y had any other incarnations together?
- Let me see a symbol to know if the changes will occur.
- Why is the relationship not working out?
- If the relationship is not going to happen, why did they feel so strongly about it?
- Why are they having such a hard time letting go?
- How were they so easily misled?
- Is X having an affair or being honest?

Questions about Creating the Ideal Relationship

I don't like to leave people hanging with no hope. So if you see that a specific relationship is not going to pan out as expected, I suggest you pose the following questions:

- How does the readee's relationship space look in general?
- What will the readee's next relationship be like?

- How will the readee meet their next partner?
- What will the readee's next partner be like?
- What does the readee need to do to heal their relationships in general?
- What does the readee need to do in order to create the ideal relationship?
- Why has this person been caught in a pattern?
- What actions or next steps does this person need to take?
- What does the ideal person look like for the readee?
- What is standing in between the readee and manifesting the relationship they desire?
- Look at a rose for the relationship pattern. Look at the rose for the person's relationship in the present or their future. Compare the two roses. What looks different?

Relationship to Oneself

For me the most important relationship we can have is the one with ourself. Therefore this is the most important relationship to look at during a clairvoyant reading. This relationship encompasses self-love, one's spiritual path, one's purpose in life, and so forth. When someone asks me for a spiritual reading or life path reading, or tells me to "just look and see what comes up," the techniques offered below are those that I usually use to begin accessing the information the readee seeks.

- Look at one rose for the readee and one rose for their heart.
- Look at one rose for the readee and one rose for their spiritual path.
- Put up a rose for readee and drop a symbol of heart of path in their rose.
- Put up a rose for them, another for their inner voice. See the relationship.
- Put up one rose for their god of the heart space and look at it.

- Put up an image of the readee and have them look in the mirror; see what happens.

- See a rose for the readee and put in it something they want—e.g., to develop their spirituality—and see what happens.

- See a path and put the readee on the path and then tell them to show you something as they walk down the path.

- See one rose for their inner child and one rose for their parent; see what happens.

- Put up a rose for the past life that most resonates with the readee's current life.

- Put up a rose that represents the readee's clairvoyance.

- Put up a rose that represents the readee's healing abilities.

- Look at a rose/receptacle for each of the readee's chakras.

- Look at a rose for the readee's clairaudience and spirit guides.

Career and Finance Questions

Questions regarding one's career aspirations or changes are very common. When a client asks you to tell them about their career, you will need to decide whether or not to do the reading "blind"—with no prior knowledge of what they do for a living or are considering doing—or if you want to ask the readee for some background information so you can get more quickly to the heart of the answer they seek.

For years I never asked for this information unless the readee offered it. I enjoyed the challenge of seeing what I got, even though it was more stressful. However, over the years I have become a little less patient. Now I will often ask readees for background just to save time, since they already know what they do (although they get a kick out of me seeing it anyway). They may be curious about other information or have some challenging issues that we'd be better off spending our time on. Also, if I already know what the readee does, I will be less inclined to misinterpret whatever information comes as information about the future when it really pertains to the present (something I do quite frequently).

Options

- Put up a clear transparent 3-D rose on your reading screen that represents the readee's present career. Look for a color. Or look for it to change or move or for a new image to appear. Ask the rose to show you whatever your client needs to know the most about their job space.
- Put up one rose for the readee and another one for their job and see what happens when the two come together.

Ask the following questions:

- Is this the right job for the readee?
- What is the right job for the readee?
- What kind of work would be most fulfilling for the readee?
- How will my readee start earning income?
- What job would better serve this person?
- What fulfilling job will the readee have in the future?
- If this person could be doing any job, what would it be?
- What energy is keeping this person from knowing their ideal job?
- What energy is keeping this person stuck in their current job?
- What does this person need to know in order to get unstuck?
- Compare two roses, one representing the readee's workspace and the other representing the readee. Do the colors and roses match?
- How can this person be happier in their work?
- Put out a rose for the readee's finances in general; see how it looks.

- Put out a rose for a particular financial investment.
- Put out a rose for a person who could help the readee with their finances.
- What is in the way of the readee earning more money?
- Put up a rose for their creative or manifestation space.

Of course this list is not exhaustive, and you most certainly don't need to memorize it before practicing or doing a reading. These questions are just here to guide you when you are stuck or need some inspiration. From the number of questions or suggestions on this list, you will see that it's really possible to read someone for hours, if not indefinitely—although I am not suggesting you do that!

Formatted Reading

A formatted reading is one that provides a visual structure to follow. I offer a few examples of these in *You Are Psychic*. I have recently begun using a new type of formatted reading that is working really well for the students in my one-on-one training program.

If you are reading someone else, establish the reading color (see chapter 4) and then ask your readee to repeat their name. As they do, visualize a diamond-shaped figure on your screen or out in front of you. Visualize a circle or a transparent rose at each point, and designate each point as one of the following: the physical body, the spiritual body, the emotional body, and the mental body. In your imagination, write the name of the body above the corresponding point. If you have a hard time remembering which point is which, you can draw it on a piece of paper first. I like to put the spiritual body at the top point, the physical body at the bottom, the emotional body to the left, and the mental body to the right, but I don't think the order matters at all. Sometimes this will change depending on the person you are reading, and might provide additional insight into what they are giving priority to in their life.

There are a few things you are looking for in this structure. The first and perhaps most important is to look at the lines in between the point. Are the lines connected to each point? Are they even? Are they smooth or jagged? Is it easier to see one part of the triangle (e.g., the top half or right side) as opposed to another part? It's helpful to look for a color for each point, and to notice if the colors are equally as bright, or if the circles/roses at the points seem bigger, smaller, clearer, or stand out in any way from the others. You can even look for a color for the center of the diamond and see what that represents, perhaps the person as a whole.

Take a look at these overall elements first, and then you can choose which aspect stands out that you'd like to address before the others. Then go through the process you've already learned by focusing your attention on the part that stands out, and asking it to show you what it represents. If nothing comes to you, you can try this: pose the question about the aspect in question to a new viewing receptacle/rose. Example questions might be "Why is the line broken between the spiritual and the emotional body?" and "Why is the point at the emotional body large but the one with the mental body small?" Notice what happens to the receptacle and then ask whatever happens to show you more information in the form of another image and/or on a knowingness level. After addressing these aspects, you can take one point (as a circle or a rose) at a time and focus your attention to see what emerges.

Lately I've been having my students use this type of reading without the readee asking any questions or giving any information about themselves, and then once the student has covered all aspects of the diamond shape, I invite the volunteer they are practicing on to ask whatever questions they've been wondering about. What we usually discover is that the person's questions were mostly answered in the first part prior to the student asking them. We also find that the energy shifts (it usually feels heavier) when the person asks questions, because the questions are often coming from the mind only and are about solving problems—which are defined as such by itself, as opposed to looking at the bigger picture that takes the person's whole being into account. Still, there is value in answering their questions, as doing so tends to quiet the demands of the logical mind.

CHAPTER 6

Psychic Hearing

A wise old owl sat on an oak / The more he saw, the less he spoke / The less he spoke, the more he heard / Why aren't we like that wise old bird?

—UNKNOWN

Clairaudience and Telepathy

Clairaudience is the ability to access information through a combination of inner hearing and thought. *Telepathy* is a type of clairaudience and is the sending and receiving of thoughts from one person or spirit to another. During a clairvoyant reading, these abilities will spontaneously emerge, but there are definitely things we can do to develop and direct these abilities. In order to give you a taste of what psychic hearing is like, I recommend doing the following exercise.

Exercise to Understand Clairaudience
Close your eyes and turn your attention inward. Silently say "I love you" ten times to yourself, inside your own head. Listen to yourself saying these words. Then do this again, but this time do it as if you were shouting "I love you," again only inside your mind. Now do this

again as if you were singing the words. Do it one more time with some kind of foreign accent.

You will most surely notice that you can hear yourself forming these words and that the volume, tone, pitches, and cadence will have varied even though you were not physically saying the words. This is exactly what telepathic or clairaudience messages sound like. The only difference is that in this exercise you were intentionally forming these thoughts. When they come in on a psychic level they will arrive unexpectedly, as if they were news to you. This is analogous to the relationship between visualization and clairvoyance. When you visualize, you are directing your mind to conjure up a certain image. When you are being clairvoyant, your visualizations begin to act outside the boundaries of what you intended or expected.

Telepathy Coming from Another Person

Clairaudient messages come from a variety of sources. They often come directly from the person you are reading or focusing on. Sometimes you may hear a voice that sounds just like that of your client or someone you are sitting close to that includes an "I" statement, such as "I can't stand this anymore" or "I want this more than anything." When this happens you will often have a very clear sense it's your readee speaking to you just as if your readee were addressing you with words.

Sometimes a message will come in from a spirit guide, a deceased relative, or some kind of entity that has a vested interest in the readee. The message might just spontaneously enter your mind, or you might request an answer to a particular or general question such as "Please tell me what my client needs to hear the most," "Why has this person really come to me today?" or "What the hell did that image just mean?!" Once you ask the questions, be as still and as silent as possible and put all your attention on your ears. The more the messages come in words or a tone unlike those you typically use, the more certain you can be the message is coming from a source outside yourself, particularly when the information surprises you.

You need to be aware that some spirits will lie to you. I haven't experienced this so much during a clairvoyant reading (except for a few occasions when the language was abusive, which sent up a red flag right away), but I have been relaxing at home when I have heard a message such as "Linda is dead." I was very worried when that happened, so I called my good friend Linda who advised me she was very much alive but had been engaged in a psychic battle of sorts with beings who seemed to be projecting death or suicide thoughts at her. If you wish to seek a message during a reading, it's helpful for this reason to direct your questions to a particular source, such as the readee's Higher Self, the spirit guide who is most loving or most knowledgeable in a specific subject, or a particular deity you feel connected with. If you get a very strong message, you can always use your clairvoyance to help you "see" its source.

Early on in my clairvoyant training, I realized I couldn't always trust the auditory messages I heard, so I got into the habit of backing up any clairaudient messages with my clairvoyant images. I have this little game I play with myself even now in which I only rely on messages as a last resort, as if to do otherwise would somehow be cheating. I think I do this because if all I have to do is listen and repeat word for word what I am getting, it is much easier than taking the time to focus, receive, and interpret the clairvoyant information and, as I've noted already, also somewhat less reliable.

Clairvoyant images almost always come from the reader and the readee. On rare occasions, an entity may throw a picture at a clairvoyant. I say "throw a picture" because that's how it feels, like an intrusion. It has a different quality than most other images or visions, and is usually unrelated to the topic or has sexual or violent connotations. If you've ever been falling asleep or meditating and, out of the blue, saw a demonic face or a sex picture flash before your eyes, this is what you were very possibly experiencing.

Although they are definitely subject to misinterpretation, clairvoyant images don't lie, whereas spirits are a lot less dependable unless you have an established connection with a particular one. In my experience, there is a depth of information that comes from clairvoyant symbols that clairaudient messages often do not match. As indicated elsewhere in this book, when you see information you can alter it, so clairvoyance auto-matically paves the way for healing to occur in a way that sharing verbal messages does not. Still, there are many times when I draw a blank with my clairvoyance, usually because I am either feeling pressured for time or concerned my readee doesn't understand me, and then I am extremely grateful for the messages that come soon after I request them. Many times I will not understand the message but my readee will.

Most of the famous psychics you have heard of and/or observed, from Sylvia Browne to John Edward to James Van Praagh, rely heav-ily on their clairaudience and the information they receive either from their own guides or the deceased relatives of their clients (particularly Edward and Van Praagh). This is why these psychics are also consid-ered mediums. Receiving auditory messages works well for them, and enables them to access and communicate information very quickly. Compare the difference between looking at a picture and describ-ing it in your own words to someone else, and repeating word for word what someone else is telling you. Describing the picture takes a lot longer. Therefore these psychics do very well on radio and TV programs, where their messages need to be delivered in short fifteen-second sound bites.

I have great respect for these psychics, although I do think, at least in the media, that there is far too much focus on communications with the deceased. This focus has contributed to a false impression that the only thing psychics do is communicate with the dead. High-profile psychics face grueling challenges that require more talent than just their psychic abilities, because they often work/perform in front of enormous groups, and along with receiving messages they need to very quickly figure out exactly whom the messages are for, all the while being bombarded with massive amounts of telepathic interference from the audience ("Pick me, pick me!") and the gallery of entities that desire to be heard as well.

Most of these psychics are self-taught or have been doing readings since they were very young. Therefore, they don't know the exact steps that anyone can utilize to perform a reading, although from their most recent books and appearances, I am noticing a trend in which many such psychics seem to be shifting their focus to teaching as opposed to merely demonstrating their own talents. I don't know if this is a sign of their own personal development or a sign of the times or both, but it's one I appreciate because it sends the message that these talented psychics are examples of what is possible for others, too.

Channeling

Clairaudience is a mild form of channeling. I am still not certain if it's possible to hear the messages from spirits if they are completely outside your body and aura and disconnected physically from you, or if they do have to be at least partially connected or corded into you in order for you to hear them. Channeling is the spiritual ability to bring another spirit into one's body. Spirits can plug into any part of a living person's body or energy field. Healing spirits often just plug into a healer's hand chakras. Spirits that wish to speak through a person will usually plug into the telepathic channels that are located on the back of the head behind the ears, and behind the neck and throat (fifth) chakra.

When I've attended channeling sessions, it's usually been difficult for me to be there because my own telepathic channels were being empathetically activated, and the pressure or pain on them was intense. I think the same spirits being channeled through the hosts were attempting to come through me, and I was not in agreement with this at all. In fact, as I write at this very moment I can feel someone or something trying to plug in. There are really millions of spirits out there that would love nothing better than to communicate with someone— really anyone who will listen! Some of these spirits also plug into the back of the head, behind the sixth chakra and also into one's crown chakras. Even when a spirit is plugged into just one or a few areas of the body, the body can be readily influenced by that spirit's emotions and thoughts. When the spirit is plugged into the throat chakra, the person's voice may be drastically altered, but usually their appearance will remain the same.

In full-body channeling, a large portion of the channeler's spirit leaves their body to make room for another spirit to completely move into their body and energy field. When the spirits have exchanged places, the channeler often takes on the physical appearance, mannerisms, and voice of the entity being channeled. The spirit that owns the body will frequently be unaware of what is being stated or will not retain a memory of what was said. Two of the best known full-body channelers are J. Z. Knight, who channels Ramtha and authored *The White Book,* and the late Jane Roberts, who channeled a group of beings known as Seth and wrote books such as *The Nature of Personal Reality* and *Seth Speaks.*

Some mediums will channel just about any being that wants to come through them at any given time, while others are committed to a single entity or a collective group of beings. It is pretty interesting to see a female medium channeling a male spirit. Sometimes I wonder if this doesn't feel just a little bit strange to the woman's husband, particularly when the session is over and it's time to go to bed!

We are all constantly channeling to varying degrees at every moment, whether we are channeling our parents' judgments or channeling dirty jokes from entities that we picked up the night before at the local bar. Some people attend schools and workshops to learn how to minimize the risks of channeling and how to recognize when they are spontaneously channeling in their everyday life, so they can avoid being affected by energies that don't always have their best interests in mind. I believe that many of the mentally ill homeless people you see talking to themselves on the streets are frequently channeling multitudes of beings at any given time. These beings like to talk and don't care whether or not anyone is listening. I also think that when people say things such as "I don't know why I just did that," "I know I did it, but it's not me," or "I haven't been myself lately," that they are being more accurate than they even know.

Some spirits are very adept at working with channelers. They intuitively understand how to effectively plug into a body, and to speak in a voice and use language that can be readily understood. Others have no clue as to how to achieve a proper connection. Until they are taught by the channeler or another clairvoyant who can see them, they will plug into the wrong body part or communicate in the wrong language. Just as with other types of spirit guides, channeling guides range from being ignorant and unconscious to being fully enlightened ascended masters.

When channeling you want to be very careful about whom you invite in; otherwise you may end up with a very unruly houseguest who doesn't know when to leave. For this reason I don't recommend channeling without proper instruction and supervision by an experienced teacher. Channeled spirits tend to have a specialty. Some are healers, other are teachers, still others are charismatic entertainers, and some are just vagabond souls seeking further experiences for themselves. Full-body channeling is very hard on the body. People who engage in this type of practice are vulnerable to illness and a shortened life span and sometimes might begin to incur karma based on the spirits' actions. This is what happens when a person goes on a rampage, committing an act of violence and then having no memory of it the next morning. People who have been drinking or using drugs are obviously more vulnerable to this phenomenon.

If you have a strong interest in channeling, I recommend checking out the Aesclepion Healing Center in Marin County, California, or the Southern California Psychic Institute in the Los Angeles area. The Berkeley Psychic Institute also has a transmedium program.

Although I never intend to channel other entities when I perform clairvoyant readings, occasionally a spirit will plug into my throat chakra, particularly when I am reading a client's deceased relative who was pushy or domineering when he or she (usually he) was alive. On a few occasions, this spirit's male voice has come through my own so strongly that I found myself talking like that spirit. My voice still sounded like my voice, but I felt compelled to speak in a manner that was definitely not my own, as if I were reading for a character unlike myself in a play. Some of the words I was using were not part of my everyday vocabulary and my readees immediately told me that I sounded just like their father or grandfather who had recently passed away. I also realized that I was speaking more emphatically and expressively than I usually do. On one occasion, I sounded like a hell-and-brimstone preacher, getting all riled up when deep inside I really was very detached from whatever I was saying.

I must admit that these experiences were rather entertaining. However, after these readings I had a more difficult time making separations from the spirits than I usually do, and it took me a few days before I seemed completely back to myself. Sometimes channeling a spirit you've just met is a lot like dancing with a guy at a bar that you're not really into; it's hard to get rid of him for the rest of the night!

It seems as though some people are just pre-wired for channeling while others do have to work at it. Those who are naturals at it often do it throughout their day, usually with little awareness. These people are called *transmediums*. The *trans* prefix indicates that transmediums can channel other spirits, and they also tend to run their own energy through other people's bodies.

The biggest challenge anyone who wishes to channel faces involves trust and fear issues. The faith healers in the Philippines channel some of the most bad-ass spirits imaginable. This is what allows them to perform the psychic surgery and other feats most people consider to be impossible or miracles. Accepting some of these beings into your body is kind of like trying to stuff an elephant into a jar or filling up a bicycle tire with a truckload of helium. It is very intense, and many of these healers cope with this by turning to alcohol or other addictive behaviors despite their unfailing spiritual and religious convictions. One of the biggest lessons I've learned are the two are in no way mutually exclusive!

One of the most striking characteristics I noticed with the healers who were performing extraordinary feats was that they all had the ability to completely surrender to the spirit working through them. I tried this a few times and had some interesting experiences, but I was very aware of the amount of fear and caution I had blocking me from completely letting go in order to let these beings take over to do their job. Years later, my desire to experience this is no longer there, particularly after recognizing my ego's involvement in that desire. For now, I am content being just me . . . at least this minute!

I am not going to include instruction in full-blown channeling in terms of inviting other entities to enter your body, since this is not my area of expertise and I believe that it should be done under the guidance of an experienced teacher and in person. However, in chapter 16 you can learn how to work with a healing guide that will plug into your hand or arm channels. Below I will give you some suggestions about how to develop your clairaudience, which could include telepathy from your readee or from spirits that remain outside your body. I also offer advice about what to do if it seems these spirits are getting a little too frisky or too close for comfort.

How to Work with Clairaudience

I suggest following the clairvoyant techniques first, and then incorporating the skill of clairaudience once you have practiced your clairvoyance a few times. That is not to say you won't naturally be receiving information on a psychic hearing level or that you shouldn't use it sooner, but since clairvoyance for some people is a little trickier, it's worked well for me and most of my students to get the visual flowing first and to use clairaudience to fill in the blanks. You can fall back on clairaudience when you are feeling stuck in understanding the meaning of your images, when you want further communication, or when you just feel ready to incorporate this skill into your repertoire. Some of you will have already experienced your clairaudience often enough at times when you were meditating, falling asleep, or relaxed—and for you it will most likely come easily and quite frequently when you are purposefully doing readings.

Telepathy

A good time to start calling forth your telepathy during a reading is when you see an image of your client or of a person or animal, and you wish to understand something about them or their intentions, desires, or actions. You can address these images with any question you are wondering about just as you would in "real life," but perhaps with even more boldness and candor. For example, you can say something to the image such as, "Hey, [name], how do you truly feel about this situation?" or "Hi, what do you need more than anything right now?"

Once you pose a question to these images (see chapter 5 for a list of helpful questions), the most important thing to do is to be still and silent inside yourself and wait for a response. Give the images time. Not every one of them will have an immediate response, although you won't usually have to wait more than a minute or two. Put your attention on your inner ears; you can even imagine your ears are becoming larger in order to take in the auditory information. Just wait, as if you were waiting for someone on the other end of the phone to pick up and start telling you something you've been waiting to hear, or as if you were waiting for a teacher who stands before you at a podium to start a lecture. Remind yourself (or pretend) that there is no difference between hearing with your outer ears and your inner ears, just as seeing with your inner eyes is as easy as seeing with your outer eyes. Part of the reason this doesn't seem as natural to most of us is because we just don't expect it to be as natural.

Troubleshooting: If you don't get a response, you can try rephrasing your question, or you can go back to the visual technique using the viewing receptacle method and then later on in the reading attempt to do this exercise again with another image. This is particularly good to do if you have a sense that you are looking at a spirit that spontaneously pops up or is one that your readee asked you to look at. Nevertheless, don't shy away from using your clairvoyance with spirits, as doing so will help you to see them as they used to look if they once had bodies.

Remember also that you can always address your client's Higher Self or spirits by sending them a hello in the form of a note, some flowers, or a little gift. Wait for them to respond, or you can imagine you are shaking their hands and asking them to tell you how they feel about something, particularly when the client is struggling with a tough decision. When a client has posed a question such as "Tell me what I should do," it is a great opportunity to put it back on the deepest, most intimate part of the client by asking that deep part to tell you what its greatest longing is.

Future self: Ask the client's future self a question.

A fun technique to use is to ask your client's future self to appear before you. You can call forth that future self at a specific date or point in time, or you can ask the future self to tell you the date they have traveled from along with whatever information you are seeking. If the future self doesn't seem to be in very good shape, you could even, before sending them back to the future, do a healing on them as you would for a person or spirit in the present time.

Instant Knowing

Instant knowing is different from clairaudience. Instant knowing will sometimes precede a clairvoyant image or follow it. It requires less interpretation than the other two abilities, and it's more subtle although it seems to be quite accurate. Sometimes it's almost as if you can feel it land within your mind, and you would barely notice it if it weren't for the fact that the information is not anything you could have otherwise known. It doesn't come in as a message; it's just somehow there.

This ability, I believe, is often at play in our everyday lives. Have you ever not been able to remember a name or fact and then suddenly the information was there, so clear it made you contemplate the nature of memory itself? That is quite similar to the experience of instant knowing.

How to Develop and Work with Knowingness

Follow the instructions for working with your clairaudience. However, instead of asking for the information to come through your ears, imagine that there is a special place in your mind you are going to. Be as quiet as possible. Instruct your mind that it will receive an answer effortlessly, and then just wait. This is going to be much easier after you've already been using your clairvoyance during a session and after meditating for a while.

Many people's minds are so cluttered and busy that it's hard for them to hear clairaudient messages or notice intuitive or divinely inspired thoughts. That is one reason why people tend to spontaneously begin experiencing their psychic abilities when they start meditating or increase their meditation time. Because clairvoyant reading causes you to maintain extreme inner focus and concentration, it is the most powerful form of meditation I've experienced. Therefore, usually by the second or third reading you do on someone else, you will spontaneously experience your instant knowingness. There isn't much you need to do to get it to happen, except perhaps visualize your crown chakra opening prior to or during the reading and also asking for your instant knowingness to work for you. Of course, when some bit of information does come to you in this way, seemingly landing in your head without warning, by all means express this information, regardless of whether it is accompanied by any visual pictures. You will most certainly find that it is quite accurate. I had a good friend when I was undergoing my own training who rarely ever saw pictures, but who received crystal-clear information on a knowing level quite often.

Again, this will often spontaneously happen as you are utilizing the clairvoyant techniques presented in chapter 4. Usually it starts to happen for most people by their third reading, sometimes sooner and sometimes later. You don't need to really understand what it is or what it's like before you experience it. It would happen even if I didn't mention it at all. When it does, you will understand what I am talking about.

Music in Your Head

Quite frequently, when a song is playing over and over in your head, particularly when it's one you think you didn't just hear a few minutes or hours before, it's very possible that the lyrics that are being repeated have a strong message for you. In fact, the way to get the song to stop playing in your mind is to listen to the lyrics and think about what they might mean for you right now. As soon as you do this, you will often find the music just miraculously stops, even if it's been bugging you for hours. This is because there is something out there that is using this method to get your attention.

On numerous occasions I have heard songs during readings, dreams, and in my everyday life that all ended up having strong significance. In fact, not too long ago I did an audition for a psychic TV show. The producer wanted to test me, so she showed me an envelope with a picture of something in it and asked me to tell her what the picture was. I was feeling nervous and didn't get much of a visual image, but then I heard the lyrics to "We Are Family," the song about sisters most famously performed by Sister Sledge. The producer ripped open the envelope and inside was a photograph of two twin girls. The producer told me the photo was of her and her sister.

Sometimes I feel as though I'm in the movie *Groundhog Day*. It doesn't matter that I have verification just about every day that I am psychic. Every time something like this happens, I'm still as amazed as if it were the very first time.

CHAPTER 7

The Future

The best way to predict the future is to invent it.
—ALAN KAY

Many people initially go to a psychic because they are curious about their future. They want to know if that screenplay will sell, when they might start their own business, if they will meet Prince Charming, if their husband or wife will ever snap out it, if they will be financially secure in their old age, or how, if, and when they will find a way to pay next month's rent. However, what people usually don't realize is that most of the information that actually appears or is accessible during a clairvoyant reading tends to be about the present or past. One of the main reasons for this is that much of the future seems dependent on one's actions, thoughts, and feelings in the present. Another reason is that our physical bodies are always in the present and can't be anywhere else. Since the person asking the question about their future is asking it in the present, we as clairvoyants naturally go to where they are, in the present, unless we consciously direct ourselves to another specific point in time.

None of this is to say that we won't ever spontaneously tune in to the future. Sometimes we will. Sometimes we will know this is what we are doing, sometimes not. Sometimes we will think we are reading the future when we are actually viewing an event that has already occurred.

Various researchers have discovered that, when given a vast array of information to view and describe, psychics and remote viewers are more likely to tune in to what is referred to as *peak emotional events*. We are all obviously having experiences around the clock, twenty-four hours a day. There is no way a psychic would have the time, the need, or the interest to tap into every action, behavior, feeling, or thought, so we are more likely to find the moment of drama when emotions were most heavily invested.

When you recall your past, you are not recalling everything you did at every second. You tend to recall your happiest moments, your worst moments, and the moments when something out of the ordinary happened to you. Actually, you aren't just recalling the moments as they happened; you are recalling your feelings and perceptions of a moment, and all the subsequent thoughts and feelings of that moment.

Your thoughts about the future really are no different from your memories of the past. You are projecting ideas and feelings onto something called the future, but the quality of these are no different from memories and not necessarily any less "real." Psychics and remote viewers tend to tune in to the most dramatic, emotionally charged events and memories of a person's life, particularly those of interest to the psychic. Sometimes we can see events in the future, but again it gets confusing. Are we seeing the actual event, or are we seeing a future memory of it? The two are not the same.

The Anxiety Factor

Many people want to know about the future because they are feeling anxious. What they forget is that even though they are thinking about the future, the anxiety is with them right now. As they allow their thoughts to fixate on unpleasant future possibilities, they become even more stressed out. For these people, the answer is ultimately not about knowing what the future will bring, for what if it is going to bring some challenges they think they'd rather avoid? Instead, the answer is to help them (or ourselves) to identify and release the anxiety they are currently experiencing. (Grounding, running your energy, and doing clairvoyant readings are excellent prescriptions for this.)

Because many people use their thoughts about the future to heal their present pain, discontent, and anxiety, they will often send their creative energy into the future and then have difficulty taking steps in the present because they don't have enough of their own life force left in their body. If you find yourself obsessing about the future, or being so goal-oriented that you realize you have not been enjoying yourself for a long period of time in the present, it is likely that a part of you is out there and may need to be retrieved, which can be done through awareness and can be initiated with the simple visualization offered at the end of this chapter.

The Future and Decision Making

A large percentage of people who come for readings ask about the future because they believe such knowledge will help them make the best decisions to achieve their goals and avoid failure. For example, they may wish to know how a particular investment will pay off in the future in order to help them decide whether or not to invest at all. They may wonder how a job prospect will work out so they can decide whether or not it's worth their time to even go through the lengthy application process.

As I noted, people may want to know whether or not the person they are in a relationship with is going to ever change so they can decide if they should end things or hang in there a while longer. This is where things get confusing to our little minds, which can really only comprehend events in terms of linear causation and effect. People are essentially attempting to change their futures by knowing them, and adjusting their behavior accordingly.

This leads us into an area that is as controversial as it is mind-boggling. I think—no, let me rephrase that—I *know* there are many people who could be helped by treating themselves to the gift of a quality clairvoyant reading but who fear they might receive "bad news" about their future. In the same way, there are a multitude of people out there avoiding development and awareness of their own psychic abilities due to the same fear. Many people even question the ethics of accessing information about the future. These same issues arise in the ongoing theoretical debate about time and time machines and the question "If you travel to the future or the past, will you irrevocably change the course of events that were really supposed to have happened?"

This debate seems to beg the question "What events were really supposed to have happened: the ones that would have occurred had the time travel (or psychic intervention) not taken place, or the ones that occurred once the time traveler influenced events or the psychic information was acted upon?" From here we can ask, "Is there really any particular set of events that are ever really *supposed* to happen?" Which leads us into questions about who is making these decisions. Is it God, our Higher Selves, some little green men in shiny space suits? To try to answer these questions is like driving on an endless network of highways that all connect and twist and wind together in your brain, but all lead you in one big fat circle to nowhere. These are interesting questions, but they really distract us from forward movement.

From my own experiences as a clairvoyant, psychic teacher, and recipient of many awesome readings, it is clear to me that yes, there are definitely times when people do alter their behavior based on a reading. Sometimes this is the most valuable thing a reading can do, particularly when those behaviors are self-destructive ones that lead to unproductive thoughts and unpleasant feelings and consequences. However, it's important to understand that most of the time, when a person is given information about the future, they will *not* change their behavior. The course they were headed on remains the same. They still marry that guy or invest that money. The difference is they have more consciousness as they experience events that had been accurately predicted, and they are better able to understand what is happening to them or why it's happening as they begin to heal from it once it has all come to pass.

The fact that many times people don't act on advice about the future makes me wonder if there is a built-in, set plan. Another possibility is that at the instant you began the reading you already began altering the readee's future, and therefore the future you are looking at is different from the one that would have been viewable had you not viewed it. Or perhaps the particular future you are seeing is there precisely because you are seeing it!

Some clients really do take into consideration the information they get during the reading, and then they are able to expand their vision of what is possible for themselves. For example, I might see a client in a leadership/supervisory position, when they have always been a clerk working for someone else. The client hadn't even considered this type of job. As a result of the reading, the client decides to stop applying for secretarial jobs and instead applies for management positions.

In one reading I did last year with a client named Katie, who lived in Florida, I looked into the future and had a sense she was going to be living on the west coast. I also saw her approaching some executives with her portfolio, and one of them seemed to be smiling and shaking hands with her. I had the sense Katie would be offered a position almost equivalent to his. This seemed rather far-fetched to her at that moment, as she was not even thirty years old and had no supervisory experience. However, just about one year later she called me for another reading. She advised me that she had in fact moved to Los Angeles, where she had been thinking of moving for a very long time, and that she had met a man at a bar who turned out to be the CEO of an advertising firm. He offered her a position starting at $90,000 a year.

However, a few weeks later, the company merged with another and they had to give the position to an executive with the other company. (I had not seen this far into the future in the previous reading.) In the second reading, which focused on her losing the position, I got the sense that Katie had raised her energy enough to manifest that opportunity, but she wasn't really ready on a number of levels to handle the demands that would be required of her. Her self-esteem was not high enough yet, and she really needed to do some general old-fashioned growing up before she was ready to take on a position such as this.

Basically, she needed to have patience and once again let the natural course of time work its magic.

While I rarely have anyone tell me I am wrong about what I see regarding their past or their present, I find it most amusing that more than a few times someone has told me I was wrong about what I was seeing for their future. (Let me clarify: they told me this before the "future" happened!) This is because they can't possibly imagine themselves having that kind of opportunity or doing what I see them doing. Why? The person asking about the future is not there yet. In order to be there they will need to raise their self-esteem, open their heart, and change their way of thinking (which might require an entire mental overhaul or paradigm shift), and most important, raise the frequency at which their energy vibrates. The helpful thing here is that I've planted a seed, shown them an outline of a new door, and perhaps even slipped a tiny wedge into the door of new possibilities so they can begin to open it wider when they are ready. As a psychic, a healer, and a person trying to remain sane, I need to allow them to grow at their own pace, even when that pace is much slower than I'd prefer.

Don't forget: reading the future, and then seeing if you were right, can be fun!

Reading the Future

Pinpointing the exact point in time of an event can be quite challenging. In fact, earlier in my training there were times I thought I was getting information about the future only to discover I was describing events that had already taken place. Now that I am more aware that this might be the case, rather than ever assuming I am accessing information about the future, I instead will consciously focus my attention on a specific point in the future and request information about a certain topic.

Future Reading Option One (General)

Visualize your reading screen. Then place a clear crystal rose on it. Underneath it, label it "the future." Instruct it to show you some future events. Look for a color first, then ask the color to show you what it represents. If you are not getting a sense of when these events will occur, once you start to describe them you can ask your rose to show you a symbol that will help your readee understand when they are going to happen or recognize when they're about to happen. Some of the symbols that come up might have to do with the weather. For example, if you see the readee shoveling snow it is likely the event is going to happen in the winter. If you see a graduation cap, this may indicate the event will occur sometime around or after a graduation.

Sometimes you may not get colors, but your rose might do something that gives you some indication—for example, it may grow very large and open up, or it might shrivel and fall over on its side. This will at least give you some indication whether or not the specific events you or your readee are wondering about will turn out as hoped. This is one reason why utilizing an image of a rose can be helpful when performing clairvoyant readings.

Future Reading Option Two (Specific)

Visualize your reading screen. Put out a clear transparent rose on it. Underneath it you can imagine you are writing the date in the future about which you'd like information. This could be a specific day, as in the case of your readee requesting information about the outcome of their immigration interview, court date, or wedding. More often, however, you may just wish to choose a certain period of time in the future, such as three, six, or nine months, or one year, three years, or ten years. Remember that the future encompasses millions of seconds, events, and feelings, so you are just going to tune in to a few events at most that the person perhaps needs to hear about now.

You can ask to see anything about the future, or you can pose any specific question to the rose about a particular point in time. For example, you can ask the rose to show you information about the readee's relationship three months from now or you can ask the rose to show you if the readee will have a relationship in three months. If it doesn't look as if they will, you can look ahead six months or a year and ask for images to appear if the readee will be alone or with someone else.

If you are seeing events that you know are not pleasing the readee, you can put out a new viewing receptacle and ask it to show you information regarding the reason the readee is not creating what they want, or what they think they want!

Is It Good or Bad to Know the Future?

Most psychics don't want to see "bad things" any more than their clients want to hear them. For this reason, most psychics don't pick these up unless there is a warning message there. This doesn't mean you shouldn't look at the future; on the contrary, you can be confident that if you look into the future you will see the things that your readee can deal with. It also doesn't mean that your readee is going to react favorably to whatever you are getting about the future. The readee may not like it at all in the moment, may deny that it's possible, or even tell you that you are most certainly wrong, but most of the time it's information that will be helpful for them at a later date. They will either be able to prepare themselves for that which you've predicted or you will help them understand it, or enable them to make changes to either avoid it altogether or lessen its impact when it arrives.

Personally, there are times when I find it very helpful to be able to tune in to future events and other times when it ruins the experience of being in the present moment. My son is an actor, and sometimes I tune in to see whether or not he is going to get a callback or a certain role. Even when I see he is going to be declined, I still drive the hour or more to Hollywood in rush-hour traffic and have him do the audition, just in case he is going to meet a contact who will pay off down the line, to give him the experience, and to appease his agent and manager who don't have as much confidence in my abilities as I do! But knowing it's not going to be fruitful takes away the fun of believing there is a chance. It is kind of like gambling with the certainty that you aren't going to win.

CHAPTER 8

Common Questions about the Techniques

When you ask for patience, God doesn't just give you patience,
he gives you the opportunity to be patient. When you ask for cour-
age, he doesn't give you courage; he gives you the opportunity to be
courageous.
—FROM THE FILM *EVAN ALMIGHTY*, WRITTEN BY STEVE OEDEKERK

Since the publication of *You Are Psychic*, I have received hundreds of e-
mails from readers. In this chapter I answer some of the questions about
reading techniques that are most commonly asked by these readers and
by students in my most recent workshops and classes. In the next chapter I will address a variety of topics about readings in general.

Question: I am confused about using the reading screen and the viewing receptacle together. Do I really need these? Sometimes I see images
before I visualize either one.

Answer: The tools presented in this book and expanded on in *You
Are Psychic* are offered as a way to help you focus and initiate the flow
of visual information. Once you get started, as long as the images are
flowing, there is really no need to use these visualizations solely for the

purpose of accessing information. However, they will be your saviors when you get stuck, confused, or are not sure how to proceed in the reading.

The screen corresponds with your sixth chakra, and it's helpful to clean it off frequently by grounding it and dusting it off, or by destroying it and creating another one. It gives you a place to focus and even acts as a hypnotic trigger that tells your unconscious mind that it has full permission to be psychic. The receptacle, particularly that of a rose, is enormously helpful because it's complex enough so that the energy/information will interact with each part of the rose and alter them so you will have lots of aspects to explore. If you just used your screen, you would sometimes get images, but the rose gives you even more to work with.

I've had some students who only wanted to use the rose. They really didn't like to use the screen at all and I told them this was fine, until I realized that there was a very specific reason why these students resisted the screen. It turned out that they weren't used to being centered in their bodies at all. By reading without being centered, they would get disoriented, have trouble seeing and communicating the pictures because they were flashing before them too quickly, or they were zooming too far out of their bodies and having trouble getting back in. At this point the screen became very useful.

That being said, these are still only tools. Some students become so focused on these tools that they forget the important thing is the end result. If you are getting images and pertinent information, who cares whether or not you are seeing a rose or your screen first? The value of using the receptacles/roses, however, is that when you are done with whatever it is you've just looked at, you now have a container in which you can deposit that energy. If you do become emotional, you can ask yourself, "Where am I in relation to my screen?" By centering yourself in your head and noticing the distance between you and your screen out in front of your forehead, you will regain your neutrality. The receptacle also provides you with an immediate vehicle to be used in clairvoyant healing (see part 3 of this book). The screen can be used on its own like an x-ray machine when you wish to look at a person's physical body or aura.

Question: I've never been very visual. The images I get are not that clear. I don't see the whole thing. I can't see very much, I just kind of know it's there. I know you say everyone is clairvoyant but maybe I'm not.

Answer: Many people are visualizing without realizing they are doing so. They believe their images are supposed to look a certain way, or they are so accustomed to their mind's images that they don't realize visualization can be that easy. And so they overlook these images.

Do the following exercise right now: Imagine a blue circle. Imagine you are taking a yellow sparkly marker and drawing a circle around it clockwise. Then draw a circle around it counterclockwise. Then imagine you are taking a pair of scissors and cutting the blue circle down the middle. Take the two parts and imagine you are rolling them into a ball. Throw the ball away or even pop it into your mouth. Imagine it tastes like a sour blueberry!

Now, if you did any part of that, you are visualizing! One of the biggest difficulties students have is with their expectations. They think that everything they are supposed to see is going to appear in vivid Technicolor images that remain there as long as they'd like them to. That might happen occasionally, but it is certainly not always the case. As you do a reading, you will likely have your images come in a variety of ways. Some of them will be vivid, others you will barely see. Some will flash before you like a shooting star, just leaving a whiff of an impression or thought (these are often surprisingly informative). Some images will disappear right away, some will reappear, some you will have trouble letting go of, some will be stationary, some will move. Sometimes you will be able to intentionally visualize something like a rose very clearly; other times you will barely be able to muster a faint outline. The thing is to accept and be thankful that you are getting anything.

Clairvoyant students who are pessimistic or perfectionistic often get frustrated with themselves because they become stuck on an expectation of how images are supposed to appear, or they will get stuck on the two out of twenty things they couldn't interpret or figure out. These are often the same people who go out to eat at a terrific restaurant and complain, without mentioning the food was excellent, that the waitress forgot to bring them their ketchup; who will point out the one spot you missed when cleaning the entire house; or who will beat themselves up because they got an A-minus on a test instead of an A.

Question: Sometimes when I am doing readings, the person I am reading gets upset with something I said or will argue with me, thinking I said something was bad when I didn't see it that way at all. How can I avoid this?

Answer: Avoid the words *good* and *bad*!

I have begun to realize that some people will categorize everything I tell them during a reading into two categories: "good" and "bad." They do this categorization on a constant basis, and it is the predominant way such people process information. Essentially, they are placing a value judgment on every word they hear, regardless of whether I intended it to be interpreted or categorized in that way.

For example, someone might ask me, "Why am I getting lots of headaches?" I might answer, "There is some red energy on your head. When I ask where the energy is coming from, I see an image of your father." So right here, we have the word *headaches*. To certain readees that of course is bad because no one likes headaches. Readees might continue in their heads, "Red energy? Not sure, but if it's associated with a headache, it must be bad, too. Hmmm, an image of my father? Okay, well my father abandoned me and was a jerk. Okay, he's bad too, I got it." But what if he wasn't a jerk in the readee's eyes? If the father gets placed in the "good" category, then suddenly there is a big problem for them. How can the "good" thing be causing the "bad" thing?!

Here's another example. A client has lost her job. She's terrified. Okay, so losing her job and the security she thought she had is "bad." This is just terrible, right? She rushes to me, insists on an immediate reading. I look and see that she may not find another job for quite a while. Oh no, that's not just bad, it's horrible! Right? To her, in this moment of sheer terror, it is. But I see in the reading that she was really exhausted, hated her job, and needed a long break. She really does have the personal resources in the form of skills, knowledge, and contacts to find work when she is ready. So I am seeing that this job loss is a blessing in disguise. Now I have helped her to see "bad" as "good," except that in her moment of panic she may not feel as happy as I do that she is finally unstuck and her life is moving along. Whether she herself can make this switch in her mind will determine the extent of her continued suffering.

Clients are not the only ones who fall into this trap. In fact, many psychics trip themselves up because they are doing this throughout their readings. The moment they see or hear something that they believe will be interpreted as "bad," they panic. This leads to them withholding information and overextending their healing energy to try and ensure their client won't feel bad. That tends to backfire; the readee wants information, not sympathy, and often the withheld information is the very thing the client needed to hear the most.

Most of us are familiar with the statement in the Bible, "Judge not, lest ye be judged." I think most people interpret this as: don't think badly of others' actions because we might be judged for our own. I suspect, however, that an even broader interpretation would be helpful: don't judge at all. Stop the constant assessment, rip up the checklist that runs through your mind: "That behavior made him a nice guy, okay, that made him a jerk; that action means we should be together; him doing that might be questionable; that behavior means she's a good mom, her doing that means she's not," and on and on. This logic is what creates pain. It gets in the way of being in the present moment. Many of us keep a running tally in our heads with our spouses or loved ones, and it very much gets in the way of us enjoying our relationships.

Question: I have been amazed with how easily I can see images, even during my first couple of readings. But there sure are times when I don't get anything at all, just black. What should I do?

Answer: Any time you are not getting anything, what you want to do is remind yourself that nothing is in fact something you can look at. Put up a new viewing receptacle that represents this nothing you are getting, and ask it to show you what the nothing represents, or why you are getting nothing. You will be surprised by what happens next!

If you find yourself getting distracted, you can always reset the reading color again by putting out a brand-new reading receptacle and asking the readee to repeat their name a few times. Check to see if your crown chakra color is matched with the reading color. You may not be getting much because the readee has zoomed out of their body. If they are not present, if their attention is somewhere else in la-la land, this is where you will end up as well. You can also ask them to pose a question to you as you look at a new receptacle. Doing this also helps bring them back to you and may elicit more information. Every question you pose to your reading receptacle acts like a button, key, or lever that releases bits of information from the universal source. Sometimes by asking your readee to pose a more specific question, or repeat or rephrase their questions, the information will begin to flow. If they are going to pose a question themselves, all you need to do is watch your viewing receptacle and see what happens to it, what color or image appears as their voice enters the receptacle.

Sometimes it helps to recheck your grounding, make sure your energy is running, or just create and destroy several neutral objects on your reading screen or in front of a particular chakra. Every time you do this it's as if you were exercising a muscle and clearing away stuck energies. I also highly recommend that you place your finger on your forehead at the location of your third eye, and double- or triple-check to make sure you are aligned back behind it in the center of your head. Remind yourself to sit in that captain's chair where the controls are located. Imagine that if you were up there looking down you'd be above your heart, so therefore you are actually able to stand above, in safety, and away from being overcome by the energy of your heart, where emotions whirl around like tidal waves, tornadoes, or blizzards.

Sometimes if you are really feeling stuck or lost in the reading, it may be necessary to ask the readee for some background information, particularly if you are feeling really compelled to do so. Recently I did a reading in which I was under a tight time frame and was not getting any clear images at all. I was hearing messages, but they made no sense to me. It felt as though I was stabbing at something blindly and erratically in the dark. I wanted to challenge myself to see if I could get more without having to ask for background information, but that wasn't going well so finally I asked—and suddenly all the messages I was getting made perfect sense and now I knew exactly what questions I needed to pose to my viewing receptacles. Sometimes our logical minds just need something to grab onto. Other times, too much information can taint the results.

Question: The images I get only last for a second and are gone. Then I get another one, but I never seem to know what any of this means.

Answer: I just had a student at one of my psychic workshops who had this problem. After spending just a few minutes alone with her and her partner, I realized that *she* was the problem. What was immediately apparent to me was that she was rushing the process. She'd see a flash of something for less than ten seconds, and then open her eyes and start trying to interpret what it meant. (She later complained that as soon as she started talking, she'd lose her concentration.) By listening to her speak, I could tell her interpretations were a creation of her logical mind as opposed to being intuitively, divinely inspired. I could tell this because of the language she used, such as "Well, it might mean this" or "It's possible it could mean this" or "Maybe it's because . . ." This is different from the language of "I am getting this" or "I am seeing this" or "I just got a flash that it means this."

Often, through a student's language, I can tell what they are experiencing in their imagination. Some of my savvier students quickly pick up on the terms I am looking for and will use these inappropriately, in an unconscious attempt to make it seem as though they are being clairvoyant when they aren't. It is not that they don't have the ability; rather, they don't have the necessary patience. Clairvoyance involves reading pictures and describing visual information. It is describing attributes such as colors, sizes, and objects, as well as describing actions and movement. If a student says to their readee, "I see you are wealthy or are going to be happy," a red flag goes up for me right away. How do you "see" wealth? How do you "see" happiness? These are concepts, interpretations.

The red flag is not there because I doubt what the student is getting, but because I know that the value of the information is in describing the pictures themselves, not in the interpretation—which is the weakest aspect of the reading and the most likely to be incorrect. So, in the example above I would want to ask the student to describe how the information came to them that made them say, "You are wealthy." They may say, "Well, first I saw the readee driving a expensive-looking car" or "I saw the readee holding a wallet with a lot of money spilling out." These images are much richer (no pun intended)! They might imply the readee is wealthy or is going to be wealthy, but they can also mean a host of other things. We are not as concerned with the meaning at this point as we are about getting the details of the pictures.

Question: I'm not comfortable with closing my eyes as you suggest. It's easier for me to just have them open, and then I just talk and words flow from my mouth.

Answer: People who aren't comfortable closing their eyes, except when going to sleep, often have certain control issues or are afraid to connect with their feelings. While you most certainly can do readings with your eyes open, it would be good for you to explore what happens when you do them with your eyes closed. During one psychic workshop I taught, a man just would not close his eyes. He had been doing healing work for a few years and insisted this just wasn't his style. During our practice together, he was giving the readee some information that was more complex than merely describing pictures, and I really couldn't tell if it was inspired or coming from his logical mind. Since the point of the exercise was to experience one's own clairvoyance, rather than merely be psychic, I had to be really firm with him. I told him that the point of him being in the class for the weekend, which had cost him six hundred dollars, was not to do things as he had always done them, but to learn something new. In his case, it was not to prove to himself or others that he had psychic talent, which he knew he did, but to experiment and discover this new specific skill of clairvoyance.

He agreed that I had a point but stated he just had not ever been clairvoyant. I had to again remind him that this was why he was taking the class, to learn a new skill. If he just allowed himself to relax, I could lead him to a place where he'd never been before. I also emphasized that if he wanted to gain a new skill, he just might have to allow himself to feel uncomfortable for a while.

It's amazing how many people will run from the first feeling of any discomfort. Any time we are stretching ourselves, we will feel uncomfortable. Try lifting a weight. If you don't feel it, it's not working. Try having a baby! Imagine where we'd be if women decided they should do away with childbirth because it's uncomfortable! My student finally did let go of his resistance, closed his eyes, and began to really concentrate. Within minutes he was stunned at how clearly his visions came. By the end of the reading, he stood up, dazed, and stated he had never had any reason to concentrate as deeply as he just had, and that he couldn't believe how vivid his images were. He then excused himself from class early to go take a walk alone, so he could process what he had just experienced.

Question: I have only done a few readings so far, but I am getting confused because sometimes I get images that seem really dumb or make no sense. I don't say anything and then it turns out the images mean something, but other times I have no clue as to what they mean. How do I know when to mention something I am not sure about or when to just let it go?

Answer: The answer to this is quite simple. It's my personal philosophy that you should always talk about every single detail you are getting, particularly before you've done your first twenty readings. Your logical brain should not be filtering out and evaluating whatever you see. This will absolutely impede the entire process and will mean that you end up overlooking a lot of very rich and important information.

While your logical mind is there to help you pose questions and decide what to do next when the information stops flowing easily, it should not be allowed to make any judgments about or censor the images. Of course you can't completely stop it from doing this, but once you become aware of any thoughts like "This is too dumb/weird/confusing" or "The readee won't like this," you need to be stronger than these thoughts and describe exactly what you are seeing. This is where the creed of the extraordinary psychic really needs to be applied. Self-discipline, courage, and neutrality are going to be essential.

When I am privately training students, this is what they rely on me for the most—to pull out of them what they are too afraid to mention. Of course there will be times when you do allow the censoring to take over. That's all right, because usually by the end of the reading you will find yourself sharing the information or see that the images reassert themselves later on, either as the same image or in a different form. Any time an image reappears more than once, you can be particularly sure there is significance there. But certainly don't wait for it to reappear before you mention it.

Talking can stimulate the flow of images. This is why it can be really helpful to give a moment-to-moment account of what you are experiencing as opposed to being silent until you feel that you have the entire picture. On the other hand, sometimes you will find that the flow of information stops as you talk, and then you may need to refocus on your viewing receptacle in order to get it going again. If this is the case, there is nothing wrong with telling the readee that you are going to take a minute or two and watch the images before you describe them. The thing to remember is that this reading is not about you. It is more important that your readee understands what you are saying as opposed to you having a clear picture of the entire story of their life.

Offering the information on a micro-level rather than a macro-level is very important. Describe attributes and details as opposed to forcing yourself to come up with the end-all picture. For example, if you see a man's face with a mustache, you should describe it exactly as such: "I see a man's face with a mustache." Now, as you see this image, you might just hear or get a flash or sense of the word *father*. In this case I recommend that you state exactly that: "I just got a sense of the word *father*."

There is also nothing wrong with telling your readee how you are feeling. If you are worried the readee will think you are weird because of what you're seeing, tell them, "I know this may sound strange, but this is what I'm seeing" or "This may not be what you wanted to hear, but this is what I'm getting." One way to help a readee feel better about something you think they will not be happy about is to expand your reading to include looking at the reason the readee is not happy or will not get what they think they want. This is when your logical mind becomes your friend again. In chapter 5, I offer a number of questions you can pose to your viewing receptacle that will eventually become second nature to you, so your readee doesn't ever have to be left hanging with bad news and a feeling of hopelessness or confusion.

Some experienced clairvoyants will leave out the details and give the final meaning. While this can save time, some of the richness can also get lost. Analogies and metaphors are very powerful teaching tools, which is one reason the Bible is quoted so often. Much of clairvoyant reading involves symbolic metaphors; when the clairvoyant keeps the metaphor to themselves and merely provides the interpretation of it, it is like a poet leaving out most of a poem and instead providing a bland summary of the poem's meaning. When you describe a symbol, image, or scene you are getting, readees can form their own mental images and pictures that will be lodged in their memories. *This* is what they will access in the future, as opposed to your interpretation.

For example, say you see an image of your readee with huge angel wings, but one wing is broken. You have no idea what this means, so you ask it to show you a clue or give you some insight. You see another image of your readee dragging a person along a path; the person is so heavy they can hardly walk. You are not sure what this means so you ask it to show you another clue, and now you see an image of their wrists with blood leaking out, or a man hungrily feeding from the wrists like Dracula.

From all these images—perhaps through deduction but also from a sense of knowingness—you get that this person is trying to help someone or perhaps many people, and that doing so is draining them and slowing them down in their own life.

Now, what is going to have more impact: merely stating "A man is draining you of your power," or describing the vivid imagery of the broken angel wing, the body being dragged down a path, a man drinking from veins? Which is more likely to get the readee to take notice and take action? Which is the readee more likely to remember? It's the difference between cooking and serving someone a hearty meal, and merely telling that person about the meal after you've digested it yourself!

Question: I can't always tell if an image is symbolic or literal.

Answer: This is one of the challenges of clairvoyant reading, and there is no easy answer here. This is another reason I suggest just stating exactly what you are seeing. Sometimes the readee will know if the image is symbolic or literal because the readee obviously has much more background information than you do. Other times it will be quite obvious, since what you are looking at is so unrealistic. Honesty is always the best policy, and there is nothing wrong with stating, "I am seeing this. I am not sure if it's symbolic or if it's literal, but I will tell you about it anyway."

For example, you might see an image of your readee hopping around on one leg, with crutches under her arm. This could mean she has really hurt her leg, or it may possibly symbolize that she is not fully standing on her own. When you communicate it to her, she might blurt out, "I just broke my leg last week!" Of course, another helpful thing to do that should be obvious by now is to ask the image to show you what it pertains to. You can put up a new viewing receptacle and tell it to let you know why you were looking at the last thing you saw. In the above example, even without the readee giving you any input, you may see an image of an ambulance, or suddenly feel a pain in your own leg, or have a sense of something medical that will lead you to the realization that the very first picture of the readee on crutches was in fact a literal representation of an event taking place.

There have been numerous times when I thought what I was seeing was symbolic, but instead I was actually looking at exactly what my readee was doing on the other side of the telephone—such as licking a spoon, putting curlers in her hair, or playing with a pet. I have the tendency to do this more with certain people than with others. For example, one time I saw an image of a friend of mine lying on her back in a strange position, with her head dangling over the edge, her leg in the air, and her toes close to her face. She was looking intently at one of her toes. I described this strange image to her, and she was quite embarrassed to admit that this was exactly the position she was lying in. Her toe was itching her, and she was trying to find the source of the irritation.

I don't know why I saw this image rather than anything else I could have been looking at, except that perhaps it would have captured my attention had I really been with her in her house. It may also be that her attention was more on her toe than on whatever I was "looking" at for her, and therefore this is where my own attention went. Had she not admitted to lying in this exact position looking at her toe, I would have never understood what I was looking at.

This example demonstrates a few things. One is that we have to be okay with not always knowing. Second, our attention goes where our readee's attention goes. Third, symbolic and literal images are often indistinguishable. Fourth, our confidence as psychics is quite tenuous. We could be 100 percent correct about the details we describe or our summation of the situation, and yet our readee could deny it all—either out of embarrassment, ignorance, or for any number of other reasons. This is why we need to have confidence in ourselves and not put too much emphasis on the feedback we get from others. One of the things I now ask of my clients who are receiving telephone readings is that they remain seated and do nothing but listen to me. Multitasking might be a plus in the corporate world, but it just doesn't work when receiving (or giving) a reading!

Sometimes the attributes we see in our visions or images are symbolic, which can be confusing. For example, you may see an image of a man with a mustache and have a strong feeling that this is your readee's father. However, your readee informs you that her father did not have a mustache. Now, you might be seeing the mustache for a few reasons. For one, her father may have had a mustache when she was very young, at a time when something significant occurred that is influencing her. He may have preferred to wear a mustache, but his wife didn't like it. Or it may be that he in fact never did have a mustache, but your own father did and therefore this is what your subconscious mind, or the part of your mind that generates pictures, conjured up so you would know you were talking about a father. In this case, you may likely have a matching picture with your readee, and you could both have similar issues with your fathers.

There are times during a clairvoyant reading with a new client that I will see images of someone I personally know. This person could be one of my friends or family members, or a famous person I have never met. This usually surprises me. I've found the best way to handle the situation is to explain to my client, "For some reason I am seeing this person that I know. They look like this and they act like this, and this is how I feel about them. I might be seeing them because they have similar attributes to someone in your life."

Question: Why do I get images from movies or see fictional characters in my readings?

Answer: In clairvoyant readings, scenes from movies, or characters or actors, will often come up to serve as shortcuts that help us describe a person or situation in our readee's life. For example, in a recent reading I saw an image of Jack Nicholson, and I explained to my client that I was probably seeing Jack because there was a person who looked like him in her life or who shared similar personality traits. She knew right away who I was talking about. I did follow this up with details such as "I see this guy with crazy hair; he looks really intense, edgy, but also has a mischievous grin on his stubbly face. He seems to have a strong sexual appetite and somewhat of a temper." Again, she acknowledged I was right on about the man she was wondering about.

I do recommend telling your readee who the person reminds you of, and also sharing the details of your image. The nice thing about seeing celebrities is that they are universal symbols we can all relate to. Even on the off chance that my readee wouldn't know who Jack Nicholson is, seeing an image of him would instantly give me an idea of the characteristics of a man impacting my client's life, and I would be able to describe that man faster and more easily than if I had to see the collection of his traits individually.

Recently, I did a reading for a woman who wanted to know about her future romantic relationships. I decided I would look about one year ahead. I expected to see a man, but instead I immediately saw an image of the comedian and talk-show host Ellen DeGeneres. I tried to push this aside because it made no sense, but a minute later I saw an image of k. d. lang. Hmmm, two strong, openly lesbian women. My currently heterosexual readee wasn't exactly ready to hear that her next major relationship in about a year might very well be with another woman, but she didn't hang up on me when I gave her the news.

CHAPTER 9

General Questions

There is nothing like returning to a place that remains unchanged to find the ways in which you yourself have altered.
—NELSON MANDELA

Below are some common questions asked by readers of *You Are Psychic*, as well as by the students in my workshops and long-distance training programs.

Question: Is someone who naturally sees things without training, perhaps at a young age, a superior clairvoyant to someone who has learned these skills?

Answer: Well, *they* might think so!

What is your definition of "superior"? Are they more special because their "gift" was already turned on, and ours took longer to unwrap? A person who can see things with eyes wide open and who has done so since early childhood may be very talented, a very clear channel, even a psychic prodigy, but as I have indicated elsewhere, doing readings for people takes a lot more than being able to access information. It involves discernment, the ability to identify what comes from one's logical mind and one's inner motivations, and an ability to effectively describe our visions in a loving but honest way. This is why therapists tend to make good psychics. These skills come with experience and with maturity, along with certain innate personality traits.

I've seen firsthand what happens when someone is very psychic but does not have the integrity or wisdom to handle being psychic: their relationships suffer and they can cause a lot of problems for those around them. This includes children and teenagers who discover a desire to read others at an early age, something I don't advocate unless the child feels absolutely compelled to do so, and is very mature and has adequate guidance from a grounded adult. (I now only allow people over the age of eighteen to attend my psychic workshops.) Younger people are more inclined to project their own pictures and judgments onto others because they haven't yet developed the capacity to monitor their own thoughts, intentions, and behaviors. Their inner parent is not yet developed enough to keep them in check. (Obviously some adults have this problem as well!) Children also tend to want to show off, appear powerful or special, and use their abilities to get their own way.

Obviously, most children and teenagers are not yet emotionally equipped to deal with or understand many issues adults struggle with, which is why we don't allow them to watch adult television programs and movies. Doing readings is a lot like watching home movies, and these range from G-rated to XXX-rated! Rather than reading other people, I encourage my son to pay attention to his dreams. I let him know when he's just expressed a thought I was thinking and I encourage him to use psychic tools to calm himself down and focus, as well as to find his missing things. I teach him to meditate (most kids like to say "om" and use Tibetan bells and drums rather than just sit there visualizing). I also teach him basic hands-on aura healing by mostly doing it on him when he doesn't feel well or has been injured. However, I will not teach him or encourage him to read other people until he is an adult and really expresses an interest. To do otherwise would be to take away his innocence.

Question: You and other psychics use the term *energy* a lot. I don't really know what that means.

Answer: *Energy* is a catch-all word used to describe something that we know is there, and we know we can influence. We know it connects people, comes from people, and flows to them, through them, up and down them, and around them. We know it can vibrate at different frequencies, and it is the building block of emotion, thought, and our own physical body. It's a smaller unit than the atom or subatomic particles. It's seen by clairvoyants and occasionally by the physical eye as colors and shapes. It sometimes shows up in photographs when it wasn't visible to the physical eye.

The word *energy* is analogous to the term *life force*. People with no energy are lethargic and depressed. People with lots of it are active and creative. People with none of it are dead. When discussing the energy of humans and animals, the origin of energy is as elusive as life itself. We know people can influence energy with their thoughts, and likewise their thoughts can be influenced by energy. Is this term overused, underdefined, and used too broadly? You betcha. But I think it's the best thing we've currently got to describe this unseen substance that impacts us every moment and every millisecond of the day.

During my readings, when people are blocked from making changes and obtaining what they long for (whether good health, prosperity, love, or insight), I often see a color, a substance that is connected to someone or a whole group of people very identifiably, which seems to be in their way. This I refer to as "foreign energy." As soon as this substance is removed, the person begins feeling very different and takes steps they have wanted to take for a whole lifetime. Sometimes, however, it can take a long time to release or move on from this energy because it's familiar, and what is familiar feels comforting and safe even when it's not.

Sometimes, when someone is very enmeshed with their family of origin, I see an image of a cut-out figure from a mold of the same color and substance. When someone is so enmeshed with their family, their life force is almost indistinguishable from the others. They are the same color, but I can see their outline emerging from the rest of the mold. These people who are enmeshed with the rest of the material in the mold have a hard time knowing what they want to do in life; they feel stuck, trapped, and depressed. Why? Because they are not running their own life force through their bodies; they are running that of a group of people who may not be very happy or motivated. The more they can separate from this glob of family consciousness, the more they can breathe, think their own thoughts, and feel their own emotions—because they will then be running their own vibration and energy.

Your own personal energy is like a signature, fingerprint, or DNA that has similar characteristics to all other humans and yet is unique to every individual in various ways. I wish I could get away from these terms because they are not always clear enough and turn some people off, but I have yet to find others that work better for me.

Exercise: Energy Flow

You can feel energy flow just by holding your two hands a few inches from each other, palm facing palm, and visualizing a current—like light, lightning, or water—flowing back and forth. After a minute or so you will feel a pulsating, and have a sense of the direction of the flow. When you direct this energy outward to someone else for the purpose of alleviating their pain, you are performing a basic energetic healing. However, if you are going to do this, imagine that the energy in your hands is going to act like a hose or laser beam, to wash or burn away whatever the other person wants to release. Consciously withdraw or pull back this energy by using your imagination, rather than expecting you are giving them this energy to remain in their body indefinitely.

Question: Is it better to practice readings on people and about topics you know or don't know?

Answer: I find there is value in both.

Obviously, when you don't know someone, it's easier to tell if the information coming to you is significant or if it's coming from your own preconceived notions of the person. For this reason, when developing your skills it is important to read as many strangers or unknown targets as possible.

However, there is still great value in reading someone you do know. Many times, having the background information on a person does help you put the images coming to you into perspective, letting you go right to the heart of the matter. Practicing on supportive friends and relatives is fun and much more relaxing than reading people you don't know, and you may find it easier to get into a flow. The more relaxed you are, the more success you will have accessing your clairvoyance.

Even with your spouse or close friends, there are many areas of their lives you don't know that much about. You almost certainly don't know every single person they know, so reading their relationship with someone you've never met could be interesting for you to explore. Even if he has complained about his boss or his job in the past, it is fascinating when you receive firsthand insight into why your hubby really is so miserable at work or why that boss is such a jerk. (Watch out, though—you might learn it's not the boss who's the jerk!)

When you begin to access information that is different from what you expected or even wanted to see, you will know the information is coming from a source outside your logical mind. The most exciting thing about reading someone you personally know happens when you gain information that allows you to see and subsequently think about the other person's life from a new perspective. You are then able to release your previously held judgments about what they should or should not be doing, and whom they should or should not be doing it with. For example, you might have been judging your friend for staying at a particular job, or for refusing to break up with a lover your friend constantly complains about. But during the reading you will see and learn information that will help you to understand that the path your friend is on is the perfect one for them, even if you would not personally choose to step one foot on such a path!

In this way, your clairvoyant work will enable you to release your need to control and exert your moral judgments over others. You will learn how to let others be who they are, and you will understand how futile it really is for you to try to change them. Just be aware that clairvoyants and spiritual seekers sometimes replace one set of value judgments with another (e.g., a holier-than-thou attitude that everyone should become psychic, or meditate, and use only the same techniques the one judging uses). Like proselytizing Mormons and Jehovah's Witnesses, or overzealous born-agains, we psychics and healers can be equally pushy or narrow-minded.

Question: I recently did a reading for someone, but I felt as though I was giving advice rather than being clairvoyant. Is this okay or should I avoid giving advice during a reading?

Answer: During a reading (and in life), the more advice you are giving, the more lit up you probably are. By "lit up" I mean you are encountering your own matching pictures; you are being driven by your own feelings. Perhaps your own pain is being stimulated by encountering similar pictures in your readee, and you are not in a neutral, grounded space that will allow you to maximize your clairvoyance or your communication.

So if you find yourself offering advice instead of being psychic, what should you do? Simple: just stop! Tell the readee you need a few moments to collect yourself, and go through your basic tools of grounding and centering yourself. Check to make sure your energy is running and that you have a separation object up. When you begin to feel like it's all on you to solve someone's problem during a reading, it's an excellent indication that you yourself are having a problem and need to give yourself a good talking-to and remind yourself that you are here to be psychic, not to solve problems. It's also helpful to understand that it's not the problem that is causing your readee's suffering; it's that they have lost themselves in the problem. When you have emotional distance from what you are viewing, then your readee can have distance from what they are experiencing, which is what they are really seeking.

During a reading it is very helpful to look at where the readee is headed and what next steps they might take to get there. This is especially important after you've been looking at their "problems," which is where they are really stuck emotionally. Offering "next steps" might seem like advice, but it really is a psychic prescription, a specific course of action that comes from a source other than your logical mind. This information might correspond with your own ideas or it might contradict them. If the latter is the case, congratulations! This is a sign that you are accessing information on a psychic level. But be careful not to throw away any information that sounds familiar, because it is very possible you feel a strong match with this person and the steps intended for them may be the same ones—or quite similar to the ones—you will need as well. If you aren't sure, just tell the readee, "I don't know if these steps are intended for you or for me or for both of us, but I'd like to share them with you anyway."

You can look at someone's next steps or the best course of action for them to take by doing the following exercise:

Exercise: Looking at a Next Step

Create a viewing receptacle. Pose the question to your receptacle, "What course of action would be best for my client?" or demand that the answer appear. Look for a color first, and then tell your receptacle to show you some images. It helps to describe the color in addition to the images because then the client will be able to conjure these up at a later date to manifest what they seek, as opposed to what they are moving away from.

You can also put up a receptacle and ask it to show you the color of the client's joy or creativity. Instruct your client to run this color through their body several times a day. Sooner rather than later, this practice will bring about the life experiences that will actually allow your client to have this joy.

Exercise: Distancing Yourself from a Problem

Go inward. Ground yourself. Visualize two receptacles or roses—one for yourself, the other for the problem. Label each one: one with your name, the other with the word *problem*. Give each one of these a grounding cord. Ask for any excess emotional energy to release. Breathe as you watch and notice any colors coming out.

Next, call all your life force and any remaining energy from the receptacle with the problem and see it go into your receptacle. Let the problem energy come out of your receptacle either through the grounding cord or by going back into the "problem" receptacle. You are not calling the problem itself, but your own energy. As you do this, be aware of how the two things are different from each other: you and your problem. You are not your problem, no matter how bad it seems. Notice how this feels.

This exercise can be done in about five minutes, and you are sure to see results. As is the case with all the exercises in this book, this exercise is not only assisting you on an intellectual level but is also impacting you energetically.

This is also a great exercise to do around something you feel you desperately want or need, since a problem indicates an obstacle to what you want or think you need. Instead of labeling the second rose "problem," label it as your want or need. This doesn't mean you won't get what you want or need; on the contrary, it will help release the urgency and emotional attachment to it that are causing you distress.

Question: What if I am wrong about what I am seeing?

Answer: A better question is "What happens *when* I am wrong?" because there will be plenty of times you will be. Clairvoyants are usually wrong in their interpretations of the images, rather than about the images themselves. Most images are there for a reason. Many of the mistakes are made in confusing the symbolic for the literal, or vice versa, or in making logical assumptions about the images you are getting.

Have you ever played the board game Pictionary? One team member picks a card listing a particular object, person, place, or action, and then attempts to draw this subject. The other team members have to guess what their teammate is drawing within a certain amount of time. In a way, as a clairvoyant, this is what you are being asked to do. Your mind draws the pictures or receives the images, and you are left with the interpretation part. Sometimes in the mere description of its attributes, you reveal what it is but sometimes it takes a lot more to get at what you're seeing, particularly if you are describing a whole concept or specific person as opposed to a thing. If you see a flag and you say, "I see something that looks like a flag," then you are right on. But if the concept is the Fourth of July and someone draws a flag but also a bunch of squiggles representing fireworks that look like waves, you may think you are looking at something having to do with the ocean. The problem is that to you the squiggles did not accurately represent what the artist intended them to represent.

Imagine that a readee asks you to do a reading on her pet named Lassie. You might see an image of a dirty animal with four legs and interpret this as a dog. But it turns out Lassie is really a pig. Such a mistake is more likely to happen if you are in a hurry or if your logical mind just naturally assumes any animal named Lassie will be a dog. If having a pig as a pet is so far out of your everyday experience that it's something you've never imagined, it may be harder for you to see the image as a pig or you might be more likely to dismiss the idea.

The way to decrease your errors is to make sure you describe the image you are getting and all its details before jumping to an interpretation. Sometimes an answer or message will just land in your mind. This is different from "figuring it out." Over time, with practice, you will learn the difference between these two things. If you are not sure about the meaning of what you are getting, you can always say, "I see this, but I don't know yet what it means." Or "I see this image (describe the image), and I think this is what it means but I'm not exactly sure."

Question: I've noticed that some psychics call themselves clairvoyants, but they are really channeling or are getting information through feelings and hearing and not through visuals. Your approach is quite different from theirs.

Answer: I believe that it's important to distinguish between the different psychic abilities so that we can better understand them and recognize their unique characteristics.

Many psychics shy away from using the term *psychic* and therefore call themselves clairvoyants even though they are not really accessing their visual abilities. Of course, some of the terms overlap because most psychics don't do just one thing or use just one single ability. I consider myself to be a clairvoyant because I focus mostly on the visual, but during the course of a reading I am receiving messages from other spirits and feeling other people's emotions, and therefore I could technically be considered a medium, transmedium, or channeler in those moments. Still, I feel these skills are augmenting my primary ability of clairvoyance.

I will now attempt to define some of the more commonly used terms:

A *clairvoyant* sees visual information through pictures and images.

A *medium* channels information from a variety of spirits, some of which are deceased and some of which may be ascended beings.

A *channeler* is also a medium, someone who allows herself or himself to be used to communicate information brought in by another source.

A *full-body channeler* is a channeler who permits a foreign being to enter their body fully, so that during the reading the being is more in the channeler's body than is the channeler.

A *transmedium* permits other beings and spirits to attach themselves to him or her or sends his or her spirit and energy out to others. A transmedium is similar to a channeler; the difference is that some transmediums don't mean to do this—it just happens spontaneously, often without their awareness or conscious consent. Many mentally ill people are transmediums. I believe that many people who "talk to themselves" are not really themselves but someone else. That's how they can become so passionately engaged in their conversations!

A *remote viewer* follows certain protocols to view information about an unknown target that is at a separate location (see chapters 10 and 11).

A *medical intuitive* focuses on the physical body and its ailments. A medical intuitive may be using any of the psychic abilities.

Finally, a *psychic* can be any combination of the above. I believe it's important for psychics to be able to distinguish between the various sources of information they receive, but doing so comes with practice and experience, so there is no rush. I really encourage students to be careful with their words!

Question: You suggest that we focus ourselves in the center of our heads, behind the sixth chakra or the pineal gland. But what about the heart? Isn't that the place where most spiritual disciplines say we should be? If we deny the heart, are we not going to become uncaring, even merciless, psychics?

Answer: Our sixth chakra (also called the *ajna chakra*) is the center of our clairvoyance. It corresponds with the pineal and pituitary glands. When we are in this place, we are not denying our hearts but instead are better able to observe what is happening within our hearts.

It is the difference between standing in the middle of a severe storm or standing at a safe distance, observing or even enjoying the storm. When we center or align ourselves with a particular chakra, or focus our attention on that chakra, we are activating that chakra's energy. It is not that we are saying, "This chakra is better than any other." There are plenty of times when it is more desirable to be in the heart center, particularly when you are on a date or having sex.

The energy of the sixth chakra has to do with clarity, observation, insight, wisdom, being present-oriented, awareness, calm, consciousness, creativity, and neutrality. Outside of readings and your psychic work, this is a great place to center yourself when you become aware that you have lost your center, that your emotions are causing you to act in ways that are not really serving you or those around you, or when you really need to be able to assess a situation without getting caught up in the drama. The heart is about drama, emotions, passion. When we are doing readings, we are tuning in to all sorts of high drama, emotions, and passions that don't need any more fuel from us than they already have.

Experiment

Designate either one day or an entire week during which you will consciously center yourself in one chakra. At least once an hour, remind yourself of where you are supposed to be. Call all your energy from wherever else it is to that one spot. Hold the intention that the energy of that chakra will be activated and that you will learn its true nature. Then move to another chakra the next day or week. Notice the difference. Another thing you can do is practice reading from your different chakras and notice what happens.

I like to imagine I am centered in the chakra, and then I imagine that I am looking out of that part of my body and I play around with what I would see from that perspective. For example, if I am centered in my second chakra I will be somewhere below my belly button. If that part of my body had eyes, I'd be looking directly at the television set in my home, or face to face with my cat sitting on the desk. This helps me orient myself.

Question: You suggest using a separation object for our readings and even in our personal lives, but doesn't this get in the way of being able to receive the psychic information? It also seems as though it would get in the way of intimacy in our relationships.

Answer: In order to love someone, we must be able to have some distance from them. Otherwise we can't see them anymore.

One of my favorite exercises I do with my students is to have them pair off in teams. I instruct one student to begin telling the other one their problems—the worst problems they can think of. The one listening is instructed to do nothing else but listen. (It's funny how some people can't do this; they must start giving advice right away. These are the students who need to use the tools the most; they give advice in order to decrease their own emotional discomfort.) Then I instruct the listener to visualize a separation object at the edge of their aura (for more on separation objects, see chapter 3). Once the listener sees this, the listener is told to continue listening and focusing on what the partner is saying.

Most students acknowledge there is a huge difference after creating the separation object. Many report it's easier to just listen without feeling as though they have to solve this poor person's problems. They get less sucked in. Even the person who is talking about their problem reports that they found they no longer felt the need to discuss their problem, that it was harder to recall the severity of it or how they felt about it even moments before. Some people even say they no longer felt like talking about their problem.

A separation object is not a wall. It is a boundary. It says, "This is where I end and you begin." There is a time and a place for being smack-dab in your wide-open heart chakra and completely merged with another, but a clairvoyant reading is not one of them. Let's look at the sort of language commonly found in romance novels: "With our bodies entwined, we were as one, my breath his, his breath mine. He swallowed me up in his eyes and I was lost forever." (Hmmm, maybe I should be writing fiction instead!) Being merged with another is a romantic notion that is a wonderful experience—until your partner becomes sick, frustrated, angry, or afraid, or until your partner's mother's illness, frustration, anger, or fear enters your partner's aura and you experience the effect of this. Even if your partner's energy field is crystal-clear and filled with joy, what happens after a passionate night of oneness when morning comes and it's time to go to work or class and you are so merged together that you can't get up enough strength to peel your body away from your partner, or you manage to get to work but can think of nothing but him or her? (Not that I would know anything about that!) I am not suggesting you forgo the merging, but rather I am offering you some help for prying your energy fields apart when your bodies need to go their separate ways.

To have an understanding of what it is like to energetically merge with someone, think about the guy or girl you are totally into, then imagine you are Siamese twins, a completely unromantic notion (at least from my perspective as an identical twin). The only difference between being a Siamese twin and being energetically merged with someone is that you can usually walk away for short periods of time; however, you will most likely have a hard time thinking about anything else. This is why we will obsess about someone or have a hard time making decisions when we get into a relationship. This is why it helps to create boundaries and to call our own energy back to ourselves and send theirs back to them. You can think better, make better decisions, and really feel better on every level.

In a reading, setting your boundaries will make the difference between you seeing the whole picture or getting sucked into seeing things only from the readee's perspective, or getting entangled in their emotions. Go stand nose to nose with someone, or with your face right up to the television set or the painting in your living room. Can you see the whole person, the whole screen, the whole picture? No, of course not! This is what happens when your energy and attention merge with your readee's. This is why a separation object is important. It's not going to block the visual information, although I suppose it may cut down on some sensory information—but that's okay because that information will only tell you so much anyway.

Question: Why aren't all or more psychics successful at gambling or winning lotteries?

Answer: Using one's abilities for gambling purposes can be tricky for a number of reasons.

First of all, as I note in other chapters, clairvoyance works best when you are in a deeply relaxed state. Usually this requires one to prepare through meditation. Obviously, the frenetic environment of a casino is the last place anyone is going to be able to relax. I suspect the reason casinos are noisier than just about any other place is so that patrons have as few quiet times as possible to focus inwardly, where they might just get more in tune with their intuition. In most of the casinos in Las Vegas, there is nowhere to sit except in front of a slot machine, gaming table, bar, or restaurant. This is not due to oversight but rather to very intentional design.

Another reason using one's abilities in a casino is tricky has to do with all the competing energies. Everyone is so elevated in their desires, their need to win, and then there are the casino employees, whose jobs depend on doing whatever they can so you don't win. Another challenge is that when you are gambling, you are so attached to the outcome that most of the time your desires are going to outweigh the psychic information that comes in. I do hear lots of stories, however, of people just walking through a casino and getting a sudden feeling to go put money down somewhere and winning pretty big. Yet it usually goes downhill after that.

Russell Targ and Harold E. Puthoff, authors of the book *Mind-Reach: Scientists Look at Psychic Abilities*, believe that neurological functioning and the differences between the right and left hemispheres of the brain may account for why many psychics tend to do poorly when it comes to gambling or predicting numbers. They point out that "the two hemispheres of the brain are specialized for different cognitive functions: the left for verbal and analytic thought, the right for intuition and the understanding of patterns and possibly music and artistic abilities . . . the left hemisphere analyzes over time and codes memory in linguistic description, the right synthesizes over space and in images." These researchers discovered that clairvoyant subjects in remote-viewing experiments were much more accurate when it came to describing color and shape, but subjects had more difficulty reading letters or words—although they might be able to tell there was some kind of sign or other written material at a remote location.

For the past twenty years I have been frustrated by psi experiments that use ESP cards, in which a subject is asked to name which of five different cards is the target. Targ and Puthoff agree that "such tasks tempt the subject into an analytical matching task, rather than coax him into the more intuitive mode that is required. That is unfortunate for us because the simple matching task is best suited for the statistical analysis favored by the left brain-oriented scientific methods. Right-brain results are much more difficult to pin down." I wholeheartedly agree!

Personally, I find ESP cards to be downright boring. Research has shown that psychics are most likely to pick up on information that is most interesting to them, and to home in on peak emotional experiences and events. Sitting in some depressing classroom or lab, feeling pressure to prove oneself, shuffling through a deck of outdated cards with meaningless symbols is about the worst way to test someone's psychic talents. Fortunately, many modern-day psi researchers have come to the same conclusion.

That being said, there are people whose brains are developed in a way that allows them to be both excellent psychics and excellent mathematicians. If you add in an actual interest and knowledge of gambling and an understanding of the best way to overcome the above-mentioned challenges, I believe you will find yourself a psychic who will do very well when it comes to winning casino games or lotteries.

Question: I've been doing Reiki for a long time, and I know I take on other people's energy when I heal them. Is this a problem?

Answer: Healing through absorbing the pain of others is not a problem—as long as it's a conscious choice and you are willing to face the consequences.

Let me tell you a little story. Not too long ago I attended a book signing for a spiritually oriented book at a local bookstore. I arrived late, and when I arrived there was an attractive young man speaking praise about the book. He kept referring to the author as his "guru." I wondered why this man was doing the presentation instead of the author himself. Something told me to look behind me. When I did, I saw a man sitting in the back row whose appearance jolted me. The only way I can describe him is that he looked very sick in the most unusual way. His belly and his eyes seemed to protrude unnaturally, and I got a horrible feeling looking at him.

The man did not seem particularly distressed, though. He was just sitting there, and another man was massaging his shoulders, which the sick-looking man seemed grateful for. However, I got this intense icky feeling and a flash of an image that his body was literally a cesspool filled with the worst kind of energy imaginable. I was reminded of the animated film *Spirited Away*, in which a character absorbs dozens of other beings into its own body until it almost explodes. It pained me to see this poor man, yet something was so odd here that I could not stop glancing back at him. Each time I did I felt a growing panic that made me want to stand up and scream, "There is something really wrong here! Someone do something!" And I had no idea why.

I was shaken from my craziness by the realization that this very man was now being escorted to the front of the room. It was then that

I realized he was in fact the author/guru who had written the book. After the presentation I turned to the pretty and cheerful young woman sitting next to me. I asked her, "Did you see that guy!? He looks really bad. I hope he's okay." I expected her to agree with me, not to say what she said next: "Oh yes, isn't he wonderful? He's really sick, he's been like that for years, but it's not a bad thing at all. That's his gift." "What!" I exclaimed. "Yes," she beamed with admiration. "He talks about it in his classes. He's here on this planet to take away suffering, and he does it by accepting it all into his body. He's taken my pain away a few times, and it never came back. He could do the same for you! Come on, I'll introduce you right now!"

Horrified, I declined, stating, "I think I'd rather release my pain somewhere else besides this man's body." I was quite shaken for a while, standing there among all those happy people. I was judging this man for making this choice that was obviously eating away his health, yet I felt such a pull to heal him that I could barely stand it. The longer I stood there watching him, wanting to heal him (by now he had another "disciple" massaging his shoulders), the worse I felt.

Finally, I realized what I was doing. I was essentially "matching" him in what he did, and I knew if I stood there much longer I would be taking away all the crap he had absorbed by downloading it into my own energy field. This is not the way I choose to heal clients, although I know I tend to do this in my personal relationships. I once ended up taking a boyfriend's Prozac for a few months while living with him, although I'd never been depressed like that, for no apparent reason, before or since.

I know I can and want to help people, but most certainly not like that. I hope you make the choice not to heal in the way this man did, as the trade-offs for most people aren't worth it. (As an aside, I think that extra weight on our bodies is often partially filled with others' emotional pain.) I know that my refusal to consciously sacrifice my own health for the sake of others might bar me from becoming a guru myself someday. Oh, well. I guess I'll be massaging my own feet!

Question: What to do if you've been healing others through absorbing their pain?

Answer: I highly recommend practicing the techniques in chapter 3, particularly grounding, and running your own energy and maintaining a separation object or creating a bubble around yourself filled with moving light, water, or energy.

Make sure you do these in your own meditation and before you do your Reiki or the healing techniques in chapters 12 through 17 of this book. When you are doing a healing session with someone, frequently visualize the place into which they are releasing the energy, whether it's into the ground or up to a divine source that can handle receiving it. Most important, make a conscious decision not to allow any other person to release their emotional energy, pain, garbage, crap, or whatever you want to call it into, onto, or around you!

Question: Do you think people's attitudes about psychics are changing?

Answer: Yes. I think attitudes about psychics are changing, and that we are also starting to witness the emergence of a whole new generation of psychics.

The old-school psychic stumbled onto their abilities either as a child or after a near-death or traumatic experience, and less frequently with the help of a teacher who intuitively knew how to bring out this talent.

"New-school psychics" is my term for the new generation of psychics. This new generation of psychics is armed with an arsenal of knowledge and trained in specific methodologies. New-school psychics include, but of course are not limited to, readers of *You Are Psychic* (and you yourself after you practice the techniques in this book), graduates of clairvoyant training schools, and veterans and students of remote-viewing programs and scientific research studies. New-school psychics have greater control of their abilities. They understand that their gifts are not as rare as the last generation of talented psychics believed them to be. Many of these new-school psychics know they can train others to do what they do if they are so inclined.

As more of these impassioned and caring psychics crawl out of the closet and bravely reclaim their identity, worth, and personal power, more and more people will begin to take notice of and accept their own abilities. This in turn creates a more permissive environment for all psychics and healers.

PART II

Remote Viewing

CHAPTER 10

Remote Viewing and Clairvoyance

One of the ways advertisers sell products that have been on the market for a while is to repackage them as new and improved. I believe this is what remote viewers and researchers have done with extrasensory perception and clairvoyance, although perhaps a kinder word than "sell" would be "legitimize."

—DEBRA LYNNE KATZ

Many people have asked me, "What's the difference between clairvoyant reading and remote viewing?" As far as I'm concerned, these are really two sides of the same psychic coin. They are two methods or disciplines for essentially achieving the same thing: obtaining information through extrasensory perception. Both involve viewing information from a distance that was not previously known. Both involve utilizing one's clairvoyant ability to see visions and pictures, but they also incorporate the other inner senses of hearing, feeling, and spontaneous knowing. The main difference lies in the methodology used and the type of information that is sought.

Remote viewing has traditionally focused on viewing or observing "targets" such as events, locations, and objects, and essentially spying on people of interest. On the other hand, with the exception of occasionally looking for missing keys or a pet, clairvoyant training and reading has traditionally focused on "reading" people who request this service. Because clairvoyant reading is so person-centered, clairvoyants frequently access information in the form of symbols at least as much as they see flashes of events, people, or things as they actually appear. (For example, you might see a bull with steam coming out of its ears to represent your readee, who will understand right away that you are describing how he has been stubborn and frustrated at the same time.)

In remote viewing, the viewers are encouraged to avoid symbols and instead focus directly on the target as it literally appears. This is because symbols are open to interpretation and can create confusion for a remote viewer attempting to pick up the real physical attributes of a place, situation, or object. Symbols don't have much meaning to your subject if she turns out to be a nuclear submarine! (Submarines and their locations were common targets that remote viewers working for the government were instructed to view.) The most distinguishing characteristics of remote viewing are the stringent "protocols" that the remote viewer must follow in order to maintain the same level of standards applied to the most rigorous of scientific studies. In order to understand remote viewing today and its protocols, it's absolutely necessary to understand the context from which it emerged.

Remote Viewing: Historical Overview

In September 1995, the CIA publicly admitted its involvement in setting up a remote-viewing program that had begun at the onset of the Cold War and had spanned two decades. This program was fueled by concerns that the Soviets were engaged in similar efforts to train and utilize psychic spies.[1] Scientists at the Stanford Research Institute (SRI) had been contracted to develop remote-viewing programs variously referred to as *Star Gate, Scanate, Phoenix, Sun Streak, Aura*, and a host of other highly classified project names. The mandate of these programs was to develop stringent protocols, based on continuing psychic research, that could be taught to specially selected military personnel

---

1. Russell Targ and Harold E. Puthoff, *Mind-Reach: Scientists Look at Psychic Abilities*, new edition. Charlottesville, VA: Hampton Roads, 2005, preface.

for the purpose of accessing information blocked from ordinary perception due to time, shielding, and distance.

Thus was born the first generation of American psychic spies, or *remote viewers*, who practice SRV, which stands for *Scientific Remote Viewing*, and CRV, which stands for *Coordinate Remote Viewing* (or *Controlled Remote Viewing*, depending on who you talk to).

Two of the original scientists at SRI were Russell Targ and Harold E. Puthoff, coauthors of *Mind-Reach*, the first book of its kind to introduce remote viewing to the world. Targ's most recent work is *Limitless Mind: A Guide to Remote Viewing and Transformation of Consciousness*.

Ingo Swann is an extraordinary psychic who should not be overlooked but often is; he has been credited as the creator of CRV protocols. He helped develop the process of remote viewing at SRI by participating in hundreds of experiments in which he was the remote-viewing subject. These experiments yielded shockingly accurate results. Swann, a prolific writer, is also the author of several books (see the bibliography) that offer lots of fantastic information. Some of this information is also available on the Internet. I suggest reading Swann's books if you'd like to learn more about remote viewing from a talented psychic and researcher.

Several of the original recruits of the CIA's program have broken their silence, and have written their own books and begun their own training programs that have exploded in popularity over the past several years. David Morehouse wrote one of my all-time favorite books, *Psychic Warrior: The True Story of America's Foremost Psychic Spy and the Cover-Up of the CIA's Top-Secret Stargate Program*. Joseph McMoneagle is the author of, among other books, *Remote Viewing Secrets* and *Mind Trek: Exploring Consciousness, Time, and Space Through Remote Viewing*. Another example is Lyn Buchanan, who has written books such as *The Seventh Sense: The Secrets of Remote Viewing as Told by a "Psychic Spy" for the U.S. Military*.

Major Edward A. Dames, creator of Technical Remote Viewing, is a decorated military intelligence officer who served as the training and operations officer for the U.S. government's top secret psychic espionage unit. He offers a very thorough and comprehensive home-study training course in addition to weekend workshops. He can also be heard as a frequent guest on my favorite radio program, *Coast to Coast AM*. I respect Major Dames for continuing to be very active in the discovery of why remote viewers are not always successful in their efforts to obtain information about certain subjects, and for finding remedies for this. Such remedies can offer all psychics insight into why they are not always successful 100 percent of the time. It's my hope that Major Dames will openly share his findings.

Unfortunately, it does seem as though some of the leading teachers of remote viewing are rather suspicious when it comes to dealing with anyone who takes a different approach in training or accessing extrasensory information. As a result, I feel that there continues to be a pretty strong wall up between clairvoyant training and remote viewing, and the students and practitioners of both end up missing out on having greater breakthroughs in their level of understanding and practice of the subject as a whole.

In the same way that clairvoyant training has spawned new generations of teachers, these psychic spies have birthed their own protégés who eventually went on to create their own training institutes. A man I personally worked for (as a clerical assistant), who has created a training program called Integral Remote Viewing, is Dr. Wayne Carr, founder of the Western Institute of Remote Viewing. This institute offers in-person classes and an in-depth home study course. Some of these newer training programs (all unaffiliated with the government as far as we know) have modified the stringent, rigid protocols of scientifically controlled remote viewing in order to accommodate some of the different needs and interests of today's students. Dr. Courtney Brown, a professor at Emory University, is the author of numerous books, including *Remote Viewing: The Science and Theory of Nonphysical Perception*. He has founded the Farsight Institute, a nonprofit organization that also offers instruction in remote viewing.

Clairvoyant Training: Historical Overview

While psychics for centuries have been performing some form of clairvoyant reading, most Americans who have received formal training in this area either started out at the Berkeley Psychic Institute or studied under a graduate from this school, which was founded in the early 1970s by a brilliant man and extraordinary psychic named Lewis Bostwick. According to the folklore, one of the reasons Lewis started the institute was in response to his encounters with people who had been diagnosed with various mental disorders by the mainstream medical establishment, but who Lewis felt were actually sick psychics who didn't know how to handle their abilities. Therefore, his emphasis was on providing tools for psychics to use in their everyday lives for self-healing and the healing of others.

Over the past quarter century, thousands of dedicated and talented clairvoyants and teachers have been unleashed upon the world as a result of the early efforts of Lewis Bostwick. My own teachers included some of Lewis's protégés, including David Pearce (founder of Intuitive Way in Walnut Creek, California), John Fulton (founder of Aesclepion Healing Center in Marin County, California), Robert Skillman, Chris Murphy, Denise Bisbiglia, and, most recently, Michael Tamura, author of *You Are the Answer*.

Today many other schools teach similar methods. Some of these include Psychic Horizons in San Francisco, the Southern California Psychic Institute, Intuitive Insights School of Clairvoyance in San Diego, the Clairvoyant Center of Chicago, the InVision School for Psychics, and my own school, the International School of Clairvoyance, which offers short-term workshops ("Psychic Bootcamp"), occasional ongoing classes in the Los Angeles area, and a telephone distance-training program.

Many of the basic techniques found in chapter 4 are hybrids of those taught in traditional clairvoyant training schools throughout North America. This book and my previous book, *You Are Psychic*, are currently the only books from a major publisher that offer a complete clairvoyant training course in one volume. However, an excellent book from the late 1970s called *The Psychic Healing Book*, which was written by two of Lewis Bostwick's students, also offers many excellent tips for psychic reading and healing.

Similarities and Differences between Clairvoyant Training and Remote Viewing

One of the protocols of the Defense Intelligence Agency's remote-viewing program mandated that a "monitor" be present for every remote-viewing session. A person acting as a monitor was highly trained and would act as the logical, left brain of the remote viewer(s). The monitor would give the remote viewers a set of target numbers to focus on and pose directions and questions to them. He would record their responses and ask them to make adjustments or provide clarifications to what they were seeing.

Traditionally, clairvoyant training schools have utilized a "control" to oversee each reading, which is usually performed by two or more clairvoyant students. The control is much like a monitor. They remain alert, out of trance, and centered in their crown chakra where their knowingness abilities can help them to observe the various energies and entities in the room that may affect the reading or the readers. They often lead the psychics through an opening meditation to prepare them for the reading, and give directions and pose questions for the clairvoyant to look at.

When I am training students, I act as their monitor or control until my students begin to demonstrate that they can do this for themselves. My focus is on them instead of the person they are reading, although occasionally I will find myself getting psychic impressions and sharing these, particularly when the readee has similar issues to those I am working on. Many of the questions or instructions I pose to my students are presented in this book.

Since most people learning on their own don't have the luxury of working with a monitor or control, they have to provide these services for themselves. They then have the challenge of having to use both parts of their mind: the part that receives information and the part that analyzes it. This is a little tricky initially but definitely doable. I believe one of the reasons many present-day remote-viewing trainers are beginning to relax their protocols also has to do with the fact that most students just don't have someone else in their lives they can rely on for help every time they want to use their abilities. Ultimately, I believe self-reliance is the best way to go.

The Starting Point

Both clairvoyant reading and remote viewing are active processes. We aren't just sitting there hoping for the information to arrive; we are following specific steps. The difference is that clairvoyants are often doing these steps in their minds, while some remote viewers are trained to do their sessions with eyes open, while writing on paper.

When we begin a clairvoyant reading, it helps if we have something to tune in to. This is why we ask our readee to repeat their name a few times. When the readee says their name we are like radios, tuning directly in to their specific frequency. Remote viewers don't have their subjects sitting three feet in front of them, or waiting patiently for them on the other end of the telephone. Often they have no idea who or what it is they are going to view.

In CRV, the word *target* describes the subject the remote viewers have been assigned to observe. SRI researchers discovered that psychics were better able to accurately describe locations when they were "blind," or did not know the identity of the location. "Blind" is a word used in psychological research to describe the awareness of the person participating in the experiment. Researchers discovered that the best way to label a target so that the viewers could have something to focus on was to assign it a set of multi-digit numbers. The target numbers don't have any meaning in themselves, but have been randomly selected. However, when the military or government needed information about a specific location, sometimes the numbers given to viewers were actual longitudinal/latitudinal coordinates.

Formulating targets is a science and an art in itself. Research and direct practice have demonstrated that certain targets and those creating them yield better results. Part of the reason for this is that the person choosing the target must be very clear. If they write down the instructions—e.g., "View my dog at 5:00 p.m."—but don't provide a specific date, then the psychic might see the dog at 5:00 p.m. on any other day of its life or even afterlife, depending on how interesting that day was or sympathetic the viewer is to what was happening on a particular day. Another possibility would be for the viewer to erroneously tune in to the target designer's other dog, if a specific name for the dog was not indicated and the target designer has another dog or once did at any time in his life. If the target designer is thinking of his girlfriend instead of his dog when he was designing or writing down the target, the psychic might just start viewing this girlfriend. Now in all these instances, the remote viewer may be demonstrating remarkably strong psychic abilities but would be missing the intended target, and therefore whatever information they have reported would be recorded as a "miss."

In clairvoyant reading, our target is often the person we are giving the reading to. When that person says their name, or verbalizes the name of another person they wish to know about, the name acts like a string of light that we can follow right to the source. Another way to look at it is that we are inviting a bit of their energy to come through this string right into our viewing receptacle where we can observe it. However, sometimes if that person has a lot of foreign energies around them, and they are more out of their body than in it, we will lock onto the strongest energy signal in or around them (for example, their husband or mother) and may begin to read that person instead. (This also will happen if the readee brings someone along to the reading with them. This is why I don't usually allow others to sit in the room while the reading is going on.)

When I first began doing readings, I would frequently have someone tell me they wanted to know how things looked with their boyfriend, girlfriend, wife, or husband. They might say the person's name, but I would begin to describe someone else. This someone else frequently turned out to be a secret lover or person of desire that they wanted to know about even more than the person they had originally asked about, but were too embarrassed or too nervous to do so. So now, when someone wants to know about a love relationship, I often ask them if they are involved with more than one person, and then ask them to say both people's names, or I will ask them to tell me who they are most interested in hearing about first.

Symbols/Ideograms

As we've covered in other chapters, the key to calling forth information is to build a specific place within your mind in which the information can be collected and then be observed—hence the reading screen and viewing receptacle. Remote viewers don't use a receptacle or rose, but many do work with a symbol called an *ideogram*. The difference here is that this symbol is created by the remote viewers themselves on paper, rather than in their minds. While focusing on the target numbers, they are instructed to begin drawing their ideogram. They relax and let their hand pretty much do what it wants. After a while this ideogram begins to take on shapes that have been found to match attributes of the target. Most of the remote-viewing courses mentioned in this chapter provide detailed instruction about how to work with an ideogram. When working with ideograms, I believe remote viewers are utilizing some of the same skills or forces involved in scribing or automatic writing.

In or Out of the Body?

Clairvoyant training has typically required students to do their readings from within their bodies, although various programs do teach out-of-body healing, and schools such as Aesclepion Healing Center offer programs in which students are taught how to rise up out of their body, and hang out in the chakras above their body, in order to let another being in, something we don't need or really want to do during clairvoyant reading. (I do teach you how to have a guide connect into your hand chakras later in this book. However, I suggest if you have a strong interest in channeling spirits through the rest of your chakras or body that you obtain specific and additional training for this.)

Some forms of remote viewing have incorporated the work of Robert Monroe, who founded the Monroe Institute and wrote some great books on the topic of out-of-body experiences. This program teaches people how to move into deeper states of consciousness to achieve out-of-body and psychic experiences through the use of biofeedback machines. The Monroe Institute's programs are highly rated, although expensive. When in these altered states of consciousness, a process called "bilocation" can occur. While there are different theories about the nature of bilocation, I believe it is a separation of part of you from your body. It's what most of us would consider an extreme conscious out-of-body experience. If clairvoyant reading is analogous to sitting at home and watching images of an event on your TV, bilocation would be actually going to that location and observing it directly, except that people can bilocate to events in different time periods. So bilocation is either time travel or it is similar to participating in a memory or hologram of the event.

Joni Dourif is president of PSI TECH, another excellent remote-viewing training institute. She describes bilocation as "the required mind state for accurate remote viewing to occur. In TRV (Technical Remote Viewing) terms it is quite literally being in two places at once. After the TRV protocols are initiated, the viewer's attention splits. One half of the viewer's conscious and unconscious attention is at the target matrix site (or the target blueprint in the collective unconscious) and the other half is with the viewer's senses tending to TRV structure. Bilocating in TRV structure induces a heightened sense of awareness referred to as 'a state of high attention.' This is the optimal mind state to effect the remote viewing process."[2]

When doing clairvoyant readings with a person sitting in front of you, bilocation, at least the conscious experience of it, is rare. This is because very often you are connecting with your readee's energy that is right there with you. Bilocation is more likely to occur when reading

2. Joni Dourif, *The Matrix Newsletter*. PSI TECH, 2007. Online at http://www .remoteviewing.com/remote-viewing-news-articles/the-matrix-newsletter/index.html.

people over the phone, and particularly when you are reading a person who is not present at all or when performing a long distance healing. Therefore, I suspect that bilocation is the effect of sending your energy to remote locations away from your own body rather than merely a result of following the protocols of scientifically controlled remote viewing as some leaders in the field suggest. Just like any other phenomenon, I believe it may occur in degrees, so that you will not be aware of it until more of you is out of your body than present within it.

Since most of my focus has been on performing readings while being centered within myself, most of my personal experience with bilocation has occurred while I was meditating or close to falling asleep. Upon reading about bilocation, I held the intention for about a week that I would be able to experience it. One afternoon while napping I found myself flying over a field of golden grass, near the ocean. It was quite fun, really exhilarating, because there is such a strong kinesthetic sense of movement. It reminded me of a few cherished lucid dreams I've had where I became aware I was dreaming and chose to fly. During my bilocation experiences, I really noticed the feeling of wind somehow on my body, even though my body was snuggly tucked into bed.

This experience was slightly different from the out-of-body experiences I've had, perhaps since during the out-of-body experiences I remained right in the room with my physical body. The problem with bilocation is that sometimes when you are finished you might feel "out of it": dizzy, ungrounded, or intensely fatigued. The psychic tools offered in chapters 3 and 4 can help bring you back fully to your body and reverse these effects. It's just important to understand, as I mentioned above, that the moment you say to yourself, "Wow, that sounds cool. I want to experience that," it is very possible you will do so to some extent.

Data Collection

Some of the most important protocols of remote viewing have to do with the rules regarding the viewer's data collection process, which includes their choices of what to focus on, methods of observation, and how information is reported and analyzed. This is where the differences between remote viewing and clairvoyant reading become most apparent. In my opinion, clairvoyants can very much benefit from understanding the research behind these protocols, because they have been designed to minimize the errors and pitfalls that all psychics encounter when utilizing their abilities of extrasensory perception. While I do not have room to present any sort of detailed course in remote viewing here, and I would not be the one to do so in any case as my training in these specific protocols is limited, I will present some general concepts below that any psychic should be aware of, whether they are reading people or coordinates.

Scientifically controlled remote viewing distinguishes between hard and soft data. The hard data are really the most important. This type of data includes observing, recording, or reporting the basic attributes of the target as opposed to providing a conclusion as to what the target is. Most of the terms in this type of data would be classified as adjectives. You are looking for colors, shapes, sizes, movements, textures, sounds, and dimensions, as well as smells, tastes, and feelings. Words like *red*, *small*, *round*, *smelly*, *fluid*, *sharp*, and *shiny* would be used here. This is the micro level.

Soft data are the larger concepts. These are useful but are more subject to interpretation that can be incorrect. Some of these terms could be *castle*, *swimming pool*, *dog*, *person*, and so on. These are all nouns. The reason these the soft data have traditionally been separated into a different category in remote viewing is because the person assessing the data needed to be aware that this type of data might not be as solid. For example, the castle might not really be a castle but could be a fancy house or a miniature golf course. The swimming pool might actually be a holding tank for chemicals. The dog might not be a dog but rather a goat or a cow. The person might be a statue. Since our minds naturally seek to classify and pair one piece of information with something we are already familiar with, this is what happens when we observe anything through either our physical eyes or our psychic ones.

As a remote viewer or clairvoyant, you certainly wouldn't want to leave these nouns out of your description of what you are seeing or sensing, since much of the time they are going to be valid and important, if not absolutely 100 percent correct. It's just helpful to understand where your own mind might be filling in the blanks. In scientifically controlled remote viewing, you or your monitor would, for future analysis, record on paper these nouns (soft data) in a different column from the adjectives (hard data).

Another type or category of data would include your final impressions or interpretations of the whole. This category of data is the least reliable because, again, it leaves a lot of room for the remote viewer's mind to fill in the blanks. A building, a cornfield, a bunch of animals in a field—a remote viewer might assume the overall target is a farm. However, it could be a zoo, or it could be a slaughterhouse, or it could turn out to be something the remote viewer has never heard or thought of, which would make it almost impossible for the viewer to effectively label it. The same is true of a person who was actually physically present at an unfamiliar location and attempting to define what it is.

One day, after hearing a radio program about the instability of Yellowstone National Park, I decided to take a peek and see what might be causing or contributing to this instability. I immediately saw an object that looked familiar, actually several of them, but I didn't know what it was. So I wrote down that it was a large, metallic (more rusty than metallic) mechanical object that was moving up and down in a steady, consistent motion and rate. It had an oblong, almost squarish "head" to it connected to something straight. It was the "head" part that was going up and down. It was large, at least three sizes bigger than a tall man (this would be hard data). The object really reminded me of a hammer, or perhaps more accurately an anvil (soft data). But why would there be a mechanical anvil moving up and down on its own accord in the middle of the desert? It seemed as though there were several of these. I had seen these before but just could not remember what they were, and it was driving me crazy.

About three days later I was driving farther north than I usually do, and along the road I saw the same exact object. "What is that?" I asked my companion. "It's an oil drill," came the reply. I thought that was strange because I had never heard of them drilling for oil in Yellowstone. However, I began doing more research about the area and discovered that some scientists were convinced that oil drilling in other parts of the country is having an enormous impact on Yellowstone, the national park that has been called the "heart chakra of America." If the area around Yellowstone ever erupts in an earthquake or volcano, most of the United States would be adversely affected.

Obviously, when reading people, particularly ones present with you, it would not be at all practical to go through the above procedure of analysis, of separating your observations into soft and hard data. I wouldn't recommend this because one of the worst things you can do during a reading is to get too analytical. Instead, I suggest that whenever possible, you should remind yourself to look for the basic building blocks first. If you see a woman, don't just say, "I see a woman" and move on. Describe instead the attributes that make you think you are seeing a woman. If you don't get any specifics, then ask your receptacle to show you these, or one definite symbol by which your readee will be able to recognize the woman.

The difficulty here is that you might be describing the actual attributes of a real woman, or you might instead be seeing a *symbol* of a woman who represents the actual woman in question. If your aunt Emma was very mean and had black curly hair, and your readee's aunt is also very mean but has blond straight hair, the part of you that generates pictures might show you someone who looks like your aunt. This may be happening because you and your readee have a strong match, or maybe because this is the only way you'd think of mentioning a mean aunt who might have had a large impact on the readee.

However, sometimes you might see the real or literal physical attributes of the person as if they were standing in front of you, and by mentioning these your readee will known exactly who you are talking about. If you are not sure, you can always say, "This is what I am seeing. I don't know if the person really looks like this because she looks a whole lot like my mean aunt Emma who I had to live with for a year when my parents got divorced." At this point your readee might exclaim, "Wow, I lived with a mean aunt too when my parents got divorced, and I've been trying to deal with the trauma I still feel. But my aunt has blond hair."

When I am training my clairvoyant students, I have to remind them frequently to go back to the building blocks of what they are seeing. This is particularly true of the psychics I work with who have been reading with their other abilities apart from their clairvoyance. If I ask such people to look at a rose and tell me what the rose looks like—is it big or small? open or closed? standing straight at attention or drooping?—and instead they give me a five-minute assessment of the readee's psychological issues and what they have to do to overhaul their life, I am frankly not impressed, even if the rest of the class is sitting there with their mouths wide open in awe.

That's not to say that such a reading might not be right on, but what I want to know for the sake of their clairvoyant training, and to help them overcome the possibility of filling in the blanks with their own assumptions and projections, is how that information came in. I slow them down. Focusing on the minute details requires a tremendous amount of focus, concentration, and mental energy. However, it gives us a better chance to obtain quality information, whether we are working with the literal in remote viewing or with the symbology that is an integral part of clairvoyance.

We've got the rest of our lives to increase the speed and complexity of our readings, which is sometimes desirable and sometimes not. Working closely with students one on one, I'm always brought back to how that which is simple can be more powerful, since the simple is usually a lot less tainted with analytical influence.

Target Design

From my own experiments and research, I believe the challenge of remote viewing is in formulating the best targets for viewers to look at. By "formulating targets," I mean determining what it is you are assigning the psychic to look at. This is why reading people is often easier. All you have to do is give a psychic the person's name, and the psychic will be locked on to that specific person. When you ask a psychic to view an event or location, you have to be specific—not about what you verbally tell them, because often all they will be given is a number to lock on to. But once they start their "mission," they could look at any aspect of the target.

For example, recently I gave my students a target that I assigned the number-and-letter combination 1A. I wrote the target on a piece of paper and described it as "Caleb's (my son's friend's) birthday party today at the Cliff Castle Casino." Several students immediately saw a large pastel-colored resort, which Cliff Castle Casino is. One student saw kids playing with balls, which is just what they do at the "kids' club" at that casino. Many others saw tropical decor, umbrella drinks, and a big swimming pool. (I didn't know they had a restaurant there with this motif so I thought these students were way off.) A couple of other students saw a wedding. The problem was that my students were all going to parts of the casino they thought were the most interesting, which were not necessarily the parts of the casino I as the target formulator wanted or expected them to see.

This experience further confirmed for me that assigning the target is the trickiest business for researchers, something many other psi/ remote viewers will also confirm. During another experiment I asked my students to look at my sister's present location. Almost all of them saw her walking through the rooms of a mountainside rustic house, opening doors and feeling bored, as though she didn't want to be working. As it turned out, my sister was en route to such a house (she was a real-estate agent about to do an open house in the Santa Barbara hills) but had not yet arrived. Since the target was where she currently was at the time of the exercise (first in a coffee shop and then in her car), technically all but one student (who saw her in her car on a winding hillside road near the water) was incorrect.

Personal Transformation and the Impact of Psychic Work

From the accounts provided by the early pioneers in clandestine remote-viewing programs, it is clear that remote viewers were very much personally impacted on every imaginable level by their viewing sessions. Their belief systems, concepts of self, emotional states, and relationships underwent enormous shifts soon after they began their training. Just about every one of these viewers will tell you the person they were and the person they became within the course of a year was very different. While this was at times confusing and painful, it could also be intensely rewarding.

This transformation is no different from what clairvoyant students experience as well. The difference here is that to my knowledge the remote-viewing protocols addressed neither the spiritual development of the viewer nor the potential side effects of time and space travel. Rather, these were unanticipated byproducts of the training and viewing sessions. This is not surprising given that remote viewing was developed in a lab, mostly by men, to be utilized by military or government personnel. You would think (hope) that the first thing soldiers trained for war would need would be a good amount of psychological support in order to know how to handle what they are about to deal with. But that is certainly not the case. Instead, soldiers are indoctrinated into a belief system that ensures they will put concepts such as patriotism and heroism over the importance of their own personal mental or physical health, which they are taught to override for the benefit of their country. The same thing is true for scientific research. When a study is designed or a project embarked upon, the only reason the researcher is considered is to ensure that the researcher does not inadvertently taint the evidence. Otherwise, no one cares about the researcher's feelings or personal experience (with the exception of research being performed with potentially hazardous physical consequences).

Since remote viewing was done as part of a team, the viewers had each other to commiserate with, and this likely saved many of them from going completely mad. However, some didn't fare so well. Fortunately, many of today's remote-viewing programs are placing much greater emphasis on the personal well-being and development of their students. As I've already noted, since their inception clairvoyant training programs have been emphasizing this aspect of personal growth, transformation, and self-protection.

Healing

Remote viewing has been used since its inception to collect information about people at a distance, without their consent. These people were not usually aware (or supposed to be aware) that they were being viewed. They could be probed for their physical attributes, their thoughts, their emotional mindsets, their behaviors or activities, and so forth. Remote viewing has also been used to influence or control the minds of other participants. It can be used to harm or help people. Although I doubt either our military or the Soviet military were too concerned about healing their unwitting targets, more and more remote-viewing training programs today are incorporating healing into their teachings and practices due to the interests and needs of current students.

Unexpected Sightings

The remote viewers working for the government probably weren't too surprised when they encountered an enemy's combat training camps, lost airplanes, captured soldiers, minefields, submarines, or assassination plots. However, can you imagine what it was like for them when they encountered deceased spirits, demons, or aliens? In reading such entities, it becomes clear that remote viewers, regardless of how skeptical or scientific they were, encountered and continue to meet the same types of entities that clairvoyants have been seeing and communicating with for centuries. They are just a little less likely to mention these to anyone who cares to listen!

Remote-Viewing Snobbery

"How dare you call me a psychic! I have nothing to do with those embarrassing fortunetellers! I am a remote viewer!" This is still a common response you get from those trained in the early remote-viewing programs. I see this as unfortunate for a number of reasons. First, it's just outright confusing. Oh, okay, sorry, of course you aren't psychic. You just use your nonphysical senses to gather information about the past, present, or future that your logical mind has no access to. But wait a second, isn't that what being psychic is? Isn't this the same thing that clairvoyants and channelers do? Hey, come to think of it, isn't this what Jesus, Moses, and Mohammed did as well? Weren't they prophets who had visions of the future and heard voices no one else could hear? Whether these religious icons were gods, men, or both is still up for debate; however, it's clear that they became famous for their psychic or remote-viewing talents. Psychics? What! How dare you, you blasphemous infidel. ESP is the work of the devil! Oh, okay. Now I understand. Yeah.

One of my best friends and a talented clairvoyant of thirty years, Rachel Mai, recently pointed out to me that, like disobedient slaves who were tarred and feathered, psychics have been splattered with the most toxic of accusations and stereotypes since way before the Crusades. This has happened despite the fact (maybe because of the fact?) they were the very people who have enacted the most change and to whom millions upon millions of people today not only pray but completely hand their lives over to ("Jesus will save you"). Every time we see a cross, we are told to think, "He died for our sins." But a deeper message is, "If you rock the boat, talk directly to God, foresee the future, heal the sick, perform exorcisms, or try to get people to see the truth, then you could end up like Jesus but worse because, after all, he was the incarnation of God. You are a mere mortal, and therefore it's gonna hurt."

It's no wonder, then, that the remote viewers, who invested years laboring in dingy college laboratories, pulling themselves up the wobbly ladder of success amidst tornadoes of hardship, who have acquired every ounce of their reputation and status with their own sweat and blood on the battlefields and within their stifling office cubicles, are extremely loath to be classified as lowly, bourgeois psychics.

That the remote viewers working for the government wanted to distance themselves from the debilitating stereotypes around the word *psychic* is therefore understandable. As Joseph McMoneagle states in his book *Memoirs of a Psychic Spy*, "The ridicule and derision encountered during contact with outside personnel on a week-to-week basis is difficult to relate." The amount of cognitive dissonance that remote viewers such as McMoneagle experienced must have been absolutely exhausting.

However, years after the dissolution of these governmental programs, there are still remote viewers today who are so concerned with their reputations and with maintaining a positive public persona that they will chastise or debunk any psychic who does not adhere strictly to the remote-viewing protocols, which in my opinion are not always practical or applicable to every situation involving the use of one's psychic abilities. If I can close my eyes, focus on a simple rose, invite the target's energy into the rose, and within thirty seconds correctly identify the target or describe its attributes; if I can describe a person I've never met down to specific physical, mental, and emotional characteristics, even occasionally getting their name, then obviously the methods I employ and teach are more than adequate for what I am specifically attempting to achieve. Are these as effective as the remote-viewing protocols for viewing coordinates or distant targets? I believe they are.

The fact is that most psychics, whether clairvoyants or remote viewers, don't have our own controlled laboratories equipped with isolation chambers lined in acoustic insulation for electrical shielding and soundproofing. We don't have biofeedback brain-wave recording equipment. We most certainly don't have Stanford-trained scientists standing by our sides, whispering instructions into our ears or piped in through little microphones sewn into our lapels. We don't have anyone handing us a list of pre-selected, time-tested targets when we meet with our clients. We must therefore do the best with what we have: the techniques offered throughout this book and a genuine desire and commitment to be as accurate as possible given the circumstances and nature of what it is we are doing.

I don't think enough research, if any, has been done specifically on clairvoyant training and on utilizing one's abilities for the purpose of accessing information about a person who requests it. I believe this is the next step in psi research, one that is long overdue, and I hope to be a part of this at some point in the near future. The reason reading people has not been the focus of psi experiments is the same reason psychological research in general lags behind other types of research in funding and support. When dealing with people, there are just so many variables that are difficult to control.

In her book *The Intention Experiment*, Lynne McTaggart outlines several studies that look at the effect of one person's intentions on another. These experiments have high validity and are extremely controlled, and they have yielded statistically significant and repeatable results. Therefore, it should not be impossible to design and implement studies that look at the accuracy and impact of clairvoyant reading by one person for another.

Clairvoyants Are Not Immune to Judgments Either

I know far too many psychics who are graduates of clairvoyant training schools, and who are convinced that any psychic who has not followed their same path is an ungrounded, unbalanced, wacky New Age sickly psychic vulnerable to all the insidious energies waiting to attack at any moment. I was programmed to believe this myself until I graduated from the school I attended, moved to the Philippines and then Sedona, and then eventually to the L.A. area. I discovered that yes, there are a lot of wacky people out there, but some of these people are also extremely talented, loving, self-taught psychics who have become my very best friends! Would they benefit from my training or the training that I received? I'm sure they would. But this isn't their path, and I am sure I would have benefited from some of their experiences, which I will never have.

Divide and Conquer— It's Worked So Far, Against Us All

Both clairvoyant training programs and remote-viewing protocols are at risk for becoming antiquated if each one continues to be conducted in a spirit of elitism, possessiveness, paranoia, and an unrelenting addiction to the way it's always been rather than the way it could be better. We need not criticize each other, but rather learn from each other to further perfect our techniques and approaches. We have formidable opponents out there in the forms of ignorance, fear, and a dogmatic skepticism that continues to deny the experiences of millions and continues to ignore the undeniable results of what are now thousands of quality scientific studies that have proven psychic functioning is as much of a reality as are the turned-up noses on our faces. The only way to disarm these enemies of truth and spiritual freedom is to sever our own alliances with them. We must stop allowing our fears, egos, and economic interests to divide us. Instead, as psychics and lovers of the innate psychic talents within us, whether latent or blatant, we must stand, sit, float, fly, dream, study, practice, learn, develop, and transform together.

CHAPTER 11

Hybrid Remote Viewing: Experiments and Techniques

If you want to be incrementally better, be competitive. If you want to be exponentially better, be cooperative.
—UNKNOWN

My Own Remote Viewing Experiments: How We Can Use Our Clairvoyance to View Objects and Events

As I've noted, I was trained as a clairvoyant reader, not as a remote viewer. Therefore, all of my training centered on reading people who request information and assistance, and most of my professional practice has as well.

However, ever since I read David Morehouse's book *Psychic Warrior*, I've been utterly fascinated with anything having to do with remote viewing. I purchased a few home-study courses and vowed to follow them step by step, but then I broke those vows almost as soon as I made them, because quite frankly I was too impatient. I wanted to jump right to viewing the targets to see if I could just use the simple methods of utilizing a rose and my reading screen. What I discovered was that most of the time, that was all I needed. Occasionally, I felt as though I did need to go into a deeper state or actually do some out-of-body travel, but many times I just focused on the target number and immediately began getting images that turned out to really pertain to the actual target. During my very first attempt, I saw an image that looked like the shape of Texas. I saw people fighting and a structure that looked like an adobe castle. The target turned out to be the Alamo.

Soon after the publication of my book *You Are Psychic*, I began getting tons of e-mails (this is the best way to contact me) from readers who were unable to find clairvoyant training programs in their area. In response, I designed and implemented a long-distance clairvoyant training program so that I could at least accommodate some of these budding clairvoyants. In order to keep the training fresh, and for my own curiosity, I decided to conduct some little "experiments." These experiments involved the remote viewing of objects, and later events, with pretty awesome results! I do want to point out that, from a scientific standpoint, they were not well "controlled" and would not stand up to the rigorous standards that psi experiments must adhere to. (Note: such requirements are far more rigorous than those applied even to studies on pharmaceuticals.) However, since my goal was one of discovery and insights for me and my students, you will see that we had what I feel are some pretty interesting results.

For my very first "experiment," I placed a few objects in a shoebox and asked Masaru Kato, one of the students in my long-distance telephone training program, to leave his body at his home in Chicago and to send his spirit over to my place in California. I instructed him to focus on a brown and orange box resting on my lap and to describe its contents. I told him to visualize the box and wait and see if he got anything about the contents. (The box in this case was taking the place of a receptacle.) He wasn't very confident in his ability to do this, but as usual he pushed himself and courageously reported that he saw a shiny black ball with something floating in it. He stated it seemed like the ball had a "window in it," and inside was something displaying a message. The message was unclear but seemed to be written on a triangle. He also stated it was reflective.

Masaru was right about almost all of these characteristics, except that I didn't think the object was reflective. However, I decided to check. I opened the box to look again, and sure enough I saw my own reflection! He had no idea what this object was that he was describing and stated he felt rather foolish. I finally explained to him that this was a toy—a black, plastic, shiny fortune-telling cue ball with a triangle-shaped cube inside floating in liquid. When you shake it up, one of eight inspirational messages written across a triangle cube appears in the window, except most of the messages had worn away over time and were unreadable. At first he didn't know what I was talking about, but then he remembered he had once seen such a ball in a cartoon.

Excited about his accuracy with the details, I asked Masaru to imagine he was freely wandering around the room and to tell me what else he noticed. He stated, "I know this sounds pretty strange, but I see a dinosaur sitting in an egg that looks kind of plastic." I assured him that was not strange at all, as there was in fact a stuffed dinosaur inside a plastic egg on the shelf about five feet from me. He later saw "two Muppets, like from *Sesame Street*" sitting on the dresser. He was accurate about that as well.

The following week I repeated the same experiment with another student named Deborah Sharif, who was located even farther away, in South Carolina. Up to this point I had been encouraging her to do her readings from within her body, but this time I gave her full permission to let her spirit venture out onto the etheric highway for a visit to my home (much faster than the Los Angeles freeways!). This time I placed a souvenir inside the box. The souvenir was a snow globe that contained a miniature of the White House in water. When you shake it up, it looks like it's snowing. It didn't take her more than a minute to report a "heavy object, like a paperweight, almost like a crystal ball, with glitter or snow swirling around." She then went on to describe my own house, admitting it looked cozy but much smaller than she had anticipated (it is rather small). She also saw it looking very clean and well-organized. Fortunately, she wasn't viewing a few days earlier, before I had cleaned up my house!

Next, I walked into my living room, stood in front of a window, and asked Deborah to describe some objects on the windowsill. She wasn't really able to get anything about these objects, but instead she began describing the view from the window. She saw a scene in which a woman who she thought was me but had red hair (she didn't know I had highlighted my hair red) and a dark-haired and dark-complexioned boy (my son, who she didn't know looks nothing like me) were "laughing and laughing" along with a "stocky guy," who she thought was my boyfriend Danny. She was confused about this last point, because during a prior session she had spontaneously tuned in to him and at that time he had no facial hair. She said this time it looked like he had a goatee, which he had in fact recently sprouted. She reported she "saw" us having a great time sliding down hills outside on something that looked like a "wooden sled with wheels." I told her that this was exactly what we had been doing the past weekend, only it was a makeshift wooden go-cart.

During a recent ongoing class held at my home with a few enthusiastic students, I invited them to meditate on their own for a few minutes, while I hurried off to my bedroom where I dug out the now-familiar box that I had been using with my long-distance students the week before. At first I placed the above-mentioned snow globe with the snow swirling around the White House in the box along with a figurine of a decorative, brightly painted horse, but then I changed my mind and decided to replace these with objects I had never before experimented with. I finally decided on an action figure of a little guy riding a toy motorcycle.

Less than ten minutes later, I sat in front of three of my students with the sealed box on my lap, and two of the three described the action figure in the exact position he was sitting in. They were not able to get a grasp on a couple of other objects that I had hurriedly placed in the box, but instead saw a "paperweight-type object, like a ball with liquid in it, and something like glitter or snow floating around a white building." Another student saw a "decorative show horse." These were the exact objects that had occupied the box during prior experiments, and that I had momentarily included in the box earlier before changing my mind and removing them. While this was very interesting, I was not surprised since it is common to confuse points in time when reading people, and similar incidents have been reported by other remote viewers and experimenters using different techniques.

Although it was now after 10 p.m., my students were still raring to go, so I retreated to my bedroom again and decided on another object, this one still in its long, narrow gift box. I wrapped the box inside a large towel so as not to give away any clues about its shape, before returning to the students in the living room. I asked them to use the same techniques they usually use to read a person in order to "view" this object, now placed only a few feet from them in the towel on my lap. They all immediately reported seeing an orange/red color. One student named Sandy saw "an orange-y reddish tulip, with lines in it with a very long narrow stem that curved a bit." She stated that it seemed like it should "be in a vase."

"Close," I advised, "but it's not a tulip; it's a rose." I unwrapped the towel, exposing first the narrow box and then its single occupant: an orangeish, reddish chiseled-glass flower with a long, skinny stem that curved a bit at the bottom. It was still in the box because I had not yet found the right vase to put it in. It was at this point the students corrected me.

"Hey, that's not a rose. It's a tulip, just like Sandy saw." I looked more closely, as it had been a few weeks since Christmas, when my son had given it to me as a gift. I couldn't believe my eyes. They were right. It was indeed a tulip!

This experiment also showed me that selecting a target or objects to view, and the way they are placed, is paramount to the perceived success of the psychic. This is why rigorous controls are needed for this type of experiment. I had the knowledge of what had already been in the box, and was aware of my own indecision about what to place in there. A scientist looking at the data would automatically record the responses of the students as incorrect, since the scientist would be required to mention only what was currently in the box. In an ideal experiment, the same box would not be used unless the study sought to understand how psychics can be confused by time and space. The person running the experiment would not be the same person who selected the objects or targets, nor would they even have knowledge of what the objects or targets were, because then it would not be clear if the students were reading the experimenter's mind or really viewing the contents.

For my next informal experiment, I thought I would try to fix at least one of the above flaws by making myself blind to the target. I asked my boyfriend, Danny, to come up with any event at any time in history and to write this event on a piece of paper. I told Danny to write a description of this event, put it in an envelope, and assign it a six-digit number unrelated to the subject matter. I then went to my bedroom to go to sleep. However, as soon as my head hit the pillow, my curiosity got the best of me. I wondered if I would be able to see what the target was. I knew that if I were successful, I would no longer be blind to the target, which would then contaminate the validity of my experiment with my students, but I told myself that I would just take a quick clairvoyant peek. If I didn't get anything in one minute, I would stop.

I created a reading screen, then a transparent 3-D rose on the screen, and instructing myself to stay centered within my body and behind my sixth chakra, I invited the attributes of the event Danny was presently writing about in the other room to appear in my receptacle, then forced myself to just watch and see what happened. Within thirty seconds I saw a very clear image of the Statue of Liberty. I decided not to look any further, and I drifted off to sleep.

The next morning I couldn't find the envelope and asked Danny where it was. Right before he handed it to me, I said, "I just want to know one thing. Does it have anything to do with the Statue of Liberty?" "Yeah," he said nonchalantly, "that's it."

He handed me the sealed envelope and left the room without another word. Since he'd been quite a skeptic, and a monumental jokester, I didn't believe him. I thought again that maybe, for the sake of the experiment, I should just not open the envelope until after I worked with my students. But that thought lasted about two seconds. I tore the envelope in half, pulled out the piece of paper, and there it was: Danny had written, "The rededication and unveiling of the Statue of Liberty, New York City harbor, July 4, 1986."

Even though now I was not blind to the target, I decided to go ahead and see whether or not my student Masaru (who had done so well seeing the objects in my room during a previous session) would have success with the particular target as well. Once again we conducted our session over the telephone, with him in Chicago and me at home in California. Several times during our session he stated that he felt as though he were traveling to New York. He did not mention anything about the Statue of Liberty, but instead began describing ships— old war ships, from many different nations. He saw cannons and gunfire on the ships. He saw the scene on Iwo Jima in which the Americans won the battle and put up their flag. Since I was mostly thinking about the Statue of Liberty, I assumed Masaru must be way off.

But something told me to go ask Danny what he was thinking about when he had written out this event. Danny told me he had actually been in New York for the rededication of the Statue of Liberty, and that the harbor had been filled with every kind of ship imaginable from every war in the history of the planet. There was also a massive fireworks display, but to him the ships were the highlight of the event. Danny is a real war-movie fanatic and can identify just about every kind of boat or plane that has ever been made.

This experience reminded me of a fact that many psi researchers have pointed out: that we will "see" the things we have the most interest in. Had I actually been physically present for the Statue of Liberty's rededication, I would have likely found the statue the most interesting aspect—and that is likely why I saw the statue rather than any of the ships.

At a recent workshop, I gave this same target to a whole group of students. It was at the end of the day, and there were numerous distractions in the room. I didn't give the students the specific date of the event, so I wasn't surprised that for the most part the results were mostly inconclusive. However, one student, an attorney named George who had been performing distance healing for several years, did see the Fourth of July in the New York City harbor and did see an image of the Statue of Liberty.

From the experiences above and many others like them, I have become convinced that the clairvoyant techniques taught in this book, with perhaps a few modifications, can be effectively utilized for remote viewing of objects and events at a distance.

Combination Remote Viewing/Clairvoyant Exercise

I suggest that you get a tape recorder and tape your session. Buy a ninety-minute tape and give yourself permission to have very long pauses on it. This is not a performance, so it doesn't have to sound good! No one else will hear the tape unless you choose to share it with them. Later, you can listen to the tape and transcribe it onto paper if you'd like.

Taping your session is of course optional. If you are going to use a tape recorder, turn it on and place it close to your mouth as soon as you begin, so you don't even have to think about it once you get started. If you don't have a tape recorder, then make sure you have paper and a pen or pencil next to you.

It helps to decide on your target before you begin. You might have something in mind that you are wondering about, such as a missing object, a specific location, or an event at some point in history, whether past or future. You can choose this for yourself, or you can ask someone to give you a target that they place in a sealed envelope and assign some number to. You can also check out the website for the Western Institute for Remote Viewing or the website for Ed Dame's company, Learn Remote Viewing. Both of these offer plenty of targets that have been selected as ideal ones for students to practice on, and as I noted above, it doesn't matter at all that you may be using different methods from these instructors.

I suggest you write down your target or target number, and hold it on your lap or under your pillow. You may sit or lie down for this exercise—just make sure you find a place where you won't be disturbed. Turn off your phone!

Slow down your breathing. Let your mind wander to a number of different times and places. For example, remember the last time you were at the beach, then immediately think of the first time you recall riding your bike, then recall your first airplane ride. Next, think of your first, last, or only kiss, then imagine what it must be like to fly on a space shuttle to the moon. The important thing here, and really the sole purpose of this exercise, is to keep your mind darting back and forth from subject to subject without allowing it to hold a thought for more than a second or two at the most. Do this for about five to ten minutes; if you start to fall asleep, sit up or go right on to the next exercise. (This exercise is actually great in and of itself if you suffer from insomnia.)

Next, imagine that there is a cord of light coming either out of your third chakra or out of your crown chakra (you can experiment to see which one works best for you). Imagine one of these cords is connected to an energy body that looks just like you but is made up of pure energy (some people refer to this as an *etheric double*). Imagine that you are transferring the bulk of your consciousness to this body. Now imagine that this body is beginning to move away from your physical body. You can turn around and look at your physical body, ground it, say something sweet to it, and tell it you will return to it soon, safe and sound, as soon as you are finished gathering information from your trip. Now imagine that your etheric body either has wings, is like a moving cloud, or is like Wonder Woman's see-through airplane. Any of these travel instantaneously through time and space. Imagine you can feel the air moving past you. Just relax.

Give your energy body with your consciousness in it the directive that it's going to go to a few places. For example, let it go up to the top of the atmosphere, then to the bottom of the ocean, then to a few different countries. Just do this quickly, making a mental note of one sensation you might feel if you actually were there or something you might see from an aerial view if you were actually flying over one of these places.

Now that you have warmed up your personal energy vehicle, give it the command that it and you are going to travel to the destination that is the target on the piece of paper resting on your body. This is the point at which you can completely relax and wait, as if you were waiting for an airplane to take off. You don't have to do anything else or think about anything else, except be aware. Give yourself as much time as you need. You are waiting for some kind of stimuli to come into your consciousness. As you start to see or experience something, just make a mental note of it or start to talk loud enough for your tape recorder to pick up your voice and describe what you are starting to notice.

If you don't feel as if anything is happening, then visualize a door, with the target numbers or your destination written across it. See the door open and imagine you are passing through it. On the other side is a tunnel that takes you directly through to your destination, regardless of whether you know what that is. Let yourself float through the door and through the tunnel.

Imagine this tunnel is dark but warm and nurturing, even soft and cushy as you pass through it. Be patient and notice where it takes you. Look for a sign of light. Once you begin to see the light or see some kind of shape, start making mental notes about what it is you are seeing. Look for colors, shapes, sizes, textures. Ask whether there is plant or animal or human life. Ask yourself if there are man-made or natural structures in this place.

Remember that just as in real life, your position, in terms of angle and proximity, will determine how well you can view whatever is there. So when you start to make observations, don't forget to tell yourself to move in closer or further away, or to go to the front or back or all around. This is very important!

Your Return Trip

Once you are ready to come back, it's important to give yourself the command that you are going to return fully, with all your energy intact. You can invite any of your energy or spirit that might have already been separated from your body before you began this exercise to join you. You can do this by assigning this energy a color and watching to see if that color comes in around you.

If you used a tunnel and door to get to your destination, come back the same way you came in. Once you reach the door, tell any energies you might have engaged with that they must stay on the other side. Make sure you close the door. Let yourself slowly reunite with your body. Imagine you are hovering above the planet, and then the city and then the street you live on, then the house in which your body sits or lies waiting for you. You can linger in a corner of the room or beside it. Using a rose or an object, you can run this from your energy body through the cord into your third chakra or head, giving it the command that it will fill up with anything you are ready to release. Check the grounding cord on your body and look for any black spots or things that look like rips or tears.

Use some cosmic energy to wash through these parts, and watch the colors release down your grounding cord. Then imagine you are floating right back into your physical body through the cord joining your energy body. Just make sure you return through the same chakra from which you left. Center and ground yourself.

You might feel sleepy and need to take a nap after this exercise, and that's fine. If you did not use a tape recorder, you may want to jot down some notes as it's likely the more time that passes, the more you will forget what you just saw. Have fun!

Alternative Bilocation Technique: Hand Focus

There is another technique I've been working on lately that seems to induce bilocation or an out-of-body experience, in which targets can be accessed on a clairvoyant level with extreme clarity.

You may try this technique while lying down. Relax your body by slowing down your breath. Put your attention on your hands. Notice how they feel. Imagine you are moving all of your consciousness into your hands, even your fingertips. Do this for a few minutes, then imagine you are stretching out your fingertips, hands, and arms further and further. Play around with this, stretching them in various directions (note that you are not really moving them physically, but postulate that you are doing so energetically).

Next, tell yourself that your hands are going to reach all the way to the target of your choice, either one you are aware of or one someone else has given to you. Once your hands have landed there, tell yourself you will either be able to touch the target, wherever it is, or your spirit will be projected through your fingertips right to the target. You can also tell yourself that as soon as your fingertips reach the target, you will be able to see through them with your psychic eyes. Notice how your hands feel now; continue to breath slowly and just wait and see what happens.

It is likely you will begin to get visual sensations in addition to bodily sensations. Just make a mental note of all you are observing. If you have a recording device, I suggest talking into it from the moment you begin putting your attention on your hands. Continue giving a play-by-play account of what you are experiencing until you are finished with the exercise. When you are ready to return, imagine you are retracting your hands and bringing them back to their normal positions. Don't be alarmed if you feel any strange vibrations in your body at any point during this exercise; I've been experiencing these in a way I never did with any other exercise. I believe this may be the same type of feeling Robert Monroe experienced and describes so eloquently in his book *Ultimate Journey*. If nothing happens with this exercise I suggest attempting it again on another night. Sometimes there is a cumulative effect, so it may take even a week of practice before you get any results.

PART III

Healing and Working with Nonphysical Entities

CHAPTER 12

Welcome to the Spirit World

Anything I've ever done that ultimately was worthwhile . . . initially scared me to death.
—BETTY BENDER

As a Psychic, You Must Deal with Your Fear

When I first began developing my psychic abilities, like many of you I was absolutely terrified by the idea of ghosts, entities, spirits, whatever you want to call them. I had absolutely no interest in communicating with any of them! I had signed up on a whim for the clairvoyant training program through a psychic training institute, after receiving a couple of readings from a teacher and some students who were able to see all kinds of things about me, my life, and even my own visualizations, all of which they could not possibly have otherwise known. I was more enthusiastic about being able to see visions and knowing things about anyone and anything than I had been about anything else in my life. It didn't occur to me that this would include seeing and communicating with spirits!

However, it only took about a week before I began seeing spirits clairvoyantly and realized that, at least in this context, they really aren't scary at all; to the contrary, it was really fun learning about them and hearing what they had to say . . . even when they were being kind of nasty.

During the course of my earliest readings, it became undeniably clear to me that there are beings surrounding all of us who can very much influence the person they are connected to. This influence is sometimes very positive, sometimes quite destructive. These entities are as varied and unique as any living human being. Some are very aware, intelligent, kind, creative, and communicative; others have the intelligence of a cockroach. Many have their own agendas and personalities, while just as many have no awareness of themselves at all. They exist at all points in time, including in the past and the future. Some entities love you more than you love yourself, while others will do what they can to bring you down.

Below I will offer some pros and cons to increasing your awareness of the spirit world through the use of your clairvoyance.

Pros

Spirits have more power over you when you don't see them or know they are there. When you see spirits, you can set boundaries with them. You can consciously choose whether to let them remain in your energy field or banish them. When you are unaware of them, you are at their mercy. You fear what you don't understand or know. Once you bring something into the light, it is not as scary.

Many spirits can assist you in your life. They can provide helpful information; they can heal you; they can protect you, teach you, help create and manifest for you, and comfort you. Many spirits are people you have known and loved in this lifetime or other incarnations. When you are aware of them and can clearly communicate with them, then you can more easily recover from the separation caused by their death, or heal aspects of your relationship with them that were not resolved at the time of their death. When you see spirits, your communication with them automatically increases, so you can better hear those that have helpful and important messages for you.

Cons

Spirits are drawn to people who can see them. Clairvoyants have to be careful not to get pushed out of their own auras even by their most well-intentioned but over-enthusiastic fans. Ever have someone give you a bear hug that almost suffocated you? This is what sometimes happens with some of our guides when they realize we are aware of them. Occasionally, clairvoyants and psychics inadvertently open doors to less savory visitors from the spirit world.

During readings, clairvoyants can be "slimed"—very mildly shocked and emotionally, mentally, and in rare cases physically abused by entities that are connected with their readees. This happens to every one of us in our everyday lives at some point; it's just sometimes more exaggerated when we are performing psychic readings, both due to the clairvoyant's sensitivity and to the entity's heightened efforts to prevent being seen. Spirits don't usually have to put out much effort to keep the average human being in the dark. A little pain here, a little punishment there, and most humans will abandon whatever activity they are engaged in that could break the game that the spirit is playing. On the other hand, clairvoyants can not only see the spirit, but they can see the game and break it up. Therefore spirits need to exert more effort in order to thwart the efforts of a clairvoyant.

Luckily, clairvoyants who use their psychic tools are better equipped to deal with any attack that comes their way than the average individual is. Often, all that is needed is to see and acknowledge the presence of a spirit and alert the readee to its presence. The spirit is released the moment readees say to themselves, "I no longer want to play with you."

We Live Within the World of Spirit

Wishing there were no spirits around you is a lot like wishing there were no insects. Give it up! Most humans can feel the spirits around them. We can hear their thoughts in our minds; we can feel their emotions and even their desires in our bodies. However, most people are unaware of the origin of these feelings and thoughts, and therefore attribute them and their overall influence to something else other than spirits. Likewise, we as humans are constantly affecting these spirits with our own thoughts and emotions.

One of the goals of this chapter is to help you understand how you can use your clairvoyant abilities to increase your awareness of that which is influencing you in your environment, so you can effectively communicate with the entities of your choice in a safe and effective manner. When dealing with the spirit world, I cannot overemphasize the number one rule: *You are in charge.* You call the shots. See yourself as a general, with these spirits as your own soldiers. If any of them gets out of line, you can throw them in the brig or toss them into outer space. If you are attacked by enemy forces from the dark side, you have the right and the power to obliterate them. This can be done through the power of your imagination and your words.

Now, I can already hear some of you saying, "Obliterate!?! Well, that's not very nice! That's not very spiritual!" You are half correct. It's not nice. In this book we are learning how to cure ourselves from *having* to be nice when being nice is an inappropriate, misguided, or self-destructive response. We are also relearning the definition of spirituality, a word that means nothing more and nothing less than "of or pertaining to spirit."

The fact is that not everything having to do with spirit is nice. Whether you want to admit it or not, in addition to the enlightened loving guides looking out for you, there are some nasty, conniving critters out there that want to keep you in pain and fear. Some want to lure you into self-hatred, suicide, addiction, physical violence, even suicide. Some can manipulate material objects, but so can you! And you can obviously do this *a lot* more easily than they can!

In *You Are Psychic* I provided examples of how I came to know about these beings. In this chapter and the next one, I will jump right to providing detailed instructions that will enable you to strengthen your communication with all spirits and better understand how to deal with them, including your allies and your enemies. You will learn how to recruit and train some of these who qualify as your healing guides.

You will learn how to examine and amend your contracts with them. You will learn simple psychic self-defense and aggressive combat strategies for dealing with the dark side. Do not worry: your battles will be swift and final. The key here is to disengage as quickly as possible and to always keep your sense of humor.

So it is above, so below: this tenet sets the stage for all other tenets.

Think of your interactions with spirits in the same way as those you have with humans. Some people are your best friends, and some are your worst enemies. Some are enlightened, some are completely ignorant. Some are respectful, others abusive. Some are helpful, others are draining.

For Any Relationship, You Set the Boundaries, Dictate the Rules, and Enforce Them

This is true regarding physical and nonphysical communication, as well as relationships with living people and with the spirit world. If someone or something is doing something that makes you uncomfortable, it is your responsibility to speak up and tell them to stop. If they don't stop, then you need to do whatever is necessary to save yourself and ensure that they don't violate your boundaries again.

Through our words and our silences, through our actions and our lack of action, we train both the people and spirits around us how to treat us. The greatest challenge is in setting and enforcing boundaries with the very people and spirits who in the past have helped us to feel safe, secure, and loved.

All Relationships Are Based on Agreements and Contracts That Can Be Altered and Broken

When you were a child, you were dependent on your parents. They were like gods to you. Most of the time you did what they told you to do, regardless of the quality or integrity of their advice. Fast forward forty years. Do you still have to do what your parents tell you to do? Of course not! (This may be news to some.) Relationships change. Now fast forward one thousand years. The spirit that was your parent, child, or lover may still be hanging on to you, or occupying a new human body in this current lifetime, loving you or punishing you, guiding or pulling you in directions you are or are not in agreement with. Do you have to put up with this? Absolutely not, unless you don't even know this is what's going on! One of the biggest, most insidious way others control you is through guilt. Guilt is an emotion that should never dictate behavior. And yet for most people, particularly women, it's the prevailing motivational factor.

Disclaimer: You can only help those who are open to your help!

It is very possible and quite easy to remove spirits from your home or to heal others struggling with negative entities. However, this is true only if you are truly in control of the environment and only if the other person is ready to be healed. If you live in someone else's home or work for someone else who has annoying entities wrecking havoc and running wild through the environment, you are at a definite disadvantage. Your ability to defend yourself or change and improve the environment will be quite limited as long as the people in charge of the environment agree to allow things to remain as they are.

If you try to clean out the entities from a workplace run by a boss who has a symbiotic relationship with these entities, then the entities may begin to attack you (or increase the severity of an attack) through this person, by manipulating the other person into believing that you have done something wrong, that you are out to get them or show them up, or by running anger through them that will be directed at you. It is important to remember that often a person has let that entity inside them because they weren't feeling strong enough on their own; it gives them power and does their dirty work, even though they then feel like a victim because on one level they feel *they* did nothing wrong (it was the being they are unaware of) and now here you are reacting to them with anger or distrust. So if you try to separate the person and the entity (whether or not that person has any idea what you are doing), you will anger the entity and send the person into a state of panic—and the situation will most likely worsen for you. The person might even find ways to turn others against you as well. The only good part about this is usually the situation gets so unbearable that either you decide to leave or in their anger the other person tells you to do so, and then you are free to find a situation that is better suited for you. Believe me, I've learned these lessons the hard way!

Your inner and outer environments set your energy and determine the types of spirits that are in your world. Drugs and alcohol can increase the likelihood of possession by evil spirits.

In this example, I am defining your "inner environment" as your mental and emotional state and physical health. Your "outer environment" includes the type of people you hang out with and the places you hang out in. Both these environments affect each other. They can be influenced by the spirits around you and they also attract particular beings to you. If you dwell on angry, stressful, or judgmental thoughts, you will be sending out an open invitation to other people and spirits that resonate at this same vibration. If you hang out in places with angry, aggressive, depressed, and unhealthy people, you will find a plethora of low vibrational spirits feeding off this energy and exacerbating it. This is particularly true where drugs and alcohol are consumed, where dissonant and angry music is played, and where sex is being sold. I know I risk sounding puritanical, but I can assure you that the only reason I can make these above statements is because I've hung out in my fair share of these places!

Many spirits feed off and instigate addictions. They can vicariously experience the drug-related or sexual energy by attaching themselves to the living through a symbiotic or parasitic relationship. They can make it more difficult to cure someone from their addiction, whether to cocaine or to a destructive relationship, because such spirits are highly invested in making sure the addict does not stop their behavior. I believe this is why wonderful people will suddenly become monsters, particularly when alcohol is involved.

Not only are alcohol and drugs lowering inhibitions and impairing judgments, they are preparing our bodies to be vessels for anything to occupy them—and that is when people commit heinous crimes they sometimes don't recall later. The point here is that if you live in a pigpen, it doesn't matter if you shower every five minutes, you will still be perpetually dirty. Likewise, if you meditate in a house filled with resentful, depressed people, you will clear yourself off and then get all slimed again. The difference is that through meditation you may very well get enough moments of respite so that you might actually wake up and say, "What the hell am I doing here?!"—and then have enough of your own energy to get out.

Some entities are even attached to objects such as sexually explicit printed materials or items utilized in rituals and ceremonies. Be wary about bringing home used objects!

Your agreements and relationships with spirits are not limited to this lifetime or to this physical world.

Many of the spirits that are around us or attached to us in some way have followed us from other lifetimes and incarnations. Sometimes we need to get clear and be firm about ending the agreements or karma that are no longer serving us, particularly if the spirit that has followed us is stuck on something that we now have no power to fix. Some spirits want to punish us, and then we walk around feeling perpetually guilty. When you feel guilty, it's easy to find any number of reasons to justify this guilt. This is really true of any emotion. Many people think situations in their lives elicit negative emotions. However, I have seen that just as frequently, if not more often, we already had the emotions, so we just glob onto and blame whatever is right in front of us. That's when fights of the worst kind are started with loved ones.

Sometimes spirits we have karma with will work through people who are mistreating us.

Be Careful What You Wish For!

When we say we want to understand or communicate with the spirit world, it takes less than a second for spirits to hear this and respond. Even just mild curiosity will attract spirits to us. When we are feeling desperate for help or answers, we send out emotionally charged calls for assistance that attract immediate attention. Since spirit works on telepathic levels, it doesn't matter if you verbally state, "Leave me alone" but in your mind you are thinking, "I don't know if I want you to go away." Your words and your thoughts must be in alignment with each other. Otherwise, it will be a lot harder to clear out troublesome entities from your life. The difficulty here is that sometimes it is the beings that are trying to convince you that you should allow them to stay when it's not in your best interest, which makes things confusing. This is of course no different from being in a relationship with someone you wish to leave, but who is doing everything in their power to convince you otherwise.

A couple of years ago, my good friend Darrah Waters invited me to work on her documentary crew filming a reenactment of the Battle of Little Bighorn and Custer's Last Stand. We flew to Montana and camped out for a week at the site of the battle. I barely slept a single night. From the moment I lay down, the images of Indians and soldiers exploded in my mind like a marathon fireworks display. Even when I returned home, it took a good week to clear out all the faces and blood and noise from my head (through grounding, running my energy, and utilizing several of the healing techniques in this book). I also found it necessary to intentionally turn down my clairvoyance. Doing so is possible by simply visualizing a gauge that represents your sixth chakra and seeing the arrow moving downward, or visualizing that chakra as if it were closing. It can always be opened right back up by doing the reverse.

House Hauntings

I have seen many people who were being tormented by beings, either through house hauntings with poltergeist activity or through overactive clairaudient communication. In every one of these cases, although the client initially presented themselves as a frightened victim, it turned out that the client who had contacted me was to some extent enjoying the drama, battle, attention, or interactions, despite the very real fear the clients also felt.

Spirits Are Passed Down Generationally

Spirits are passed down generationally, including both those whose only desire is to help us and those who enjoy feeding off pain. If we have been abused as children, we will be more vulnerable as adults to victimization by human and nonhuman spirits alike.

When a child is abused at a very young age, or grows up with extremely controlling parents, the child is taught that they don't have control over their own bodies or a right to say no. They are then more vulnerable to becoming victimized by subsequent abusers, those with physical bodies and those from the spirit realm.

It has become absolutely clear to me that many adults who abuse children are possessed or at least strongly influenced by angry entities at the time they are doing the abuse. The beings that are instigating this abhorrent behavior often attach themselves to the children. (After twelve years of working with so many people, I don't have an ounce of doubt about this.) The children aren't really able to distinguish between the being and their parent although many of my clients, even those who don't really believe in spirits, do recall that during the abusive episodes, they had a sense their parents were being possessed in some way or acting like a completely different person. This makes it extremely difficult for the children because they love the parent when the parent is just themselves, and are absolutely horrified of the parent when the parent is leasing themselves out like a timeshare. This is why victims of child sexual abuse often need healing of a spiritual nature, in addition to psychological counseling.

Many times when children are being abused, it is too painful and frightening for them to remain in their bodies, so they vacate the premises. Obviously, anyone being mistreated is going to be angry, but it's not safe for a child to be angry at a parent who is beating the crap out of them, so they call in another being to help them with these emotions. This is one of many reasons why those who were abused often don't really remember the abuse; they weren't quite all there either.

Abusers often see themselves as victims because they weren't fully present during the abuse (due to intoxication, leaving their bodies, and channeling foreign beings), and because they choose to focus on the subsequent reactions of the victim to the abuse the abuser is denying. This lends itself to what psychologists refer to as a dissociative process. What most psychologists don't realize is that disassociation, which I define as "various parts of an individual being closed off to awareness of the other parts," is as much a spiritual, transmedium process as it is a cognitive and emotional one.

Many schizophrenic people are also major out-of-control mediums. The boundaries between their mind and the astral/spirit realm are so ill-defined that it's like living in Grand Central Station. I've always wondered why mentally ill, homeless people tend to congregate in overcrowded and chaotic urban locations as opposed to the open wilderness. I believe their outer environment mirrors what is happening to them on a psychic level, where they are bombarded by throngs of parasitic entities on a constant basis.

Spirits plug into our pain pictures. This means that they will literally attach themselves to the areas of our body and energy field where we carry emotional pain or that were the location of some kind of physical trauma. As we release this pain, the stronghold of spirits plugged into this pain is either weakened or severed. This can happen naturally or can be facilitated with the help of a healer or counselor.

As spirits in physical bodies, we are far stronger than spirits without bodies.

While some spirits can impact or manipulate physical matter, this is fairly rare and most of the time even these exploits do little more than create fear. Fear is the primary modus operandi for abusive spirits, actually those both with and without bodies. If their hosts or victims become fearful, then they can be easily manipulated. Many beings feed off this fear, which is why they seek to create it. Most people aren't aware that they are being influenced by troublesome entities. They just hear upsetting thoughts about all the bad things that could possibly happen to them or someone they know, and they fall into a perpetual cycle of anxiety. When that happens, the being that projected the thoughts or exacerbated them in the first place has a lifetime meal ticket.

The good news here is that as long as you are aware this is what is happening, then you have won 99 percent of the battle. You can do whatever you need to get yourself in the vibration of good humor or enthusiasm, and the spirits will tire of the game and go find someone else to harass.

The Haunted and the Haunter: Which Is Which?

One of the most shocking revelations of my clairvoyant training came to me during one of my early readings as a clairvoyant student. We were reading a woman who seemed to be suffering from irrational fears that were keeping her from achieving certain goals. It soon became apparent that there was a spirit plugged into her aura that was somehow connected to these fears. One of my teachers asked me to work with the spirit to "help it take its next step."

My earlier preconceived notions of disembodied spirits (which were based more on horror movies than on my clairvoyance or any direct experience) led me to assume that this was an evil spirit that was victimizing my readee. I felt as though it was my job to save the poor woman from this big, bad spirit. However, when I clairvoyantly looked at this spirit, I was surprised to find that not only was he scrawny and timid-looking, but he was also actually wearing shackles and straining to break a chain that bound him to the readee.

In my vision, when I asked him why he appeared this way, he looked at me with pleading, frightened eyes, and began sobbing. He looked so miserable that my imagination began breaking apart the chains to free him even before I consciously realized what I was doing. I described this scenario to the readee and explained that I was in the process of conducting a healing in which I was helping the two of them make separations, and was shocked when the woman yelled at me for interfering with their relationship! She explained that if she let him go she would feel too lonely; she needed him. She ordered me to terminate the healing at once. For the first and only time in my work as a clairvoyant, I ignored her demands and continued with the healing, because I realized that I was here for him, not for her. He had brought her here. He was my true client. She had just come along for the ride. In my healing, I did my best to break the karmic agreement that had bound this being to this woman for centuries. I saw him break free and fly off toward a bright light. However, her will was very strong, and I still don't know for sure whether he managed to escape her entirely.

When you are performing clairvoyant readings and healings, it is imperative that you do all that you can to put your judgments and pre-conceptions on hold. Many people will come to you complaining that they are being victimized when the opposite it true, just as there will be those people who blame themselves for situations and other people's behavior that they could not possibly be responsible for. You will also encounter spirits and other energies attached to them that want you to think the client is bad, so you will be less inclined to help them. Fur-thermore, if you see that being victimized is a pattern in your client's life, regardless of how much they have truly suffered, it's always most helpful to see whether or how this state of victimhood is serving them, or how they believe it's serving them, because therein usually lies the greatest answer to helping them out of their situation.

CHAPTER 13

Specific Types of Entities

An idea, like a ghost, must be spoken to a little before it will explain itself.

—CHARLES DICKENS

In this chapter I am going to discuss energy forms that have a certain level of consciousness that I have personally come into contact with. These energies include those that are commonly referred to as spirits, beings, entities, guides, ghosts, alien life forms, angels, demons, spirit councils, ascended masters, and orbs. Names are of course symbols we assign to things, so I don't want anyone to get stuck on what I am calling the entities I've encountered. When I see these entities, like anyone else I ask myself, "What is this? What do I call it?" I then look for something that has the most comparable characteristics to that which others have named.

It's not as if these things walk out to me with an outstretched hand and state, "Hi, I'm an alien" or "I'm an angel." Instead, I see them, observe them, and decide which category they seem to fit into. I am most certain that many entities will take on a particular façade in order to achieve a certain effect on the viewer, whether to ease our fears or to scare the pants off us, so it is important not to get too caught up in appearances or in labeling. Still, for simplicity's sake, in this chapter I am using the common names for these entities with the hope that my observations or experiences will add more data to the unofficial collection that has been accruing on the subject for centuries.

Spirit Guides

My definition of a *spirit guide* is an entity that desires to offer guidance in some way. Like the millions of living people who serve others, spirit guides are a diverse group of beings that exhibits an enormous spectrum of personality traits, motivations, and altruistic behaviors. Some spirit guides exist for the sole purpose of aiding humans. The extent of their love, purity, and selflessness is at a level that we cannot even comprehend. (This includes spirits in and out of physical bodies.) Some spirit guides are deceased relatives and friends. However, not all of these guides are enlightened.

One of the first eye-opening realizations I had as a clairvoyant student was that many deceased spirits who pass over to the other side remain just as ignorant, judgmental, opinionated, and messed-up as they were when they were alive. It seems as if many of the spirits that fall into this category do want to assist the living, but their methods of problem solving and communication can be dysfunctional, disruptive, and sometimes just plain silly. People who were particularly controlling, domineering, stubborn, and authoritarian when they were alive seem to hold on to these characteristics for quite a while after they die, perhaps because their staunch thinking does not permit them to accept the new reality they are in. These beings are likely to continue to pass judgment on their living relatives and to boss them around, out of the "goodness of their hearts."

As a clairvoyant reader, you will want to use discernment when receiving messages or advice from spirit guides, since the advice may be earth-shattering or it may be akin to what you'd find written on a bathroom wall (which I guess is sometimes exactly what you need to hear at a particular moment, even if it's crude!).

Deceased Relatives and Loved Ones

As a clairvoyant, once you realize you have the ability to tune in to the spirit world, it's quite normal to want to check up on someone who has just died. This is a fantastic way to gain insights into life after death and beyond. However, I advise you to be very cautious with what you do with the information or communication you receive. One of the biggest mistakes psychics make is to tread upon others' grieving processes by providing information that has come to the psychic either spontaneously or by intentionally tuning in. I am not saying this isn't sometimes welcomed. In fact, it can be the one thing that saves the grieving person from having a complete meltdown. Conversely, it can be taken as a gross intrusion into something very private that could serve to destroy your relationship.

Sometimes the grieving person thinks, "Why would my deceased relative or friend come to you and not to me?" These people obviously aren't able to understand that perhaps they are not objective enough or clear enough to receive the information at that time, particularly if they don't even believe in psychic communication with spirits or they have been programmed by their places of worship to believe this type of communication is evil. Sometimes the grieving person just isn't ready to share their feelings or memories with the over-eager psychic, particularly if they haven't been that close to the psychic before. So if you do have some information for a grieving person, I suggest you use your clairvoyance to determine whether or not they would be open to your communication. It may be a matter of timing. This is pretty much true of psychic information you've received about any topic. After making a couple of painful mistakes in my early days as a clairvoyant student (mostly due to overzealousness), I have a general rule: I don't share unless someone asks. That being said, many times people ask and I just haven't taken or don't want to take the time to look.

It seems as if there are countless paths a soul can follow upon discarding their physical body. Just as living people will have totally unique reactions, responses, and effects after undergoing similar experiences, there are limitless potential responses and effects on a spirit that experiences the death of its own body. A deceased person's personality, philosophy, and understanding of death; their attachment to the physical body and to possessions and relationships; their vulnerability to others' feelings and thoughtforms; and the circumstances that surrounded their death all play a role in how their spirit is affected and where the spirit goes after death.

Sometimes a client will be upset because they feel they are unable to communicate or connect with the spirit of a deceased loved one, and many times I have had the sense that the reason for this is that the deceased really no longer exists as we understand existence. I have seen in my readings that some spirits pass over into a realm that is so far away from the physical plane that all that remains of them or their connection to the physical world is an echo. This echo is like an inanimate hologram of the deceased spirit's body, personality, and voice that a clairvoyant can see and describe, but there is no conscious interaction in present time. The many brief glimpses I've seen into the places spirits go after death have been only shadows, and I had to be careful not to project my own perceptions onto the experience, particularly since my readees are usually quite inclined to do this as well. Some readees will even try to corner me into agreeing with their limited perceptions and argue with me when I refuse to do so.

During these experiences I've had the feeling that my mind was only able to comprehend about 2 percent of what really was going on way out there. I hope this will change as I continue to grow as a person and as a psychic. On the other hand, when a spirit is quite present around a living person, there is usually no way for me to miss them, and information about these earthbound spirits is a lot easier to comprehend.

Our Attitudes Toward the Dead Determine Their Next Steps

A few years ago I gave a reading to a woman whose five-year-old son had died after a lengthy illness. She wanted to know that his spirit was all right. When I tuned in to his spirit I saw that he was not all right.

I saw an image of him lying in a bed, with all kinds of tubes running in and out of his body. He seemed to be in an uncomfortable, groggy state of confused unconsciousness, somewhere between a sleeping and waking state. I felt he was stuck in the trauma of his death.

His mother confirmed to me that her son had died in the hospital and that she feared he had suffered more from the treatment than from the illness itself. When I asked his soul along with God what would help to free his spirit, I was told that his mother's thoughtforms played a significant role. Her unhappy thoughts were actually pinning him down and trapping him in a repetitive reenactment of his traumatic death. She needed to visualize him being all right, at peace.

When I told the woman this information, she admitted that the only way she could ever picture her son was as he was during those final weeks in the hospital. She never pictured him happily playing with his toys or laughing; it was almost impossible for her to recall how he looked when he was healthy. I saw and told her that she must, for both of their sakes, train her mind to visualize her son in an absolutely perfect state of health and happiness whenever she thought of him. One thing that would help her was to look at photographs of her son that had been taken prior to his illness. She admitted that she had many such photos but had not looked at them since his death.

This reading continues to haunt me because, just as any other mother would, I wanted desperately to see that the spirit of this woman's son was all right. No matter what I see in my readings, emotionally I want to believe that when anyone dies they immediately go to a better place—a beautiful, wondrous place where they find peace. At the same time, I am thankful for the understanding my readings have given me regarding the power we as spirits in physical bodies hold over disembodied spirits. We are actually as much their guides as they are ours. We have the ability to free them or to hold them captive. We can affect their destinies.

There are many people who are meant to die a pain-free death but who are chained mercilessly to their failing bodies by the selfish grief of their loved ones. We need to rechannel our love for the dying into saving their spirits rather than their physical bodies. The greatest gift you can give to a dying person is to celebrate their passing and the life they have just accomplished, as the Tibetans (read *The Book of the Dead*) and many indigenous cultures do.

As a clairvoyant reader, you will be presented with plenty of situations in which your natural inclination will be to provide assurances that everything is all right when it's really not. Such statements may make your readee feel better in the moment, but ultimately no one will be served—because whatever problem is occurring will continue and ultimately your client will realize you were not being honest, which will create a whole other level of pain. When you are faced with giving upsetting information as I was in the above example, use your clairvoyance to generate feasible steps that your readee can take to alter or mend the situation. This is ultimately why your readee has come to you, whether they know it or not.

Angels

I did not start out believing in angels; I used to think Catholics and New Age enthusiasts put way too much stock in them. However, from time to time I do see angels in my meditations, as well as figures that look like angels standing behind my clients. These angels seem to have a very different vibration from other spirit guides. When I think of them I hear a single musical note, about two octaves above middle C. Their energy reminds me of the energy of certain mountainous areas where there is a lot of open space and clear skies. They seem unencumbered by the thoughtforms, emotions, and agendas that many other spirits carry. They actually seem to be less obtrusive and invasive than any other beings I have observed.

The angels I've observed seem to be prepared to help, but they won't step in until they hear a call for help. This call could come in the form of a willful silent prayer, or from the screaming heart of a person in need. I wish I could say angels make up most of the population of the spirit world; however, as most of the psychics I know will agree, they only make up a very small percentage. If you see an angel in a clairvoyant reading, say hello to the angel and ask it what its purpose is, what its favorite name is, and how the readee can better communicate with it.

Sometimes I see my clients with angel wings, and I have the sense that this client is an earthbound angel. Occasionally, I see clients with broken wings. These broken wings seem to symbolize that this soul came from a place where evil was not known and they've had an especially hard time coping in this lifetime, not just with the ugliness on Earth but with the very fact that ugliness exists at all. They are also vulnerable to being taken advantage of by others who are not coming from the same place. These souls seem to have a lot of catching up to do when it comes to managing their finances, or with successfully meeting the physical needs of a human body that they may feel quite trapped in.

Healing Guides

Another common class of spirits can be referred to as *healing guides*. These guides are spirits whose main mission and talent is to heal. They are as diverse as the healers within the living human population, with an assortment of methodologies and approaches. Some seem to work individually while others work in clusters. Just as there are surgeons, psychologists, and massage therapists, so there are healing guides who do intensive operations, those who work more on a psychological level, some who are very subtle and gentle in their touch, and some that are quite aggressive and intrusive. Some merely work in your energy field, while others dive right into your body and yank out the energy that is not working well in there.

This latter group includes those healers that I have been working with most closely for the last decade or so, the psychic surgeons. These spiritual surgeons can pull out diseased matter and foreign energies from a specific location in the body. They also fight against lower astral energies and work with students in their dreams to rid them of troublesome entities. I've had quite a few experiences during which clients and even young children, who had no idea that I or my students were using guides in our healings, have seen these spirits and describe them as looking like doctors, with surgical instruments in their hands.

For most of my life, I was pursued, chased, and haunted by any number of lower astral beings who took a variety of forms in my dreams, including those of monsters and criminals. After one week of working with these psychic surgeons and asking them to enter my dreams to assist me, I had a series of dreams in which these guides appeared and helped me to wipe out my attackers. By the next week all signs of any troublesome pursuers in my dreams had vanished. It's been well over a decade since then, and I rarely have dreams of being pursued.

Filipino Psychic Surgeons

When I lived and studied in the Philippines with actual living healers known as psychic surgeons, people with the rare ability to extract physical matter from a person's body by making an actual incision with their bare hands, I was approached by a strong-vibration group of healing spirits of the type that I also refer to as psychic surgeons. These spirits are more aggressive and intense than ones I had worked with previously.

In my own training, I learned to allow spirits to only plug into my hand chakras and to call upon them when I needed them. However, this new group of spirits would plug further into my arms, usually up to my elbows. Sometimes they are so bent on performing a healing with the use of my hands that I find myself wandering around with my arms outstretched, looking for anyone to heal! I usually know I am about to encounter a person who will need and request a healing because my hands, and sometimes my arms, begin to vibrate and twitch as if they have a life of their own. (They just started to do this as I began writing about them!)

It is important when working with any kind of healing guide or spirit guide, no matter how evolved or impressive, that you remember you are ultimately the boss of your own energy field. You call the shots and set the boundaries when it comes to your own body. These spirits are very enthusiastic, and if permitted will infiltrate your aura or chakras and set up camp indefinitely. I recommend only allowing these spirits to plug into your hand chakras until you gain more experience working with healing guides or channeling. (This is good advice to follow in regard to your spiritual teachers in bodies as well!)

Spirits have a number of ways in which they can communicate with you. Just as some of your psychic abilities are more developed than others, the same could be said of disembodied spirits and healing guides. Some communicate through clairvoyance, others communicate through mental telepathy, some communicate through telekinesis, and still others will actually attempt to speak to you on a verbal level. We will be working with the psychic surgeon guides in chapter 16.

Ascended Masters or Gods

I am certain from firsthand experience that God figures, saints, and yogis such as Jesus, Mary, Buddha, and Paramahansa Yogananda continue to exist in spirit form. (Fortunately, they don't care what religion you are!) They will often spontaneously appear to clairvoyants, healers, and even laypeople when their type of energy is needed and welcomed. They have the ability to be everywhere at the same time, so they can be available to many people at once. They have strong healing abilities. They vibrate at such a high frequency and carry such a tremendous amount of light that merely visualizing their image or stating their name is a powerful tool for protection, transformation, insight, and healing. I recommend calling upon one or more of these figures when you are faced with a challenging situation in your healings, particularly when lower astral spirits or energies are involved.

Telekinetic Guides

Another class of spirits are *telekinetic guides*. These guides have the ability to influence physical matter. They can generate sounds that range from a baby's cry to laughter to people chattering to deafening hammering noises. They can beat on drums, turn on children's electrical toys and kitchen appliances, and open and close doors and windows, and so forth. They can also create smells that range from the pleasing aroma of flowers or sage to the noxious odor of feces or spoiled milk. (I have personally experienced this entire spectrum.) These spirits range from lower astral forms (poltergeists) with the mentality or consciousness of a baby to healing spirits of a very high vibration.

Spiritual Councils

During a few readings and in several meditations in which I have practiced astral travel either consciously or inadvertently, I have clairvoyantly encountered councils. These councils seem to be a collective group of spirits that are gathered together for a specific purpose. They seem to have a leader or gatekeeper. These spirits have usually appeared to me as older, arrogant men who took themselves very seriously. They always have the same message for me: "You are not supposed to be here. Go back." They seem to be guarding certain dimensions or information.

Alien Beings

During readings and occasionally during a meditation, I've encountered the traditional-looking Gray aliens. A couple of times they appeared as a group, which reminded me of the council I've just described. There seemed to be numerous miniature Grays, only knee-high, who seemed to be controlled by larger Grays. They appear to operate on a hierarchy, which is one reason they remind me of ants, except for their eyes and the fact I don't like them any more than I like ants.

The first time I ever saw them I was doing a reading for a close friend who was also a clairvoyant student at the time. We were tracing some emotional problems he was currently having that apparently went all the way back to his birth, when suddenly I saw some unusual objects that reminded me of outdoor furniture. I then realized I had never seen furniture like this, and that somehow I was in a place I had never seen before here on Earth. As I had this realization, a gray alien face popped up in my mind, and in no uncertain terms demanded that I get out of where I was. It startled the sh— out of me that the image was actually talking to me! My clairvoyant images almost never interact with me, any more than an actor on television interacts with the viewers. But this one did. He was pushy and controlling, and I have to admit I heeded his instructions and terminated the reading. I felt the consequences of doing battle with him would not be worth the effort.

In 1997 I was traveling by jeepney to the remote terraced villages in the Mountain Province of the Philippines with my son's father, Manuel Lukingan, who was one of the only acupuncturists in the country at the time. We were visiting people who had no access to medical care. Some of them were dying. I was assisting Manuel with clairvoyant diagnosis and doing energetic work on those who could not tolerate the needles.

One early morning I was taking a cold shower, which consisted of dunking a little plastic cup into a barrel of frosty water and pouring it on my head in spastic, agonizing intervals. After a minute or so of this, I felt a pain creep up my spine and settle in the back of my neck. I knew in a way I never had before that I was about to become quite ill, and then I did, with severe flu-like symptoms. What I didn't know at the time was that I was also pregnant.

Yes, I realize that sounds silly coming from a psychic, but I just wasn't ready to admit it yet. (If it makes you feel any better, I did have a psychic dream prior to this in which my son came to me as he looks now and told me, "I am your future child, but you aren't ready to accept this yet.") Anyway, in one of the towns, which consisted of three roadside shacks posing as stores, someone handed me a dilapidated copy of one of Sylvia Browne's early books. I can't tell you how thrilled I was to find a book written in English by a fellow American psychic! Toward the end of the book, there was a healing exercise that instructs the reader to lie down and visualize a room in which the ceiling, floor, and each wall is a different color. (I still love this visualization, but now I am wary of it for reasons you will soon see.) I believe, if I recall correctly, that the next step was to imagine a table or bed in the middle of the room and to see yourself lying down on it.

Since I was feeling so sick, I decided to do this exercise before bed one evening. However, before I read the next steps, I fell into a restless sleep. Sometime after that I woke up and seemed to go right back into the vision of the multicolored room. But now someone else was there with me. It was a tall entity that was unmistakably alien. This alien seemed more feminine than masculine and had a pointed, sloped head that reminded me of the Coneheads from *Saturday Night Live*. I could only see its back or side, and it seemed to have a tray with something on it that was to be used for the healing. There was something very scientific or clinical about its attitude, even though I was pretty certain it was there to heal me. I was really torn about allowing it to work on me; I was feeling so sick, but at the same time I did not totally trust it. Finally, I decided to allow it to work on me, if only for a minute, to see how I felt as we proceeded. However, I immediately fell asleep.

The next thing I knew, I was lying there in my room, looking into the very black, slanted eyes of several gray or greenish aliens. They seemed to be staring at me, extremely close up. I was terrified! I screamed and woke up, freezing cold, only to have the sense they were still right there, only now I couldn't really see them. My screams woke Manuel up, and it took me quite a while to fall back to sleep. However, as soon as I did drift off to sleep, exactly the same thing happened again. I didn't go back to sleep after that. We packed up our few things and moved on to a warmer place. Since that time, I've only seen flashes of these guys in meditation or during readings. I know it's not very neighborly, but I really can't even stand to look at funny pictures of them.

Several years ago I gave a reading to a sweet, innocent-looking college student in Berkeley, who had a part-time job as a prostitute (well, *dominatrix* was the term she used, but only after I described a vision I received of her donned in black leather undergarments and whipping some sorry-looking sap). What disturbed me more than her occupation was that I saw her hungrily chowing down on what seemed to be psychedelic mushrooms. These seemed to be causing her a slew of problems in school and with her thought processes. When I told her that it appeared her unusual addiction to these mushrooms was keeping her from reaching her educational goals (something I was afraid to mention for fear she'd tell me I was wrong and nuts), she became quite angry and adamantly insisted that even though she was having a lot of personal problems, she would never, ever, *ever* stop eating these mushrooms! She stated this with such conviction that I almost fell off my chair!

I looked to see what was contributing to her addiction and was surprised to see what appeared to be an entity turning a switch on her back as if she were a wind-up doll. He was quite grotesque and had a bulbous, ugly white face and a big transparent head displaying an oversized brain. I somehow knew at once this was an alien being. In my vision, he had her tied up in ropes and was feeding her mushrooms. I had the eerie feeling that it was he who was speaking when she told me she would never give up her drug habit. I wondered if he wasn't somehow participating in her role as a dominatrix as well. That was one of the oddest clairvoyant experiences I've had, and really the only one in which I had such a strong sense that an entity involved in promoting someone's addiction was an alien.

A couple of years ago I had a dream that I was lying in bed embracing a tall female alien that seemed to be very sick—actually dying of something like cancer. She was mostly white but had some other colors in her as well. I seemed to be doing a healing on her by using my whole body, but I was rather uncomfortable with the whole thing. The strange thing was that her face seemed to be covered with these large rock-like jewels that were embedded in her, and I knew if the jewels came out she'd have large holes in her face. I woke up from this dream very disturbed and not feeling well.

More recently I had a very vivid dream of an alien: this one also had a head larger than felt normal for a human. His eyes were not like that of the Grays; instead, his eyes reminded me of the eyes of a fish. They were spread out so that they almost seemed to be on either side of his head. In the dream I specifically told him that I wanted more than anything else to remember this experience when I awoke. He assured me I would. He then approached my partner, Danny, who in reality is about as skeptical as you can be about aliens, and stated very clearly, "Someday you will know for sure that we exist." Danny says he's still a skeptic, but he seems to get rather perturbed when I remind him of this message (which I like to do quite often)!

Baby Beings

Baby beings are a particular group of spirits that have a strong desire to experience life as human beings on earth. They are desperately seeking parents who will bear them, and they will stop at nothing to achieve their goals. Some of these beings are in fact meant to be born. They have strong agreements with certain individuals, and it is only a matter of correct timing before the proper body is created for them to inhabit. These beings are usually conceived easily and born without much trauma.

These beings can be both of service and annoying. They can actually help create relationships, as they are able to indirectly introduce prospective parents to one another. They can also stimulate people's sex drives and help manifest anything on the physical level that will facilitate their conception and birth. These beings can convince people to say no to safe sex and cause the most conscientious women to forget to use birth control. Some of these beings are actually the leaders behind the right-to-life movement! At least a couple of them, at this very moment, are sending pain into my third eye, causing me to get sleepy all of a sudden! They are probably doing this so as not to alert the world to their presence.

(Okay, I'm back. I had to clear them out, and then I took a long nap!) Then there are those beings that, for whatever reason, are unable or not meant to inhabit a particular body or any body, no matter how much they think they want to do so. Sometimes these spirits are just too weak or uninvolved; some of them are essentially alien beings whose energy would not be compatible with that of a human body. In my readings I have seen that many miscarriages and abortions involve this latter of group of spirits.

Sometimes, when the spirit's efforts to be born are thwarted, as in the case of a miscarriage or when the targeted parents fail to meet each other or stay together, the spirit can become very frustrated, angry, fearful, or panicked. These feelings are easily transmitted to the targeted potential parents, who are usually unaware of the presence of these beings and therefore naturally attribute their feelings to a problem within themselves or their relationship (which causes the beings to become even more frantic). People who are obsessed with having babies are often being tormented by frustrated baby beings. Someone's obsession with a particular person is often also connected with the influence of a baby being.

Women who have had miscarriages or abortions are often hammered by confused beings that don't understand they will never and can never be born. I have seen this in dozens of readings with women whose past histories I knew nothing about. Sometimes these beings are literally trapped with the women's body or aura. These beings could wreak havoc on the woman's self-esteem and emotional, mental, and physical health throughout her lifetime if she is not aware of them. Most people are constantly surrounded by a multitude of baby beings, although they may only have strong agreements with one or two of these beings, agreements that may or may not pan out.

Not all baby beings are cute and cuddly. They are more like reckless toddlers with a ferocious appetite and little regard for others. Just like their potential parents, some are very capable, intelligent, loving, and evolved, while others possess none of the qualities you would want in your own offspring.

Creating, Updating, and Healing Agreements

You can create agreements with baby beings that you would like to bring into this world, as well as break strong agreements that have not come to fruition, by using the same methods you would to create or break agreements with living beings, as discussed in chapter 12.

Simple Methods for Moving Out Most Baby Beings

Many baby beings are pestering you merely because you have the ability to create a baby, or they think you do (some don't understand the meaning of menopause or infertility!). You can unwittingly pick them up from anyone, particularly members of the opposite sex who are attracted to you or to whom you are attracted. Clairvoyant readers also tend to inadvertently attract them during readings and healings. You will have little connection with most of these beings, so it will be easy to extract them from your aura with some simple visualization techniques.

You can easily perform the following healing on yourself or someone else. Ground yourself. Create and ground your reading screen. On your screen, visualize your body surrounded by your aura. Postulate that every baby being that you are not in agreement to bear as a baby is going to light up as a sparkling blue balloon. Imagine that you are collecting all these balloons and tying their strings together to make one large bundle of balloons. Say hello to these balloons and explain to them that you cannot be their mommy or daddy, and that it is time to move on. Let them know this is an order, not a suggestion.

Tie this bundle of balloons onto the railing of a special crib that is nicely decorated with fluffy down pillows and shiny quilted blankets. Ground this crib into the center of the planet with a heavy-duty grounding cord that is decorated with pictures of cute fuzzy animals. Turn on the mobile attached to the crib that plays soothing music so they will have some entertainment on their journey. You can ask the spirit/balloon that is the strongest of these beings to rise up above the others, and appoint it the task of protecting and overseeing the other spirits/balloons. Then take a giant imaginary scissors and cut the grounding cord of the crib. Watch as the crib floats upward, out the window, into the sky, past the horizon, past the atmosphere, past the stars and the universe to a place that is commonly referred to as God or heaven.

Following this exercise, it is vital that you fill up your body and aura with your own energy, particularly in any areas where the baby beings were plugged into. These areas will be more vulnerable to reinfestation from other beings who will be less able to plug in if you are adequately running enough of your own energy through these areas. Also, destroy your grounding cord in case any baby beings are hanging on to it, and create a new one. As you do the above healing, on yourself or someone else, you will likely experience sensations of pain, pressure, or temperature change as the baby beings are stimulated and released. It is advisable to repeat this healing at least once a week (this is something you can easily teach to your clients) or whenever you feel you are being affected by these beings.

Lower Astral Entities

A plethora of parasitic beings are attracted to and feed on the energies of pain, fear, hatred, and addiction. Some have almost no consciousness or self-awareness, while others are highly intelligent but lack a conscience. I have witnessed in my readings how these beings gravitate toward abuse of drugs, alcohol, violent films depicting demonic images, some heavy metal music, sadistic/masochistic sex, and physical and sexual abuse. People who engage in or subject themselves to these activities are more vulnerable to attack or infiltration of these beings, or seek out these activities due to the influence of these beings. Many people see these beings as snakes, spiders, rodents, and roaches.

In my readings I occasionally see images of snakes, spiders, and roaches nestled somewhere in the readee's aura, chakras, or physical organs, where they cause pain and disrupt the flow of energy. Sometimes these beings are sitting on eggs. Sometimes they scurry away and hide when they see me; other times they do nothing. When I utilize the technique of erasure (see chapter 14), often both my readee and I can physically feel pain as the being is eradicated.

I have witnessed, during readings and in my personal life, the surprisingly detrimental impact these beings can have on relationships. They interfere with communication, causing confusion, doubt, and mistrust. I have seen over and over again how these beings can disrupt and destroy even a strong relationship between two people who love one another. When the beings are eradicated from the relationship and energy fields of the individuals, instantaneous healing and rejuvenation of the relationship often occurs.

Demons

Demons are similar to but slightly more intelligent or aware than those beings that appear as snakes and spiders. Often in my meditations and when falling asleep at night, I have clairvoyantly seen the faces of demons. Through the years I've come to understand that these ugly, disfigured faces are projections sent by an ill-intentioned group of entities for the purpose of scaring me. On a couple occasions that I am aware of, they infiltrated a reading and tried to turn me against my readee, who was suffering from a variety of drug addictions. They did this by projecting negative, derogatory thoughts. Since I rarely have judgmental thoughts during a reading, it was easy to realize what was happening, step out of these thoughts, and find the source of them.

Demons or other nasty beings will sometimes throw sex pictures at people. I use the term *throw* because that is the sensation, as if something being thrown at you is abruptly landing in your mind. The quality of these pictures is different from other clairvoyant images. They are quite sexually graphic and rude. It's as if an angry guy who wants to throw you off balance or anger you were to throw a hardcore pornographic photo into your lap and laugh at you. This is not going to happen often. But I mention it because these pictures can be thrown at professional psychics and unsuspecting people who are unknowingly being psychic by receiving these pictures. I believe spirits are often at the heart of sexual addictions as well, and can cause us to do some pretty silly, self-comprising things.

I am also mentioning these beings here because I have learned how to destroy and eradicate destructive entities, and now their scare tactics only backfire on them by alerting me to their presence—and I hope to help you learn to do the same. These beings are sometimes connected to a living person who has ill intentions, and the beings' presence alerts me to the fact that I am about to encounter such a person, or that such a person is presently up to no good. I may not know who this person is, but they are usually revealed over the course of the next few days, at which time I am prepared and equipped to clean up any damage they have done.

Mind Eyes

There are also beings whose eyes I see only when I close my own eyes. I don't know if these eyes belong to one specific group of beings or if a variety of beings appear to me in this way. I see these eyes surprisingly clearly. They feel mean and cold. It's as if they are in my head, watching me. They appear sporadically, unexpectedly, and most often right at the beginning of a reading with other people, so they actually alert me to the fact that there is a spirit I am going to be contending with soon. Usually I will ask the being to introduce itself. If I don't get a response (I rarely do in these cases), I then tell the being in no uncertain terms to leave. If it still doesn't leave, I threaten to erase it. If it still does not leave, then I hook it up to God, give it a grounding cord, and wait to see if the eyes disappear. If they do not, then I do use the technique of erasure, at which point the eyes always disappear.

Dwarf Tree Spirits

Another group of spirits I have clairvoyantly encountered in readings, dreams, and in waking life are those I refer to as *dwarf tree spirits*. These are boxy, homely guys who stand only two to three feet tall. They dwell outside, near trees and sometimes water. They are very mischievous and even mean-spirited. I never get the feeling that they will do too much damage, but they do like to trick and toy with people for their own entertainment. This is how they have fun.

When performing readings outside or in a building that is near a wooded area, be aware that these and other kinds of nature spirits may attempt to interfere with your reading by distracting you or the readee, or by playing around with the images you see. By now you have learned enough tools to adequately deal with varmints such as these!

Walk-ins

Walk-in is a common term among psychics, referring to a spirit that has taken over a body that did not originally belong to the spirit. Most of the time there was another spirit who gave up the body, either before the new spirit arrived or at the same time. Sometimes when a baby is born, the baby's spirit is not fully connected into the body or the spirit departs or is forced out of the body during infancy or early childhood. This commonly happens when the baby or child is placed in a dangerous and traumatic situation, such as during a physical accident or in a domestic-violence situation. Often, during a near-death experience or during a severe psychotic episode, the person's spirit will actually take its next step and vacate the body. Sometimes there will be a period of time before another being moves in; at other times the transfer will happen immediately. This is one reason why many people seem significantly changed after they have recovered from a near-death experience.

Walk-ins are often fairly easy to identify because they seem to have greater difficulty operating the physical body than spirits that have been born into a body and matured with it. Many mentally ill people and street people are walk-ins who can't operate the body well enough to handle maintaining a job, paying rent, or even conversing in an intelligible manner. Some walk-ins are more adept at handling the physical body, due either to experience or to having a better body/being connection, but even they will still have difficulties dealing with other people. People who are high-functioning walk-ins often explain that they feel different from others, and have a sense that they don't really belong here. Some walk-ins seem to come from other planets or dimensions that are very different from our own. I've also suspected that some people who are obsessed with aliens and UFOs may be walk-ins from places other than Earth.

During your clairvoyant readings you may occasionally encounter a walk-in. You will begin to get some clues during the initial stages of the reading when you are attempting to tune in to the readee's spirit, although the situation may not become totally apparent until much later in the reading, when your clairvoyant images unexpectedly reveal information about the exodus of the original spirit and the entry of the one sitting in front of you.

Some people who are walk-ins tend to change their name soon after the transfer. They also tend to remember less than other people do about their past. Some people who are walk-ins realize exactly who they are and are even familiar with the term. Others don't realize this but are actually relieved when they find out, because it explains so many of their feelings and difficulties.

If you suspect that the person sitting in front of you is a walk-in, use your clairvoyance to help them understand why it is they chose to come into that particular body at that time, what their agreement was or is with the original occupant of the body, and what actions they can take to help themselves cope with life on Earth. Don't try to remove that spirit (your readee) from the body unless it is clear that the original owner is still very much present within the body and fighting with every ounce of its being to regain sole ownership of the body. Otherwise you may end up with an unconscious body on your hands!

Space Invaders

Space invader is a term I have coined to describe a walk-in that is either in the process of kicking out the original owner from their body or is cohabitating with them within their body. I have done several clairvoyant readings in which I have encountered these types of beings. These readings were particularly difficult. I had a sense something was going on, but I couldn't quite put my finger on it until the being sent an electric shock through my third chakra, at which point I suddenly became very aware that there was a very large spirit that was dominating most of my readee's body, one not at all happy that I was seeing him.

I am not sure why this being chose to shock me in this way, other than to try to scare me and chase me away. However, this kind of response always has the opposite effect on me, in that it motivates me to investigate the source of this attack. Although the shock is uncomfortable and, well, shocking, it is not really any more painful than receiving an electric shock from static electricity so it doesn't scare me in the least, even though it tends to fill up my entire solar plexus. When I become aware that another being is cohabitating within my readee's body, I will often clairvoyantly look to see what the agreement is between the two spirits. I will then gingerly address the subject, and test the waters to see if the readee has any level of awareness of the situation. I will usually ask them if they would like a healing on this situation. Sometimes they will say yes. Other times they will refuse, telling me they think they need this spirit.

In my early days as a clairvoyant student there were times when I earnestly attempted to talk the readee into removing such a spirit from their body, only to discover later that it was the invading spirit that I had been addressing all along. I would open my eyes and see this being staring angrily at me from behind the readee's eyes. On a few occasions, the readee's spirit actually vacated the readee's body and another spirit took over during the course of the reading. It became clear that the invading spirit was not at all open to any kind of communication from me, and the most prudent course of action seemed to be to end the reading and get out of there as quickly as possible!

Sometimes a readee will share their body with a number of spirits. A few years ago a very sophisticated-looking woman who owned her own business and appeared very confident sat down in front of me for a reading. I spent several minutes describing her personality characteristics, and then suddenly I began describing other characteristics that seemed to contradict the ones I had just mentioned. I felt as if I kept losing my connection with her spirit, so I frequently asked her to state her name to regain that connection. I began to realize that I was not actually reading her; I was reading instead at least two if not several spirits who seemed to be flying in and out of her body at their leisure.

In order to make sure I was still tuned in to the woman's particular vibration, I asked her to say her name one last time, but I got no response. My eyes were closed so I could not see her to determine why she was not responding. I asked her again to state her name, but she still remained silent. I asked her if she was not responding because she didn't want to repeat her name. I still got no response. I then got the eerie feeling that maybe she was not able to respond, and I asked her if this was the case. I opened up my eyes and saw a look of complete horror on her face. She began crying, and she explained that she literally could not remember her name. I performed a clairvoyant healing to move out the beings enough so her spirit could come back in, and she was once again able to say her name. She later admitted that she had been diagnosed by two therapists as having multiple personality disorder, although she had felt this was not an accurate diagnosis.

My reading later revealed that she had been severely abused as a child and had called in these spirits to help her cope with the abuse. This is a common scenario among people who suffer from possession by multiple spirits, as well as people who are diagnosed with multiple personality disorder, which I have found is always related to possession. Although this client acknowledged she had been abused, she began to get very condescending and hostile toward me and I realized she was not emotionally able to handle addressing these issues at that time.

I believe that the reason some patients diagnosed with multiple personality disorder actually test positive for physical illnesses such as diabetes or hypertension when they are exhibiting one personality, but test negative for these disorders when exhibiting another personality, is because they are actually channeling other entities. These diseases are linked as much if not more so to the spirit within the body as they are to the body itself.

Extrasensory Emotional Energy

Emotions are one form of energy. Such energy is generated from within our bodies but is very often projected outward to other people and our environment; this is the primary way people release their emotions. This release might make someone feel better, but it can make those around the person miserable and even sick. Just look at the spouse or long-term partner of an unhappy person who doesn't know how to deal with their own emotions, and you will almost certainly find someone who has or has had cancer or another equally unpleasant disease, particularly if they never really knew how to block this invasive energy.

The emotional energy generated through a heated argument or a violent or traumatic incident can linger inside a room or building for decades. Anyone, but particularly a sensitive person, will feel and experience this energy as they step into this area. Most of the time they will not understand the dynamics involved, but they may experience the emotions as their own. In this case they may feel and exhibit anger, fear, or depression more intensely than usual.

I've seen and directly experienced how this energy can impact people on a physical level by making them weaker, causing them to lose their balance, drop things, and become nauseous or dizzy. It can interfere with electrical equipment, computers, and lights. This extraneous emotional energy can also seep into furniture, clothing, and especially jewelry. Sometimes it is mistaken for an actual entity. More often than not, it's found in the same locations where other entities are having an impact on the current occupants.

CHAPTER 14

Battle Techniques

The victorious strategist only seeks battle after the victory has been won, whereas he who is destined to defeat first fights and afterward looks for victory.

—SUN TZU

Techniques for Handling Troublesome Entities

In your readings you will undoubtedly encounter troublesome entities at some point. They may appear as I have described them in this book, or they may look totally different; however, you will know what they are when you see them. Evil occasionally disguises itself behind the appearance of a loved one or loving one but can only do so for so long before its true nature betrays itself. If you ever see an image of a loved one in your readings, meditations, dreams, or waking life but something seems slightly off or makes you feel uncomfortable (e.g., a look in their eyes, the color of their hair), you can be fairly certain a being is trying to imitate that person in order to lower your defenses or trick you.

In one of my dreams several years ago, a spirit disguised itself as one of my respected teachers and told me that my boyfriend at the time was cheating on me and that I should break up with him. The teacher took my hand and asked me to follow him. I felt a level of devastation

I've never before felt in a dream. However, as I walked down a corridor with this teacher, I suddenly became aware that my teacher's eyes were brown instead of their true color, blue. The moment I noticed this, the spirit could no longer maintain its disguise and its diabolical face was revealed.

On another occasion I entered my front door and saw this same friend standing in my hallway. I was confused because he didn't have a key and I had just left his house. Then I realized I was looking at an image of him that was not entirely solid, and I thought, "Oh, he must have decided to pay me an astral visit, maybe he misses me." But then I felt a cold chill wrap around me, and I saw his eyes. There was something off about his eyes, something evil. That's when I knew it was not him; it was an evil entity trying to impersonate him. I told the entity that I knew he was not who he was pretending to be and ordered him to leave at once, which he did.

It is important to remember that you always have the advantage over disembodied spirits because you have a physical body that is connected to the earth. They use scare tactics to control you because fear brings you down to their vibration. If you are not scared, they ultimately have no power over you. When you see such entities, say hello to them. Let them know that you see them. Some of them are like bullies; they put up a good show of being tough but the moment they understand that you really do see them, they get scared and flee.

These lower astral beings are antisocial; they lack the ability to empathize with and respect human life. Acknowledge their presence but don't try to reform them or get them to understand you. Don't argue with them. Trying to change their nature is like trying to reason with a hungry man eating a tiger. If you try to talk sense into them, you will merely make yourself more vulnerable to their tactics.

If a misguided entity has invaded your territory, then by all means kick it out. However, if you have inadvertently trespassed into their territory (as I did with the Grays and the spiritual council), I recommend turning back and leaving them alone. You actually don't have a right to go anywhere in the universe you please, even if you think you should have such a right.

A few years ago I performed a reading on a man who had recently been diagnosed with schizophrenia. My reading revealed that he was infested with a multitude of parasitic entities that were projecting all kinds of horrifying pictures and thoughts at his sixth chakra. This man was extremely clairvoyant, and he saw these images as clearly as if they were really there. He was also extremely clairaudient; he could hear the thoughts of spirits and living people as loudly as if they were standing inside his head. His complaints that things were crawling over and around his body and his paranoid thoughts of persecution were actually astute perceptions of the energies that were in fact attacking him, rather than the unjustified delusions his doctors naturally assumed them to be.

When I attempted to remove these beings during a healing, I clairvoyantly saw that this man did not really want these beings to go. He had some kind of fascination with them. I saw that he spent hours on the Internet researching subjects like aliens and ghosts, and that this was opening up doors that were attracting the beings to him. When I suggested that he get rid of all his books on the subject and avoid the Internet altogether, he adamantly insisted that he was not going to abandon his favorite pastime just because these beings were upsetting him; he was going to make it his mission find them and fight them until his death. It looked as though death would not be too far away for him if his combative attitude persisted.

When you choose to actively go into battle with a person or entity, you become intimately entwined with that spirit. (This is what happens when you sue someone; you end up engaging with them and perhaps suffering more than if you just took the loss and severed that unpleasant connection.) Self-protection or prevention is one thing; an offensive invasion into their territory is a whole other ballgame and some people just don't know when to back off! Whenever you think about an entity (or person), you give them your energy. I suggest that you don't talk about them or even think about them except when you spontaneously see them and need to deal with them.

The high vibration of amusement or a sense of humor is your greatest weapon.

When you see or sense an unpleasant entity, use your great imagination to dress them up in funny clothes. Pretend that they are wearing a sparkly-pink baby girl's dress with a matching frilly bonnet and sunglasses with little birdies on the ends. Throw them into a pink baby carriage, plop a bottle of milk into their homely mouths, and take them for a ride through a lovely garden while you tell them silly monster jokes. Many spirits will automatically depart because they won't be able to breathe in the vibration of amusement you are creating. If they are vibrating in fear and you are not, it's like being on two different floors of a building. You can take the elevator up just by pressing the amusement button with your thoughts and feelings.

Esther and Jerry Hicks' book *Ask and It Is Given* is an excellent resource for understanding the vibrational scale of emotions. While the authors of this book present this information in order to assist readers with manifestation, I think it's also helpful in terms of breaking free from all the entities that feed off and instigate the lower emotional vibrations of humans.

If these entities don't disappear, then there are several other tactics you can apply. But you must ensure you do your very best to apply these tactics while holding on to your sense of humor and amusement.

On your reading screen, see this spirit connected up to God with a cord of brilliant light and connected into the planet with a strong grounding cord. Imagine that God has giant hands, and you are gently placing the spirit into God's hands. Thank God for taking this spirit away.

As you do the above, feel free to call in help from an ascended master or one of your guides. Whether or not you consider yourself to be a Christian, the name of Christ is a powerful symbol that has been used for centuries in exorcisms. (I'm Jewish and it works for me!) In the name of Christ, demand confidently with every ounce of your being that this spirit is now banished from your kingdom. State this demand out loud.

You can also create a large viewing receptacle, such as a rose, a glass bubble, a boat, or a cage. Visualize the entity inside the receptacle. Send the receptacle far away, into outer space or across the globe to the bottom of the ocean, and then watch the receptacle as it explodes into a trillion specks of light that ultimately will be returned to the source of all creation.

The Power of Repetition

Religions and spiritual disciplines have long understood the power of repetition for prayer, manifestation, and protection. Just about all religions utilize repetitive words, sounds, or phrases known as mantras; others put these to music, which is called chanting. Roman Catholics utilize a beaded rosary called a chaplet that helps them say the prayers that they must repeat over and over again. Tibetan prayer wheels (called *mani wheels* by the Tibetans) are devices for spreading spiritual blessings and well-being. Rolls of thin paper, imprinted with many, many copies of the mantra (prayer) *Om mani padme hum*, printed in an ancient Indian script or in Tibetan script, are wound around an axle in a protective container, and spun around and around. Tibetan Buddhists believe that saying this mantra, out loud or silently to oneself, invokes the powerful benevolent attention and blessings of Chenrezig, the embodiment of compassion.

Repetition accomplishes a few things. It builds up energy in a person's psyche; that energy and the thoughtforms can then project themselves more powerfully. By repeating an intention, affirmation, or prayer over and over again, we reaffirm it, energize it, implant it. Doing so also seems to clear out whatever is opposite to that which is being repeated. Repetition can clear our minds, and it eliminates matter from space.

Make Your Own Prayer Wheel

Choose a prayer that states your intention, and repeat it over and over again. You can make your own prayer wheel by writing down your prayer over and over as many times as possible, then taking a lint brush that you can get at any store, taping the prayer to the brush, and spinning the wheel. This can be done with any prayer to evoke any desired intention and is effective with difficult entities.

One prayer that I like to say—sometimes in full, sometimes just in part—is "The light is all-powerful, powerful is the light. It shall dissolve all and anything not of the light. I am all-powerful, I am the light. God is all-powerful, God is the light. Together we generate the power of one million lights that will turn all darkness to light, darkness to light, darkness to light. So it is, so it will be, for now and forever more." (An abbreviated version is "The light is all powerful, powerful is the light.")

Remember that darkness is only the absence of light, so on the spiritual plane, as soon as you increase the light, darkness ceases to exist. As you repeat your prayer or mantra, imagine the brightest light you could ever imagine pouring from the wheel and zapping and consuming the negative entity, like a lightsaber from *Star Wars*. You can also use this technique for moving out any kind of negative energy from another person's body or aura as well as for dealing directly with entities.

Weapons of Mass Destruction

While the word *mass* may have startled you, I use it here to refer to matter! The following techniques can be utilized when extreme measures are called for. These techniques are designed to instantly weaken and ultimately eliminate the structural building blocks of an entity so that it will no longer exist. It's important to understand that the following steps must not be done on living people. Instead, these techniques are intended only for those demonic or low-vibration entities in spirit form that are attacking you, draining you, or causing you to have violent or obsessive thoughts. These can also be utilized as mini-exorcisms or to remove parasitic beings during your clairvoyant reading/healing sessions with others.

Establish Communication If Possible

Visualize your reading screen. Create a viewing receptacle. Demand that the source of whatever it is that might be causing you discomfort or unease show itself in your receptacle. Watch it and see what comes up. Look for a color. You can either see how it affects the rose you are looking at or see if you get an actual image.

Once you get something, you can communicate telepathically and ask it what it wants or why it is there. See what response you get, but it is important to understand you may not be able to trust it and you will want to use your clairvoyance to evaluate the communication. If you are working on yourself and you have determined you definitely want the spirit or entity to vacate your premises, you can first politely tell it to leave. Then demand that it *must* leave.

Imagine you are opening up a door in the receptacle or on your screen and tell the critter that it either has to leave on its own or you will destroy it. If you like, you can visualize a symbol for God and create a tube or column of light running from the door to God; imagine that this tube or column is an elevator or a teleportation machine like the transporter in *Star Trek*.

Show the spirit the light and see if it goes or if God takes it. You can also call in some of your backup spirit guides. See these as glowing yellow figures there to help escort the critter out, up, and away. Remember to keep up your sense of humor and amusement. Tell yourself some jokes and dress up the spirit in funny clothes.

When Working with a Client

If you are reading someone else, then I suggest that you describe the spirit and your clairvoyant findings to them, asking your client if they would like you to help them get rid of the critter. If your client is confused, you can do a reading on that confusion by putting up a new receptacle on the screen and inviting the energy of confusion into it so you can take a look at it. Sometimes the confusion is the being not wanting to let go. If you have not done one already, you can also do a relationship reading at this point (as discussed in chapter 4) around the agreement between the person and this entity. Doing such a reading will help both of you decide how to proceed.

If your readee objects to you evicting the spirit, you can ask your readee if they'd be open to you moving the spirit out of their body or aura enough so they can make a clear decision, or you can refer your readee to this book, so that when they are ready they can do it themselves. Sometimes it can get confusing in your readings, because if a person has a strong entity attached to them and you are discussing that entity, the entity may be using more of your readee's body than the readee is and will therefore do whatever it can to hide by making it hard for you to clearly see them or the situation and by convincing the readee that you are the enemy.

Such a scenario only occurs in very rare cases, but I have had the experience in a few readings of spending two hours with a person only to realize in the last five minutes that I was addressing the wrong spirit in the body. I compare these experiences to what Little Red Riding Hood encountered when she arrived at her grandmother's house. She thought she was talking to her grandmother, even warning her grand-mother to look out for the big bad wolf, but instead she was really just addressing the wolf dressed in her grandma's clothes.

If you feel as though there is more of the entity than the original spirit in your readee's body, it is important to remind yourself that it's not up to you to break any agreements for your readee but rather to look at these agreements and the situation, communicate them, and do what you can to bring more awareness so your readee can make the changes.

Call in reinforcements. Give them the option of going to the light. Ask God if God will take them for you.

If it still feels as though the entity isn't leaving, then proceed with the next set of instructions:

Technique #1: Rearrangement

I've been doing this technique lately and getting excellent results. The entity is made of energy. Imagine this energy has finer particles, smaller than atoms and molecules. Your imagination is strong enough to rear-range these particles and essentially reorganize or break down the cur-rent organization of this being.

Imagine you are separating the particles and then rearranging them in new places. So if a scary face is popping up, imagine the atoms, molecules, and particles are moving all around, getting jumbled. You could even see the larger elements, such as the eyes, mouth, and other features rearranging themselves to look like a funny face or a fuzzy, cute animal. You can also see these particles breaking up and splitting apart, which is essential as you rearrange this being and it is breaking down. Continue watching until all the particles have broken down and dissipated. This technique should never be performed on a living person. And the other methods should be employed before this step.

Technique #2: The Black Hole Method

Gravity is the most powerful force on the planet; it pulls matter toward the center of the planet. A black hole is thought to be an area where the force of gravity is magnified to the extent that anything coming into its realm will be sucked in at such intensity that it will implode on itself.

Keeping the above in mind, we can either visualize a black hole as a place to send the entity where it will collapse into itself, or see the entity itself as a black hole, collapsing into itself and thus imploding. For this first method, use the power of your imagination to place the entity on a spaceship. Send the spaceship into an image of a black hole and postulate that this black hole you are creating actually does possess the real qualities of a black hole. See the entity inside the spaceship implode over and over again until it disappears.

Another way to do this technique is to visualize the entity itself, or a receptacle with the entity inside, and see this imploding into itself over and over again until the entire image is gone.

Technique #3: Erasure or Duplication

The erasure method is currently taught at a variety of clairvoyant training schools throughout the United States. It was first introduced to the Western world by Lewis Bostwick in the early 1960s. A very powerful method that destroys lower astral entities, it essentially erases the entities' information so they no longer exist. I can't exactly explain the mechanics behind it, but it really seems to work and often elicits a powerful shift in a person who has been bothered by a disembodied spirit or entity. This is a great exercise to practice during your own meditations, even if there is not presently an entity you wish to get rid of.

You can replace the word *entity* in the directions below with any kind of energy you'd like to rid yourself of (such as pessimism, doubt, hate, and so on). Also, note that just performing this exercise can cause a strong shift in your own energy field that you may consciously experience.

Step 1: Once you are certain that you wish to evict an entity from your space or the space of someone seeking healing, visualize a clear transparent rose. Either see the entity inside the rose, or ask the rose to take on/fill up with the energy of the entity. Watch to see what happens to the rose; note its appearance in terms of color, shape, and size. Next, see a symbol for God above the rose and draw a column of light running down from God, straight through the rose and into the earth. This is grounding it to the light and to the earth. Tell the entity that you have placed it inside the rose and tell it that this is it's one and only opportunity to take a hike. Show it the column of light leading to God and invite it to go there. You can also ask God if God is willing to take this entity off your hands, or if this is something you have to take care of yourself. If you see the entity leaving the rose, or the entire rose moving towards God, or some other image indicating the entity is leaving, then you are done—just visualize the rose dissipating. However, if you still have a sense the entity does not want to go on its own, proceed to the next step.

Step 2: Visualize the rose containing the entity (i.e., spirit) or energy of the entity. Take a good look at it, and then right next to it, create a duplicate version of that rose. So now you will have two of the exact same roses side by side. They should appear identical. Take the second one you just created and imagine you are tossing it right into the first. Notice what happens. The goal is to have both roses disappear, which they quite often do via this process. If they don't disappear, whether both or just one still remains, repeat the process, tossing the second rose into the first until you have a strong sense they are both gone, that you can't see them anymore. If the images are changing on you while you are attempting to perform this technique, imagine that you have a bucket of something called "frozen energy." Pour the bucket over the rose and imagine that the rose absolutely has no power to move or change. Sometimes the entity will impact your visualizations or your confidence about your visualization in order to prevent you from carrying out this technique. I believe most of the time that before the entity can be absolutely destroyed, it ends up leaving on its own accord.

Alternative steps to erasure: If you don't wish to use an image of a rose, you can visualize the entity directly, or you can visualize a card, such as a tarot card, and place the entity on the card. In this case, you will be duplicating the card, and tossing the duplicate of the card into the original.

If you feel you are having trouble with this exercise, you can simply do step 1, and then imagine you are moving the rose with the entity inside off your screen and sending it to a faraway place. Then imagine that the rose with the entity inside is exploding. If there are any remaining pieces, roll these up into a ball and explode the ball. Repeat this process until all pieces seem to be gone.

CHAPTER 15

Basic Aura Healing

*Of one thing I am certain, the body is not the measure of healing—
peace is the measure.*
—GEORGE MELTON

What Is Clairvoyant Energy Healing?

To me, healing is merely replacing something undesirable with something desirable. It's transforming that which is out of balance into a
greater state of equilibrium. Healing includes replacing pain, disease,
and discomfort with a state of health. It also includes replacing mental
and emotional distress with a state of peace, enthusiasm, and excitement. Healing can also mean opening a closed mind, releasing limits
to expanding one's range of possibilities, transforming one's negative
sense of self into a more positive sense of self, and transforming one's
apathy into creativity.

It doesn't take long for an clairvoyant to realize that not only is
there a mind/body/spirit connection, but they are also really all parts
of the same thing. The concept of "we are all one" takes on new meaning when we see for ourselves how people are sharing the same thoughts
and emotions, and how strongly one person, with or without awareness,
can influence another through thought or emotion alone. Clairvoyants

209

see firsthand how there is a very real correlation between our physical pain and our thoughts, emotions, and even our relationships with others. When you enable someone to release thoughts and emotions that are no longer serving them, this can significantly impact their physical body. Conversely, changes on the physical level can drastically impact our thoughts and feelings. Our mind/body/spirit connection is not a closed system. To the contrary, it is very much connected with the minds and spirits of everyone around us, including people we no longer have physical contact with, people we have not actually met yet, and people we may never meet.

When you as a clairvoyant even just begin to "look" at someone, doing so spontaneously effects a change in them, and that change resonates outward to all the people both of you are connected with. As noted elsewhere in this book and in *You Are Psychic*, we all carry the energy of others around with us. Their ideas, their judgments, their needs, doubts, and pain become lodged in our bodies and we experience them as our own. So releasing these can have a significant impact on our overall state of well-being, and even on the well-being of the people who have so generously shared the energies with us that we are now trying to release.

We Need to Place Less Emphasis on Cognitive Understanding

Many people think that if they can just figure out the right answer, then everything will be okay and they will broaden their spectrum of what they believe is possible for themselves. Healing can occur when one undergoes a shift in consciousness, and it can also occur through the manipulation of energy. Far too many people try to heal their emotions through thought, and this just doesn't work; it only creates an excess of unproductive mental activity that causes more suffering.

The Power of Simplicity

Because people's thoughts, bodies, problems, and lives are so incredibly complex, it's helpful for us as clairvoyants and particularly as healers to keep things as simple as possible. This is sometimes hard for students or those interested in learning about energy healing to accept. In school we are taught that the more "facts," the more details, and the more complex information we can cram and hold in our minds, the better we will be at any given profession or task.

When it comes to healing, the two most important things are that the intentions of the healer and healee are in alignment with one another, and that the healer can allow herself or himself to be both an active participant and a watchful recipient at the same time. This requires the healer to be able to get out their own way, something that is also the hardest thing for most healers. This is why healing can be particularly powerful in traditions of healing or prophecy in which the healer goes unconscious or leaves their body and allows in another spirit to do the work.

Still, that's not to say the type of healing we are learning here cannot be as powerful; it just requires us to be able to have an intention and let go of that intention at the same time. This is really what's required of us in life. We are always going to have desires and goals, and it's important for us as humans to do all we can to achieve them. At the same time, we need to let go of our emotional attachment to them. When it comes to healing or even saving lives, this is quite a challenge.

The simplest yet most effective healing technique that I've used, received, and now teach to others, is to reduce every issue to its smallest energy component. I define *effective* as achieving both the intended result and unintended consequences that ultimately bring the healee into greater balance. The technique I am about to share can often be felt by the one being healed through a variety of physical sensations, even when the healee is unaware of the healing. However, as a healer it is important not to get caught in the trap of wanting to prove to your healee or yourself that you are actually doing something by putting your energy, efforts, or attention into getting them to feel it.

Color, the Smallest Visual Component

Whether someone is dying of cancer, feeling suicidal or stuck, or suffering from obesity, alcoholism, or boredom, we can ask ourselves three questions: What is the color of the energy that forms the foundation/basis/core of this problem? Where is it in the body or the body's energy field? Does this color need to be released or removed, and/or is there a different color (representing the desired state of being) that needs to be increased or flowing through this area? Once we know, or even just have a minute sense of these things, all we have to do to effect change is to visualize the flow and release of the colors.

Some people are just not going to believe it's this easy. Many are not going to believe that through simple visualization you can impact another person's health. If you have these beliefs, I highly recommend that you read Lynne McTaggart's book *The Intention Experiment*, in which you can learn about the hundreds of fine experiments that have been done according to the strictest protocols, which show that through mere thought, even at a distance when the receiver is unaware of the thought, thoughts can impact, and be perceived by, the receiver's mind or reflexes. Even more importantly, I also encourage you to exercise some faith, suspend your skepticism long enough for you to try these techniques, and observe the results for yourself.

Working with Color

We really are only concerned about color insofar as it gives us something to latch onto for further exploration and manipulation of energy. I recommend that you first utilize the clairvoyant reading method of conjuring up a viewing receptacle and asking it for the color of the thing you are wondering about. You may see a color quite vividly, even before you begin to imagine your receptacle. You may just get a vague sense of a shade, or you may not get anything. If the latter is the case, then you can always assign the subject a color of your choice, and alter it later in the process if you get a color later on.

Remember that the color is really just a way of visualizing invisible energy. This is the same thing that is done in imaging technology, in which an image's colors are assigned to frequency bands that are normally invisible to the human eye (such as infrared radiation or gases), in order to enhance contrasts. This helps to differentiate features or convey information. In clairvoyant healing, we work with colors so we can differentiate one energy from another. When performing readings, it gives us something tangible to work with as a foundation for further exploration.

Aura Healing

The more students I work with, the more I am learning to appreciate the simplicity and power of working with the aura to access information and healing. The beauty of doing an aura reading is that you see and describe the energies that need to be released and/or increased, and then you can switch into healing mode by facilitating the readee to do this themselves at that moment, and also give them something to do once they've gone home or hung up the phone.

How to Perform an Aura Healing

1. *Get an overall picture of your readee's entire aura.*

   Follow the directions for how to begin a reading and establish a connection with your readee. On your screen, visualize an image of your readee as a silhouette figure; even a stick figure is fine. Ask to see the overall appearance of your readee's aura, including shape and size, and the texture and color of the energy filed around them. Just sit back and see what first impressions you get. Notice if one side of the aura looks any different from the other. You can imagine you are seeing both their front and back, and look for differences there. Feel free to communicate or investigate what you are noticing by posing further questions to the spot of interest, or by putting up a viewing receptacle and asking it to show you information about what you are looking at. If you have trouble seeing the entire aura, don't worry; that is common. Instead, just proceed to step 2 below.

2. *Investigate your readee's own energy in this layer.*

You will be working with the seven layers of the aura, one layer at a time. Some people like to think of these as energetic bodies and that's fine too. I realize one's aura might have more or fewer than seven layers and that these layers may not be very distinct. I've seen hundreds of Kirlian photos, and while I could see lots of colors, none of them depicted very distinctive layers at all. Honestly, I've never actually spontaneously seen distinct layers apart from when I chose to visualize them this way. However, intellectually dissecting or categorizing the aura into seven general layers does seem to yield excellent results, and that's what we are going for here. If you don't have much time, you can mentally divide the aura into three layers. (This is kind of like taking a pie and cutting it up any way you want. You could cut the entire pie into three big pieces and then taste the three and describe how they taste, or you could cut it into seven smaller pieces and then describe each of those pieces.)

I recommend starting with the first layer of the aura closest to the body since this layer will contain information most relevant to your readee's body. Put up a receptacle such as a rose on your screen and ask it to show you the color of your readee's energy in the first layer. Make a mental note of this color, or write or draw it on a piece of paper. Notice if the receptacle or rose is showing you any other attributes. Then you can ask the color or attributes to show you further information, in the form of images. If you aren't getting anything, ask your readee to say their name a few times and repeat this step. Some good questions to pose in this part of the reading are, "What does this color represent?" "Why is this color in this particular layer?" Take about five minutes or so to do this part of the reading.

3. *Investigate the foreign energy in this layer.*

Next put up a new rose, or revisualize the figure on your screen, putting your attention on the area just outside the body, asking it to show you a color that represents any foreign energies in this layer. Repeat the process above of investigating this color. If you see a color, some good questions to pose to it are, "What does this color represent?" "Who or what does it belong to?" "Why is this color/energy there in this particular layer of the aura?" "In what specific way does this impact the readee and their life?" "Is the readee ready to release this color/energy?" and "What would best facilitate this process?"

Spend another five minutes or so reading the foreign energy in this layer (if there is any; there may not be).

(*Optional*: Instead of, or in addition to, looking at the readee's own energy and foreign energy, you can look at the "masculine energy" and "feminine energy" in each layer.)

Before proceeding on to read the next layer, you can ask the readee if they'd like you to help them release the foreign energy and bring in more of their own. If they say yes, which 90 percent of people who are receiving aura readings typically do, then tell them that together you are each going to visualize the color representing the foreign energy release from their body. You can give them a grounding cord first. Then remind your readee of the color of the energy that seems to represent their own in this layer. You can also decide to use the color you established as the overall reading color at the beginning, or choose one that seems to represent a vibration they need more of. Then visualize this desirable color coming into the area, or increasing or circulating, and watch as it washes away the color representing the foreign energy.

You can invite your readee to do this visualization along with you, by merely instructing them to visualize the color representing their own energy (which you can share with them, or ask them what color they would choose) and by visualizing the color of the energy that isn't working for them to release. If they don't know about grounding, that's okay; don't get caught up in a teaching session, just let them know you are imagining the color leaving through a cord that connects their body to the earth and trust that they will do fine from there. (If you feel your readee really needs and is ready for these techniques, then recommend either this book or *You Are Psychic*. That's why I wrote these books, so I would not have to leave my reading/healing mode and go into teaching mode, and so you wouldn't either.)

You can of course teach these techniques yourself, but it's best to wait until you've got some practice and experience under your belt first. As a teacher, it is important for you to create boundaries for yourself so you know when you are in teaching mode and when you are in healing or reading mode. This is healthier for you, and your readee will appreciate it, too. I find it annoying when someone is supposed to give me a reading but instead it turns into a lecture, although I must admit I have quite often been guilty of this myself!

4. *Repeat this process for each layer.*

As noted above, you can break the aura into three main layers: the one closest to the body, the one in the middle; and the one furthest from the body.

CHAPTER 16

Advanced Healing and Psychic Surgery

Practice acquiring the consciousness of childhood. Visualize the Divine Child within. Before falling asleep suggest to your consciousness, "I now realize that there is within me a spiritual joy-body ever young, ever beautiful. I have a beautiful, spiritual mind, eyes, nose, mouth, skin—the body of the Divine Infant, which now, tonight, is perfect."
—BAIRD T. SPALDING

Supreme Being, Holy Spirit, and Ascended Master Healings

When someone is very ill, to the point at which it seems they have no life force energy left, or is so stuck because they have so much of other people's energy in their body and aura, or they have so many issues that it seems to be overwhelming (if not to them, then to me), then I perform a healing with the energy of the Supreme Being, the Creator (God), Jesus, Mother Mary, Buddha, Holy Spirit, Archangel Michael, or any other deity I or the readee feel a connection with at the time.

No matter how powerful the deity is that you are working with, if you don't acknowledge the power within yourself and your healee (particularly in your healee), then something is going to be missing in the healing. This is because it is not even so much the power of God or Jesus or Mary as it is the power of the relationship between these ascended beings and the one receiving the healing. These figures are the unexpressed potential of your healee. They are the embodiment of all that your healee is. Creation, health, love, strength, faith, perseverance, courage, power, and so forth have been expressed and emanate from these beings, but their core is made of the same stuff as your healee. By bringing the two together, your healee can begin to express these aspects, which may lie dormant or may have been forgotten within himself or herself. This expression will manifest itself either in a healed body or a transformed emotional/mental state.

This is where the concept of the Holy Spirit comes in. Most of the faith healers in the Philippines use the energy of the "Holy Spirit" in their healings. You can think of the Holy Spirit as being the energy between God and the manifestation of God.

When the Creator (a name by which you can call God or the Supreme Being, if you like) of a tree creates a tree, the force or energy that was used to create the tree is the Holy Spirit. It is the same energy that comes from our Creator and creates us. By evoking the Holy Spirit, we are evoking that which created us and the same energy within ourselves. If we were created once, we can be re-created, either back to the state of health we once had, or to a state of health we may never have had in this lifetime but that we know is possible because other human beings exhibit it. This is what we must hold on to.

One other important thing to remember: the moment we think about healing energy (sometimes even before it's a conscious thought), that energy is activated. Even at this moment, I can feel it as soon as I think about it. Perhaps that's because it's always there, just out of our awareness. It's that easy!

Visualization Technique #1:
Working with the Deity of Your Choice

This technique uses visualization only. Once you have run through your psychic tools and are in the center of your head, well-grounded with your earth and cosmic energies running, you are ready to begin the healing. If your healee is present, sit directly across from them and make sure both of you are in comfortable positions. Ask your healee to say their current name and date of birth a few times.

If your healee is not present, then repeat their name, date of birth, and current address to yourself if you know them (it is not essential to know all of these, but it can help you to establish a clearer and stronger connection if you do), and visualize your healee. If you don't know what your healee looks like, you can physically put a chair across from yourself and invite the healee's energy into that chair and conduct the healing as if they were sitting a couple of feet from you.

Next, say a prayer invoking God, the Holy Spirit, or the deity of your choice. Usually, when conducting a God or Holy Spirit healing, I will imagine a very bright shimmering ball of light above the healee's head. When conducting a Jesus, Mother Mary, or Buddha healing, I will imagine the faces and bodies of these figures and see them floating above the healee. Once you have a clear image or symbol of the deity of your choice, using your imagination you can either draw a column of energy (i.e., a ball of light) from the image to your readee's crown chakra or you can pull that ball right into your healee's heart center or solar plexus.

See sparkles of the deity's light pouring into the healee's head, and down or out through every cell of their body until it is streaming from their feet and down their grounding cord. See their aura filling up as well. See the healing light fill up your healee's arms and fingers, spilling out of their spinning hand chakras. See their organs, their chakras, their brain, their eyes, and their bones becoming energized by God's light. Remind yourself as you do this that this is the creative energy that created your healee in the first place. It is all-knowing, all-loving, all-powerful, and can perform any miracle. Know that it is not you performing the healing; you are merely an observer. Know that the moment this energy touches any part of your healee, the unhealthy or foreign energy stuck in your healee's body will immediately be released or transform into God's light. Finally, ask the deity to transmit or infuse your healee with the qualities and powers that the healee is ready to accept. Look at your healee and watch to see what happens when you do this!

Technique #2: Visualization and Touch

If your healee is present you may wish to add touch to the above technique, which will intensify the effects. Touch is a very powerful aspect of healing and one that we don't have time to address in great detail in this book. Sometimes your healee will be in dire need of touch, either because they have not been touched in a long time or because their body is very ungrounded or has incurred a trauma that makes it feel unreal. Touching your healee or readee lightly on the shoulders or arms will help ground them, providing they trust you and welcome the physical contact.

During a God or Holy Spirit healing, your healee can either sit upright in a chair, with their feet resting on the floor, or they can lie on their backs on the floor, on a bed, or on a sofa.

Place your hands on the healee's head. Reground yourself, including your aura, and check to make sure that you are centered. As discussed above, choose an image that represents God or the Holy Spirit or whatever deity or figure you'd like. Let's say we are going to visualize the Holy Spirit as a glistening golden star. Draw a column of energy from the star to your own crown chakra. Then draw columns of energy from the star to your hand chakras, forming a triangle or pyramid shape. See sparkles of light pouring down through these columns—this time through your own head, down through your throat and circulating through your heart, down through your shoulders, then down through your arms and out of your hands, into the crown chakra of your healee. See this energy wash through every cell of your healee and watch as it effortlessly flows out through their feet chakras. Watch this flow of energy for a few minutes as you continuously thank God or the Holy Spirit for their assistance.

Next, you can physically move to the healee's feet. Cradle the healee's bare feet in your hands (it's okay if the healee is wearing socks, but ask them to take off their shoes prior to the start of the healing). Make sure the center of your palms, where your hand chakras are located, have contact with the center of their feet, where their feet chakras are located. You may want to visualize that your hand chakras and their feet chakras are spinning and opening wider. Many foreign energies and entities enter through the feet, even through the big toe. Gently place a finger or hand over the big toe and demand that any spirits or negative energies occupying this body drain out from the toe. In your mind, or out loud if you'd like, yell at these energies to release from the toe. Don't be surprised if your readee experiences pain here. It should subside within a minute, and you can explain that this is part of the healing. If your healee does feel pain, talk them through it and tell them it will subside within a minute or so. Encourage them to continue, and do not stop this process until the pain is gone.

Then, once again, visualize God or the Holy Spirit and draw a column of light from this deity to your own crown chakra and hand chakras. See sparkles of light rush down through these columns, down through your crown chakra and out of your hands into the feet chakras of your healee. This time see God's light as it rushes up through the healee's feet, legs, torso, chest, arms, shoulders, neck, and out the top of the healee's head. See the light cleaning out every layer of the healee's aura. See every cell growing brighter and brighter as God's healing energy transforms illness into health, darkness into light. Let this energy run for a minute or two. Then you can thank God or the deity of your choice for sharing their energy with the two of you. From time to time, tune in to yourself and notice if you feel your body going into any effort. If you feel yourself "trying" to do anything, this means you are overextending yourself. Healing is not really about *doing* anything; it's about witnessing the energy flow. You are merely acting as a channel for God's light. You are merely an observer. Nothing more, nothing less.

When you feel you have finished (this entire process shouldn't take more than ten minutes), you can ask for the light to give you a healing on any matching issues you have with the person you were working on. Just relax and notice what happens. Finally, imagine that you are disconnecting the columns of energy from God to yourself (know that you are always connected, but you don't need this much of an energy rush all the time; it could overwhelm your chakras and body). Say out loud to your healee, "With the blessings of [God, the supreme being, the Holy Spirit], my role in the healing is completed. May the deity continue to work with you for the next twenty-four hours as needed."

With healing, particularly long-distance healing, it's really important that you are clear about when you are beginning it and when you are finishing it. Otherwise your own energy can become depleted very quickly.

Clairvoyant Psychic Surgery

At times you may be conducting a reading and healing, and you will become aware of a strong foreign energy that has invaded the healee's body or aura. You might even see a color or an image of an object that seems to be stopping the flow of energy from one part of the body to the next. One very effective technique to remove this foreign energy is what I call *clairvoyant psychic surgery*.

The method of clairvoyant psychic surgery I now teach is based on experiences gained from my own personal practice as a psychic and healer. It is also very much inspired by techniques I learned during my own course of clairvoyant training with a variety of teachers in the United States, and from the hundreds of healings I observed, received, and participated in while studying with several faith healers in the Philippines in the late 1990s. Some of these healers, known as psychic surgeons, had the extraordinary ability to make an actual incision in a patient's body with their bare hands, reach into the incision, and pull out the foreign energy, which would then manifest into physical matter such as tissue, blood clots, tumors, stones, fluids, and the like. (To learn more about some of the most popular healers of the Philippines and Brazil, I recommend reading any of Jaime Licauco's books about the Filipino healers, such as *The Magicians of God* or *Jun Labo*, or *John of God: The Brazilian Healer Who's Touched the Lives of Millions* by Heather Cumming and Karen Leffler.)

One of the most extraordinary things I have ever experienced was when one of my Filipino teachers, Brother William, made an incision in a patient's chest with his bare hands and held the incision open while he instructed me to take a pair of tweezers and extract a large tumor from inside the incision. The tumor was connected to tissue, and I had to yank on it a little before it would come out. I was terrified that I would pull out the wrong thing! As soon as I removed the tumor, Brother William took his hands away and the incision immediately closed without a trace of a scar. This specific operation was observed by no fewer than twenty people.

When doubt from the multitudes of doubters around me sets in about the dozens of healings I received myself, or the hundreds I observed by numerous healers, I always go back to this one experience, which is why I believe I had the experience.

Clairvoyant psychic surgery mimics the techniques used by these healers. In fact, I believe there is not much difference between the two, except that in clairvoyant psychic surgery, the diseased energy does not typically manifest as solid physical matter, as it does in traditional psychic surgery.

How to Perform Clairvoyant Psychic Surgery

You can actually have your healee lie down, or you can merely visualize your healee lying on a table. You can then imagine that a white sheet is covering the healee's body. Wherever healing is needed, in your mind's eye look for a dark spot to appear on the sheet. (This is also a popular diagnostic technique among the psychic surgeons of the Philippines.) Choose one area of the body that seems to be in the greatest need of help. If you feel uncertain as to what part of the body is in need of healing, or if you feel that there is a systemic problem, you can work solely with the healee's third chakra, located at their solar plexus. Simply postulate that all illness, pain, or negative energy in the body will be magnetically pulled to the third chakra, where you will soon help it to release. (This is another technique commonly used by the healers in the Philippines, and I have heard that the very popular healer John of God, in Brazil, often works with the third chakra in this way as well.)

Next, imagine that you are looking at your hands. See columns or cords of energy running from your hands to either God or the Holy Spirit (you can visualize God in any way that works for you). See sparkles of light traveling from God down through these columns/cords and bursting out of your hand chakras. See tiny, dancing, healing flames flickering out of your palms and fingertips. Feel the heat of these flames pulsating through your hands and your arms.

Now imagine that you are taking your glowing hands and making a clean incision into the affected part of your healee's body. You can do this seated at a distance from your readee, or you can actually lay your hands on the location of the body you are working on. In your imagination, reach in and grab hold of whatever foreign matter is ready to release. You may need to gently pull on it, or it may glide out effortlessly. Observe the color and shape of whatever is coming out. If it is attached to a particular organ or chakra, you may need to imagine that you are cleaning that organ with the use of your imaginary hands. See the brilliant lights beaming through the layers of the inside of your healee's body, penetrating deep beyond the areas that need attention. Know that this light is strong enough to dissolve anything that is no longer conducive to your readee's well-being. The matter may disintegrate before you pull it out. If the foreign matter does not want to release, give that part of the body a grounding cord and watch the color of the resistance as it releases, and then try again.

Once you have pulled out the foreign matter, imagine that the healee's incision automatically closes up as if it never existed. Then take the matter you extracted and throw it into a fire pit that exists somewhere outside the room. You can also send the matter up to God. See it landing in God's hands and watch to see what happens to it. This will usually give you insight not only into what your healee is dealing with but also into the very nature of God and the Universal Laws.

As a final step, make sure you fill up your healee with the color of their own healing energy. When you are finished, you and your readee can discuss both your observations and your experiences with the healing. You can then disconnect yourself from God or the Holy Spirit, say a prayer of gratitude or words of thanks, and state out loud, "May it be with the blessings of God that this healing is completed."

Working with a Psychic Surgeon Guide

When practicing clairvoyant psychic surgery, you may find that when you go to picture God, you will see another figure in God's place. This will most likely be a healing guide or psychic surgeon. It is up to you whether you would like to work with this guide or work only with God. Psychic surgeon guides are extremely powerful guides that can be very helpful but also very domineering.

If you experience twitching in your hands or eyes, if your hands or arms begin moving without your intending them to, if you feel an overwhelming urge to go and find someone to heal, and if you hear ringing in your ears, these are signs that these guides are seeking to work with you and are plugging into your body. Pressure on the back of your neck is a sign they may be plugging into your telepathic channels. Most likely, these spirits will not approach you if on some level you are not open or ready to work with them. If you choose to work with a healing guide, I recommend undergoing the steps below.

The healers in the Philippines who can actually operate on a body with their bare hands have the ability to do so because of the powerful guides they work with. These healers not only form a connection with these guides at their hand chakras, but they actually let the guides take over their entire body—which works for them but is totally unnecessary for the type of healing we are doing. Full-body channeling is complicated and risky, and should be done only under competent supervision and after extensive training. That being said, there are some people who spontaneously do this channeling with little awareness, as they go about their everyday lives. A small minority of people are absolutely compelled to do it. I wholeheartedly believe that you will know if you are meant to do healing in this way, or meant to do any activity for that matter, by your degree of interest in it and natural inclination to do it or try it.

Meeting Your Healing Guide

This method can be used to establish a relationship with any type of healing guide. First, imagine there is an empty chair facing away from you, about eight feet from you. Invite the guide to sit down in the chair. See a light above the chair and, at the count of three, turn on the light. Tell the guide that as you turn on the light, you would like the guide to turn around and show you what it looks like. Ask it to show you both a color and its physical characteristics. Once you have an idea of what the guide looks like, say hello to it, introduce yourself, let it know why you are tuning in to it, find out what the guide would like to achieve by working with you, and ask if it has any messages for you.

Some guides have certain specialties, certain talents that they can bring to a healing. For example, they might be particularly adept at removing other entities, they may have extensive knowledge about healing cancer, or they may be very good communicators. Ask your guide to clairvoyantly show you what its specialty is. Chances are, you will share some common talents and interests.

Next, you will want to establish some simple boundaries. Tell the guide it may only plug into your hand chakras, and only for the duration of the healing. After that it will need to step outside your aura and wait until you call upon it again. If you don't set these limits, the guide might stay plugged into you indefinitely, and while the guide may be good at healing, it is not going to know any better than you how to get along in your everyday life (many of these guides have never had the experience of having a physical body), and the guide may have an agenda of its own that can interfere with your goals, desires, and overall health.

Furthermore, let the guide know the best way to communicate with you. You can tell it to communicate with you through images and pictures. It is also important to give the guide notice that if at any time you wish to do so, you can fire it and it will not be allowed to approach you again without your permission.

There are as many spirit and healing guides out there as there are people, and a lot of them are desperate to work with you. The more you interact with them, the clearer your communication with and understanding of them will be. These guides usually know when you are going to perform a healing well before you do, and sometimes the way you will know that someone is about to ask you to perform a healing is that you will feel your guides plugging into your hands or buzzing around you. If you aren't comfortable with your guide, you can always fire them and recruit a new one. The nice thing is that you won't have to pay them unemployment insurance!

Connecting with Your Guide

To actually connect with your guide, first ground yourself, then ground the guide. Then hold up your hands. Direct the guide to plug into one or both of your hands. Imagine that there is a cord of energy that runs from your hand chakras to the guide's hand chakras. The color of the cord is the same color that the guide showed you previously. As the guide plugs in, notice how your hands feel. Now ask the guide to give you a two- to five-minute healing. Ask the guide to specifically clear out any blockages in your hand chakras and any other part of your body that might be inhibiting your healing energy. Sit back, relax, and notice how you feel. Feel free to watch the healing clairvoyantly. At the end of the healing, ask your guide if it has any communication for you. If you are immediately going to conduct a healing on someone else, keep the guide plugged in and begin the healing. Otherwise, thank the guide for the healing, and let it know you will call upon it again soon. Then visualize it unplugging from your hand chakras, cut its grounding cord, hook it up to God, and see it floating away.

Technique #3: Clairvoyant Psychic Surgery with a Healing Guide

You can utilize the help of psychic-surgeon healing guides when performing clairvoyant psychic surgery. You can go through the same steps described above, but instead of merely seeing your own hands, you can see the hands of your guides working alongside or though yours. For a particularly tricky healing, you can just sit back, relax, and clairvoyantly watch your guides as they fly around the healee. You can let them make the decision about where and how to perform the healing. Occasionally you will want to clairvoyantly check the connection between your hand chakras and those of the psychic-surgeon healing guides. As your guides conduct the healing, you can help by observing and communicating which colors are being released from the healee and which colors the healee is using to fill up with. Another option is for you to take responsibility for one part of the healing, while assigning the other part to your healing guide.

Clairvoyant Psychic Surgery Using Touch, with or without a Guide

If you would like to use touch for your healing and your healee is receptive to this, you can physically take your hands, gently lay them on the area of your healee that you wish to address, and perform the visualizations discussed on the previous page. When you get to the point of visualizing yourself (possibly with the help of healing guides) removing the unhealthy matter, you can pretend that your hands are actually pulling out the matter. Let your hands move in any way they desire, just avoid actually touching any areas of the readee's body that could make them uncomfortable (you can always wave your hands above these body parts to work in their aura).

Whether you are plugged into God or into a Filipino psychic surgeon guide, you can sit back, relax, and observe what happens as the guides or God/Holy Spirit perform the healing. It's likely you will be

picking up some impressions through your clairvoyance or clairaudience or through instant knowing. This is great, and feel free to communicate this information. However, don't get too much into doing an
intensive reading here because your attention really needs to be on the
healing. When someone tells me they want a reading and a hands-on
healing, I tell them I really need to do these separately. They will then
be pleasantly surprised when I give them some psychic insights, but
these will be minimal.

Remember that at the end of the healing it will be very important
to clean out your hand chakras and any other part of your body that
may have absorbed energy from your readee or your guides. You can
either ground your hand chakras or see tiny roses circulating inside the
chakras until the roses become so full with the foreign energy that they
explode. If you are near a sink, it is always advisable after a reading to
physically wash your hands well, and to take a shower before going to
bed that evening.

CHAPTER 17

Female Healing

American women expect to find in their husbands a perfection that English women only hope to find in their butlers.
—WILLIAM SOMERSET MAUGHAM

Soon after I moved to the Philippines I met the man who became my favorite healer, David Oligoni (aka "the Exorcist of Pangasinan"), in his little chapel adorned with a mural of a blue pyramid with an eye above it, and an assortment of village dogs sleeping in the pews. I observed and personally experienced David's exorcisms, which involved pulling evil spirits from a person's toe. David would lightly touch the healee's big toe and yell at the spirits to leave while his wife stood close by, usually laughing at the spirit or the healee. (I was never quite sure which!) Within a few seconds of this, the healee would usually experience a searing pain that might last for a minute. For me, this pain was almost unbearable.

Sometimes people would have other reactions: I watched nearby as a friend of mine almost levitated off the table. Another talent of David's was to clear people's nasal passages. He did this by taking what appeared to be a pair of tongs and jamming it up a healee's nose. A moment later David would proudly extract something that resembled a large wad of chewing gum. Some of these people later reported that David improved their breathing and alleviated their sinus problems. Another common practice was to ignite oil in a glass jar and place this jar on the healee's bare skin, creating a tight suction. This was supposed to draw out the toxins in that part of the body. Those who received this treatment reported that it didn't hurt; however, the jars did leave a blazing red ring for more than a couple of days following the procedure.

So when I visited David for my own healing in November 1997, I was more than a bit apprehensive. I was experiencing an irregular menstrual cycle and thought he might be able to help. I did not tell him why I was there and he didn't ask. However, he immediately placed his hands over my pelvic area for about ten seconds (something he had never done before), and then asked me a question that seemed quite odd at the time but that has been perhaps one of the most important questions ever asked of me. The question was "Do you enjoy being a woman?" He repeated it two more times before I responded enthusiastically, just to get him to lower his voice, "Yes, I do enjoy being a woman." "Good!" he and his wife laughed and shuffled me out the door. That was the last time I ever saw him. Less then four months later I was pregnant with my son Manny, who is now nine years old.

I wondered for quite a while about what exactly David was getting at. Almost a decade later I think I might have an inkling. I now realize that I can either enjoy what I have—what my body can do, how it can look and feel, what it can create—or I can despise these things. It's a choice. When I remember to appreciate the fact that I am having the rare opportunity to experience life in a human female body, I feel excited and overjoyed. When I feel oppressed, exhausted, vulnerable, crampy, or burdened, and I curse such feelings, I begin to feel worse and worse. The more I celebrate being a female, the more fun I have and the better I feel. Recently, a reader of *You Are Psychic* e-mailed me and directed me to her MySpace page. It turns out she is a he. She wrote at the top of her e-mail, "Being a woman is 100% priceless!" and on her webpage there were several pictures of smiling transvestites with figures most women would envy. This was one more reminder that if men can enjoy being women, then why can't a woman?

One of the reasons many women don't enjoy their own bodies is because their bodies are filled with everyone else's energy (quite often men's energy or that of the woman's disapproving or angry mother). As women, our bodies are extremely absorbent and receptive. They are designed to receive a male's sperm and even the soul of an unborn baby. Unfortunately, our bodies do not discriminate between whose energy they take in. Even if we are far past our childbearing years, our female organs act as magnets with just about every man we encounter and from other women who are comparing themselves to us on a body level. Furthermore, many women, somewhere along the line, were taught their bodies were not truly their own, that they had to put everyone else before themselves. This unconscious belief makes many women feel resentful of their lot in life.

While the women's movement has given us many freedoms, it has given us twice as much responsibility as we had before, since now we are expected to do all we did before, plus be the breadwinners of our families. Of course, given the fact that there are trillions of dollars being made by corporations who profit solely from ensuring that women find fault with themselves, it's no wonder we are all more than a bit dissatisfied with our bodies. In fact, in most of America it's really as though there is a covert and relentless assault on our psyches and self-image from hundreds of sources each day.

In fact, we literally cannot leave our homes or turn on our television sets, computers, or radios without being assaulted from every direction with the message that we are defective, not good enough, not enough. This is in such stark contrast to the reality of the situation: that we as women possess a force within ourselves that enables us to be creators of life itself. To downplay our power or allow ourselves to be degraded by the people around us (here I am talking about a comparatively small group of people hiding behind the fortress of the "corporation") is akin to God herself allowing Satan to suck out her soul. Whether or not we are actually able or interested in bearing children, we posses a creative energy within our bodies. When this creative energy is focused—whether to create a new life or art or for the purpose of healing—it is a force of unimaginable strength and beauty. However, when this creative energy is suppressed inside ourselves or is misdirected, it can be devastating—mostly for ourselves but also for our children and others around us.

When a woman has sex with a man, or is an object of another person's sexual desire, energetic cords form between the two individuals that often make it difficult for her to focus on herself or to emotionally separate from a relationship. When a woman becomes obsessed with a man, it is often because these energies have become entwined or enmeshed. The more entrenched she becomes in his energy field, even when his motivations are purely to protect or provide for her, the more she loses herself. The more she loses herself and becomes like him, the harder it is for him to find her, the needier she becomes, and he begins to appreciate her less and less.

Not only do we as women have to contend with the plethora of foreign energies we carry around (sometimes literally as extra pounds), but many women are also dealing with their own unexpressed emotional energy that is trapped within their bodies, as a result of societal or family programming that says it's not polite or caring to express these emotions. When a woman fails to express anger or disappointment, they become toxins that often contaminate her own female organs, such as her ovaries, uterus, breasts, and so on. Many women don't realize that emotions like anger or disappointment are actually there to protect them. When expressed in a healthy manner, these emotions serve both as shields and as warning signals that not all is good in paradise. Without these she is vulnerable to sacrificing too much of herself and she can never be in her own power; she will play the eternal victim because these feelings will always manifest within someone close to her who will project them back onto her.

As mentioned above, women have the profound ability to create life. This creative process is fueled by a vital energy that is always active within a woman's body, regardless of whether she is physically able to create a child. This creative energy can be directed into any number of creative projects, work, and even relationships (that's why many times men become our creative project, something to transform). When a woman is running this energy in full force within her own body, she will feel particularly at peace and will even appear more attractive to herself and to others (hence the pregnant woman's "glow"). When this energy becomes stifled, misdirected, or ungrounded, it can cause women to become bored, depressed, hysterical, neurotic, hyperactive, and sexually dysfunctional.

Female healing is a clairvoyant technique that helps women release foreign energy and unexpressed emotional energy of their own, and to overcome the illnesses, diseases, and pain that result from these misguided energies. Female healing also helps women stimulate and redirect their female creative energies.

Female Healing Technique: Female Grounding

The first thing to do when embarking on a female healing is to give the woman healee both a regular grounding cord, as discussed in chapter 3, and a female grounding cord. A female grounding cord will ground her female organs as well as her creative energy. This is an excellent exercise to do if she is feeling overwhelmed with too many tasks, or is having a hard time approaching or conversing with a particular man. To create this cord, draw a line of energy from each of the woman's ovaries and connect it into her main grounding cord at the base of her spine, to form a triangle or pyramid shape. Then imagine that you are writing the name of your healee on her ovaries and ask the ovaries to show you the color of the healee's own female energy in the ovaries. Then ask them to show you the color of any foreign energies that are ready to release. Next, watch as these foreign energies slip down the grounding cord. You can give them a push by circulating some earth energy, or a mixture of cosmic and earth energy, in order to rinse her ovaries as well. Invite the energies of guilt, shame, and fear to light up as black spots, and watch these release.

Once you are satisfied that her ovaries contain only her energy, you can continue to ground out and rinse the healee's other female areas. You can also use a viewing receptacle such as a rose as a type of clairvoyant washcloth. See the rose circulating around in her uterus. Imagine that the rose has a sticky surface and is collecting up all the foreign and emotional energy that needs to be released. Once it is full, take a look at the colors inside and then imagine you are sending the rose out the window and over to a large open space where you can see it exploding into a million pieces. Continue the process with the woman's breasts as well. During a female healing, you can utilize other healing techniques discussed in this chapter and the next.

One of the important steps in a female healing is to help a woman ground her female creative energy. You can imagine that this energy is located around her baby-making organs. You can imagine that she looks nine months pregnant but instead of her tummy being large, it is really just a ball of female creative energy that is swelling out in front of her. See this ball of energy as swirling, pulsating, dynamic. Ask the energy to show you its true color(s). Then imagine that you are giving this vibrant ball of energy its own grounding cord. Ground it into a soft, peaceful, dark place deep within the earth. Write the woman's name on this bubble of energy and command any foreign energies that are no longer serving the woman to release from the grounding cord. If the woman has been dealing with a particular man or relationship, you can state this man's name and specifically order his energy to release as well. Next, look for energy such as competition, envy, doubt, guilt, or anything else that is keeping the healee from being in her true power—anything that is keeping her from expressing her full creative energy—and help her release these down the grounding cord as well.

Then, for the most important part of this process, visualize the woman's creative energy rising up and circulating abundantly through her entire body and aura. You can use your clairvoyance to see a color for this, or you can ask the healee which color makes her feel creative, happy, and passionate. See the flow of this energy begin to circulate and vibrate faster and faster, and as it does this, see it getting brighter or more sparkly.

Help Her Separate from Baby Beings

It is always important to help a woman to separate from any baby beings that are connected into her female energy, unless she is trying to become pregnant and feels that she wants to keep the beings near her. (See chapter 13 for a more in-depth discussion on baby beings and additional techniques for working with them.)

A simple way to locate and move these pesky spirits out is to simply imagine that you are throwing some neutral purple or cobalt-blue energy into the healee's bubble of creative energy and watch to see if any white cords appear. Then create an imaginary pair of scissors and cut the cords. Imagine that any baby beings or other spirits that were attached to these cords are now flying off into outer space. If you are concerned about their well-being, you can show them an image of God (located at a far distance from your healee) and reattach to your image of God the ends of the cord that were formerly attached to the healee, so that the beings will have a safe and comforting place to go to and will be less inclined to turn their attention to you! Chances are that your healee is going to feel physical sensations in her body as you move out these spirits.

Working with the Umbilical Cord

Finally, during a female healing I like to work with the healee's own energetic umbilical cord. While every baby's umbilical cord is physically severed at birth, many people, particularly women, remain energetically attached to their mothers throughout their entire lives. On one level this gives them a sense of comfort and security, but on another level it keeps them from ever fully coming into their own full power.

During a female reading or healing, you can clairvoyantly look in the area of the woman's belly button to see if there is an umbilical cord, and follow it to see if it is attached to anyone or anything. You might find her mother or you might find someone else. If you find a connection or sense one, then put up a viewing receptacle on your reading screen and ask the question, "How is this connection serving or not serving my client in the present moment?" If the images show you that your client is not benefiting from this connection, you can do two things. First, write the current day and time across the healee's stomach with an imaginary pen, then imagine a timeline with the current date and time in the middle of the timeline. Next, imagine that this umbilical cord is placed in the middle of the timeline. Watch to see what happens to the umbilical cord. If it does not detach, then take out your imaginary scissors and cut it close to the healee's body. Watch what happens when you cut it.

Next, tie off the end of the cord, making a strong knot. Now take the end of the cord that is still attached to the healee's mother and tie it off. Then give the mother a general grounding cord as well as a female grounding cord. Complete the healing by describing the work you just did and explaining that both your healee and her mother may feel the effects of the healing over the next several days (whether or not her mother is even aware of the healing). This technique is helpful for women whose mothers are still around as well as for those whose mothers have physically passed on.

PART IV

Understanding and Improving Your Own Life as a Psychic

CHAPTER 18

Healing the Healer Within

The important thing is this: to be able, at any moment, to sacrifice what we are for what we could become.
—MAHARISHI MAHESH YOGI

Most of Us Are Healers

Chris was a client of mine whom I worked with every few months over the course of two years. He came to me because he wanted to make sure he was on his "spiritual path." He was a gay man in his sixties. During one reading I was surprised when I saw an image of him turn into a big piece of . . . *Kleenex.* Then I saw an even funnier vision of his partner picking him up and blowing his nose in him. "Hey," Chris said excitedly, "do you know what I just picked up right before you said that?" Since this was a phone reading, I obviously did not. He continued, "I was just looking at a big Kleenex box, reading the words on it, and wondering about why they named it Kleenex."

I told him I couldn't answer that question, but that I did know why in my vision he turned into a piece of Kleenex. "Your partner has been emotionally dumping on you," I told him. "He uses you to release his toxic feelings." Chris wholeheartedly agreed that this was a strong dynamic in their relationship, which at that point had lasted more than a

241

decade, but he stated he didn't know why he allowed this dynamic to continue or how he could even change it. I told him that it wouldn't be impossible but it would be hard, because he is such a healer. "Healer?" he asked me, surprised. "You think I'm a healer? But how can I be a healer? I don't even know how to do healings!" I suggested to Chris that his problem is that he doesn't know how *not* to heal.

Except for psychopaths, most people are healers. Whether or not people choose to consciously perform healings—by working with energy, touch, herbs, or allopathic medicine—is irrelevant. When we have the desire to help someone or make someone feel better, and we talk to them or extend them a helping hand, we are in a sense healing them. Some of us are absolutely driven to help others. We feel pain the moment we see someone else in pain, or the moment we assume they must be in pain, because if we were in their situation, we know we would be in pain.

The biggest challenge for any healer is having to live with the fact that others around us are in pain. The next biggest challenge is to live with the fact that many of those in pain are unwilling or unable to take the steps they need to take to get out of their situation. That situation usually includes subjecting themselves to toxic people, toxic substances, or toxic thoughts, and engaging in other self-defeating behaviors. Have you ever had a friend or family member who had the following ongoing problems?

- They refuse to leave an abusive situation.
- They refuse to let a relationship go that they are no longer in.
- They are drinking themselves to death.
- They are abusing drugs to the point that their body is falling apart.
- They weigh so much that they can hardly get out of bed.
- They weigh so little that they look like a skeleton.
- Their spouse left or died, and now they don't know how to support themselves and refuse to do anything except rely on relatives.

- They keep making bad financial decisions and are always in a state of crisis.

Doesn't just reading this list give you a knot in your stomach? Doesn't it make you sad, irritated, and frustrated to the point that you can actually feel your blood pressure go up? Why is this? It is not because the person you care about has a problem; it's because that person does not seem to have the capacity to make the changes you want them to make within the time frame you want. It might take them half a century to get to where you'd like them to be now. It's important that you give them the room they need to take the steps, or not take the steps, they need to take. This doesn't mean you abandon them, but you do need to understand that some people—lots of people, adults—want to be taken care of by others. They are afraid, and you could give them every ounce of your energy and they still would not have the courage or determination that you do. They want the easy road, the shortcuts, and therefore they will not even consider choosing the road that has led to your own awakening and healing.

Those feelings that you feel from reading the list above are toxic. They come from overextending yourself, literally. This is because you've crossed the line. You've jumped from your path to theirs, and you are fighting a fight that you cannot win because it has nothing to do with you. Essentially you are taking on their karma. You are trying to overshadow their self and will with your own, hoping to transfer your power into them. No wonder you are exhausted, frustrated, depressed, or worse!

I know it's bad writing to use clichés, but the expression "You can lead a horse to water, but you can't make him drink" is completely apropos here. Imagine if you did try to make the horse drink. He'd be spitting the water out at you and messing up your clothes; he might kick you, bite you, or trample you. He might go berserk and disturb the other horses in the barn. I suppose you could anesthetize him and give him an IV. That might save his life. But what happens when he wakes up? Will he now be ready to drink?

What happens when the horse is your husband or parent?

How do we deal with people who are not ready to change in the way we want them to change? Do we just abandon them? Do we give up? Do we avoid them? Do we remain in this agonizing situation?

I am starting to realize that the people I heal most often and lose my energy to are those who aren't willing to do the same work I am to change my life. They are scared, and they are convinced they need a greater level of security, even though some of them have a lot more security than I do with regard to long-term jobs and savings. Some of these people are actually looking at me to do the things they don't want to do themselves or don't feel they can do. It is as if on one level they are screaming out "Save me!"—but then they shoot down every way you come up with for them to be saved. This can make you absolutely crazy. It happens with some clients and, as you know, it can happen with those closest to you.

Time Does Make a Difference

As a forty-year-old psychic, now with twelve years of reading under my belt, I am finally beginning to see shifts in some of the people I've been trying to heal for years, including my own friends and family. In some cases, I am seeing glimpses of change now that I had yearned to see decades ago. Patience is the answer to just about everything.

Reasons People May Not Be Healing

1. The person is not ready to heal.

2. The person is actually benefiting from the illness or problem— e.g., getting disability, attention, or time off from work.

3. What you are defining as a problem is not one for that person.

4. You have lost your neutrality. You might be leaving some of your pain with them or making them feel worse.

5. It's the person's life lesson, destiny, or karma.

6. The person doesn't really believe they can be healed or that you can help.

7. The patterned, programming energy is really ingrained, and if you just ripped it out the person couldn't function normally; their reality would be shattered and they would feel as if they were going nuts, so they must do this at a much slower pace than you would have.

8. There are changes happening but you can't see them.

9. You are not giving the person enough time to go through the process of changing or healing.

10. You are only seeing half of the story.

11. The person's physical body has gotten to a point at which there is not enough healthy energy to regenerate.

12. The spirit is ready to depart from the body; it is preplanned. You are trying to play God.

Hold the Vision, Even When Others Can't See It

I am only beginning to understand the power of holding a vision for someone who can't yet see it themselves. Many people suffer because they are locked into a fixed idea of who they are and what they want and need. They are afraid of the unknown or can't imagine a different reality.

Sometimes, as soon as I communicate a different version of how a readee's life could or will be, they are relieved, even excited. However, sometimes they are upset, confused, frightened, and occasionally angry. They want what they want now and nothing other than that, while as a clairvoyant I can see that there is really something much better out there for them. This is true whether the person is an isolated seventy-five-year-old woman who has done nothing but watch TV for the past twenty-five years and now is facing (and resisting) moving into a retirement home where she will have new opportunities for friendships and fun activities, or a man who is being told that he won't have the woman he's obsessed with but that there will be someone else out there who is perfect for him, perhaps when he's "ripened" a bit.

When my client or someone I meet can't yet comprehend this alternate reality or future, I will focus my attention on their spirit, and postulate that I am mentally showing them this picture. I will keep sending hello to their spirit. I will sometimes advise such a client, "I understand what I am saying doesn't make sense to you right now. That's fine. File it away in the back of your mind, and when you are ready it will be there for you."

Most important, I remind myself that it's perfectly okay that this person's ego or mind is not yet ready to grasp a greater version of reality or an expanded notion of possibilities. It doesn't mean I am a bad healer or psychic. On the contrary, it means that I can see what is, rather than what others want me to see.

CHAPTER 19

Overcoming Limits to Manifesting

No one in the world was ever you before, with your particular gifts and abilities and possibilities. It's a shame to waste those by doing what someone else has done.

—JOSEPH CAMPBELL

Surpassing Limits

In every area of our life, including relationships, money, freedom, and success, we develop and operate from conscious and unconscious parameters around what we believe is possible or not possible for ourselves. These parameters can also be considered "limits." These limits may be quite low in one area and quite high in another. Our parameters or limits are based on many factors, including our belief system, our past experiences and memories, the emotions and programming that we've internalized from parents and society, and the energy of others in our body and aura. The "limit" is whatever line is drawn at the top of this threshold that says, "Stop. It's not possible or safe to go beyond this point."

Often, our limits are set at the same levels as those of our parents and the culture we grew up in. If we are ready on a soul level to exceed these limits, then we may encounter our parents' resistance on an energy level (if they are deceased or unaware of what we are doing) or on the physical plane, as when they try to tell us that what we are doing is not possible or is dangerous, selfish, or won't work. If we demonstrate that it *is* possible for us, then it suggests perhaps it could be possible (or could have been) for them. This knowledge could inspire them, or it could make them angry and fearful if it means letting go of excuses that they have talked themselves into believing.

One of the main ways we can help a person in a clairvoyant reading is to help them recognize, identify, understand, and move past their limits. This is the primary reason I get readings myself. However, this is also what makes clairvoyant readings quite challenging at times. You as a clairvoyant must access information about and for a person who believes this limit is absolute reality and who may be very emotionally invested in holding on to this reality. This person's entire existence may have been a self-fulfilling prophecy that demonstrates over and over again that this limit is real, and now you are about to require them to look at a whole new range of possibilities outside that limit.

When the readee is close to tearing down these walls and overcoming blocks and limitations, the clairvoyant will often be able to see the information about the situation quite easily and clearly. However, this can be confusing and difficult even for a person completely committed to their personal growth, one who has been praying for insight and change. So as a clairvoyant, you may begin to encounter their resistance, confusion, or any number of fears and energies even before you sit down with them and set the reading color. You may find yourself dreading the reading and having no idea why. You might feel nervous or overwhelmed. Or you might lose your confidence. You may find when you put up a viewing receptacle on your screen that you are unable to see anything, or that you just see black.

During a clairvoyant reading with someone who is hitting a limit or has something blocking them from achieving a goal, I will often see an image of a wall, which represents the limit. However, sometimes the readee has been doing a lot of work to break down the wall, and the moment I see and describe it, the readee's spirit is able to push down this weakened structure (in my visualization and also in reality) and is flooded with insights and a fresh perspective on a situation that may have seemed quite hopeless. This can be followed by sudden changes, new opportunities, and a huge influx of energy and movement. It is as if the wall were a dam, and the person's life force that was collecting up on the other side of it all that time is now released with tremendous gusto. Since our ability to create and manifest is dependent on how much life force we have in our bodies at any given time, people are often able to manifest really big goals, even miracles, at this juncture. I also suspect this is why occasionally the things we manifested after getting unstuck in a big way don't always last (e.g., sudden fame or fortune or an opportunity that seems unbelievable). Sometimes, the energy loses its momentum before the person has had a chance to assimilate all the changes, or the person doesn't have the self-esteem or wherewithal yet to handle the thing they were able to manifest with the excess of energy, and so they lose that physical manifestation. The good news is that even when this happens, the person doesn't lose what they have gained on the inside, which is a new awareness and an expansion of their limits or parameters, and they are able to re-create that miracle again further down the road when it is more likely to last.

Sometimes our readees come to us because they are just in the initial stages of this process of releasing limits and expanding their parameters. They are not ready to open the floodgates of consciousness completely, even if they say they are. This may be because they have conflicting desires. If they really had an awareness of their entire situation, they would have to make the changes they are afraid of or are unwilling to make. In this case, the clairvoyant has been called into their life to unlock the door and allow in just a glimmer or light. The readee will then go back to their life, and likely encounter similar patterns, but they may begin to respond to these differently than they did before.

Please be aware that we might be talking about just one aspect of the readee's life—say, their relationships, finances, or the way they operate from a need to control or in response to fear. In other areas they may be very conscious, happy people.

We all have our own walls and limits. The nice thing is that we can help each other become aware of them. Anytime there is someone in your life who seems to have a lot of limits or a really big one they can't seem to crawl over, it can be an indication that you also have some, or at least one, really big wall yourself that you are working through as well.

Matching Pictures

There is another reason why reading someone's limits or walls can be quite challenging for a clairvoyant. The psychic is being asked to look at information that they themselves have been unconscious to. They may have the same limit themselves, and now it's as if their subconscious mind is presented with a major dilemma: if the clairvoyant is absolutely not ready to see it or handle it, they may just not be able to get any images, or they will see an image but its meaning will completely elude them.

This is probably the main reason why people sometimes just can't get the answer they are seeking. The clairvoyant wants to see what is behind the wall, but if they do so they will see the very thing they have protected themselves from. If the clairvoyant is actually ready to see this, has in fact been chipping away the bricks or stones for quite a while, and has attracted or been attracted to do a reading on this person for this very reason, then the subconscious mind or another part of the clairvoyant will permit or bring forth the illuminating images, visions, and/or messages that will move them forward. Even then, the clairvoyant may have difficulty communicating what they are seeing because they are too "lit up"—there is too much emotional charge on what they are looking at because they are encountering their own limits or pictures, underneath which there may be a lot of fear or control.

If fear has been a factor, the clairvoyant will feel it now but within the context of the reading, so they will become fearful that whatever they are looking at will not be well-received, will be misconstrued, or that they may just be wrong.

Most of the time, if you as the clairvoyant work past this fear and deliver the information, the readee will accept it and benefit from it. However, occasionally the readee will respond unfavorably by insisting that you are wrong, that it's not possible for them to do what they say, or the readee will give you lots of excuses as to why they don't have the options you are seeing for them (for example, leaving an abusive relationship, applying for a management position instead of a clerical one, searching for work they might enjoy, and so on).

If this is the case, then what I usually do is look at the part of them that is resisting what I am saying as the stuck part. I will then imagine I am sending greeting notes to their spirit, or the part of them that is really receptive and wanting to move past the stuck part. I will direct my communication to that part and point out the fear. I may look to see where in their body the fear is, because usually it's the fear that is doing the talking. Sometimes I might tell the readee that there is "a lie in your space that says this is your only choice." I won't say, *you are lying* since they aren't; they completely believe themselves and their own excuses. That is the nature of being stuck. I will just clairvoyantly look to see why they are so fearful or wanting to avoid the other options, or I'll look for where the lie is located.

It is always helpful to ask your clairvoyance to show you the actual location where any emotion, energy, or issue is, because then your attention and that of the readee can go to that exact spot. Our attention is like a powerful laser that will immediately zap the spot and burn away whatever is ready to go. This is why a clairvoyant reading is also considered a healing.

Solution: Havingness Gauge

"Havingness" is a concept that indicates the degree to which we can love ourselves and permit ourselves to have our goals, dreams, and desires.

Step 1: Close your eyes and ground yourself. Visualize a crystal-clear rose out in front of you. Choose one goal or desire for yourself. This can be an object, such as a specific amount of money, or a particular quality, such as peace or more fun. Somewhere above the rose, imagine you are either writing the name of this single goal/quality or visualize a symbol for it. Next, imagine you are dropping the name of the goal or the symbol into the rose. Then be silent for a minute or two, place your attention on the rose, and wait to see what happens to it. Does it take on a color? Does the bud get bigger? Smaller? Change positions? Does it open or close? Grow brighter or shrivel?

Step 2: If you don't like how your rose looks, destroy this one and create a new one. Ground the rose by seeing its stem go deep into the earth. Next to it visualize a gauge that goes from 1 to 100. This gauge will represent how much permission you are giving yourself to fully have this thing or quality for yourself. Visualize the gauge and notice where the arrow lands. If the arrow of the gauge lands on a number lower then you'd expected, then go ahead and raise the arrow to the number you'd like it to be at. This could be 100, but it doesn't have to be. Do this very slowly, and postulate that you are going to release anything from the rose that might be in the way of allowing yourself to receive and keep this creation for yourself. Watch the rose and stem, and notice if any colors or even images release out of either one. Then take the gauge with the new number and drop this revised gauge into your rose. Notice what happens to the rose.

You may need to repeat the exercise a few times before you are happy with the results. Anything that comes up that is not to your liking can always be dropped right down the stem into the earth. It doesn't have to be a problem, and if you are feeling that there is a problem with this rose or are struggling with any feelings of effort, hopelessness, or frustration, then just see a color for this struggle or for the feelings, and release these down the stem of the rose and/or your own grounding cord.

Step 3: Finally, see an image of yourself receiving the rose into your heart. See yourself jumping around with absolute joy and enthusiasm because you have already received what you wanted. Imagine what you are doing now that you have attained your goal, and imagine yourself telling someone who is supportive of you how happy you are that you were able to manifest, receive, and have this for yourself. Thank yourself for allowing yourself to have this wonderful gift.

Note: This exercise can be intense, can bring up strong emotions, or make you sleepy. Take a nap as needed.

CHAPTER 20

Overcoming Psychic Stage Fright

It is not work that kills men; it is worry. Work is healthy; you can hardly put more upon a man than he can bear. Worry is rust upon the blade. It is not the revolution that destroys the machinery, but the friction. Fear secretes acids, but love and trust are sweet juices.
—HENRY WARD BEECHER

Fear is one of the first things you will encounter when exploring your psychic abilities. Whether you are just taking you first baby steps on your path of psychic development, or whether you have covered millions of miles along that road as a professional psychic, you are susceptible to the many factors that may put you into resistance to doing further readings and that diminish your joy and enthusiasm for readings. Fear is an emotion that may keep you from ever attempting to consciously use or develop your abilities, and particularly from practicing readings on or for other people.

Most psychics, if not all (including the most famous), battle with this fear their whole lives, sometimes falling prey to it but then wrestling out of its tangled clutches and finding their way back to their certainty and passion, soaring, and then being sucked back into it through an endless cycle that becomes quite familiar. Others fall into the muck and never find their way out. Still others learn to identify the enemy of fear so that each time it rears its ugly head it's easier to sidestep. This is my hope for you. Every time a psychic takes a new step—whether expanding their clientele, raising their rates, or moving into the public spotlight—they must grapple with the fear all over again.

The most renowned psychics don't speak about this fear because they are in it. They fear that by talking about it, they will seem less capable, less in control, less confident. I certainly fall into this trap myself. I took out the chapter on this subject from my first book, but now I understand that it has really got to be included in any discussion about the mastery of psychic skills.

This fear results in what I call *resistance*. Resistance is a feeling and attitude, sometimes with accompanying negative thoughts, that you just don't want, or even can't do, something—in this case, clairvoyant readings. I emphasize readings instead of healings because for most people it's a lot more threatening to verbally communicate something to another person, since there is greater potential for the person to say, "You are wrong." Keep in mind that sometimes you will be completely aware of the fear and its impact on you, and at other times it will morph into excuses and justifications that seem logical at the time but really are doing you a disservice (fear of anything does this, by the way).

Sometimes you will interpret your fear as a "gut feeling" and wonder if it is not a premonition telling you to stay away from this odd fascination you have with your psychic abilities. The problem with gut feelings is that they can be right on, but at other times they are nothing but nervous butterflies or indigestion. (That's one reason to turn to your clairvoyant images, which can be a lot more informative than a simple feeling.) Sometimes you may feel nervous before a reading because the reading will in fact be a challenging one, either because the person you are reading is challenging, or their issues are, or because your own issues, pictures, or blocks are going to come to light.

Some of the most challenging readings turn out to be the ones that serve to remove the first or final brick in the wall keeping you from the life you really want to have. Would you avoid this opportunity just because it's going to be challenging? When it comes to clairvoyant readings, it's really not very common to find yourself in a situation in which you really wish you had not done the reading. (If this does happen to you, it has more to do with your choice of clients and your decisions about how you wish to work with them—for example, the frequency, the compensation, or the boundaries you've set.)

Resistance will fluctuate from person to person, from one end of the continuum to the other, and it may be so strong within someone that they are not even able to contemplate the possibility of psychic talents in themselves or others (this category includes professional skeptics). For others, resistance might hit them as they contemplate doing readings, or once they start charging money for their readings. Still others might hit their resistance after a particularly trying reading or after receiving some kind of negative feedback or response. The important thing to remember when you hit your resistance is to not let it stop you from doing another reading because, ultimately, continuing forward is the only thing that will help you to work through the resistance.

Below are some of the thoughtforms through which the fear expresses itself for both those who have not even begun to explore their own abilities and for seasoned professionals who have been doing psychic reading or healings for years. It is important to understand that these come up for even the most talented, successful psychics, so it's not a matter of just gaining a certain level of skill or confidence. As you read this list, it would be helpful to put a check mark next to any of these that may have ever crossed your mind or that might ring true for you.

I am afraid I might not really have psychic abilities.

I am afraid I might not see anything.

I am afraid I might be wrong in what I see.

I am afraid I might see something that will scare me.

I am afraid I might see a spirit, even a bad one.

I am afraid I might tell someone something that will upset them.

I am afraid I might influence this person in the wrong way.

I am afraid of what the readee might do with the information.

I am afraid I might be messing with something I shouldn't.

I am afraid I am dealing with an area I don't know enough about.

I am afraid this readee will think I am a bad psychic or a bad person.

I am afraid if I am charging money that this person will feel cheated.

I am afraid they may not believe I am really psychic.

I am afraid I may not be able to convince them I am psychic.

I am afraid the person might get angry if I tell them what I see.

I am afraid my parents or friends will think this is all ridiculous.

I am afraid that people from my church will not understand.

I am afraid I might get psychically attacked.

I am afraid I might take on too much of this person's energy.

I am afraid I will be too vulnerable right now.

I am afraid if I get into this stuff too much I will lose my relationships with people in my life who don't believe in it or approve of it.

I am afraid because my church says it's the work of the devil.

I am afraid I can't explain what this is all about.

I am afraid I am doing something I should not be, but I don't quite know why.

When we are not conscious of the above thoughtforms and fears (and even when we are), the fear can easily impact out behaviors. Some of these behaviors may be accompanied by feelings of nervousness, or even dread, particularly before you've begun your reading. These feelings are really not any different from good old-fashioned stage fright or performance anxiety. Some of the most common are as follows:

Resistant Behaviors before a Reading

- Canceling the readings
- Failing to do anything to solicit readings, or to let people know you are available

- Rescheduling readings because you are too tired, too emotional, or too sick
- Avoiding calling back interested clients

Resistant Behaviors during a Reading

- Excessive apologizing for the things you are not seeing, as opposed to just stating what you are seeing and experiencing
- Failing to do further exploration when you see something you don't understand
- Withholding information you are seeing out of fear of disapproval or a negative response on the part of the readee
- Consciously making things up or guessing during your reading to get through it, as opposed to making yourself be patient and concentrate more
- Making emotional statements such as "How am I supposed to know?" or "I don't know"
- Failing to creatively ask your viewing receptacle the right questions to elicit a response
- Asking your readee too many questions
- Constantly asking your readee to validate or confirm too much of what you are seeing
- Refusing to look at something with the excuse that it can't be done without trying it out first
- Giving advice based on your beliefs as opposed to waiting for information to come to you
- Falling into a teaching mode as opposed to a reading mode
- Falling out of a clairvoyant mode and into a counseling mode

Resistant Behavior after a Reading

Note that these behaviors can cycle back into the above thoughtforms and behaviors.

- Obsessing about how you should have done something differently
- Wondering if you did the right thing
- Beating yourself up for not having stated something
- Feeling like you are not a very good psychic
- Feeling like you might not want to do readings again
- Feeling fear about doing another reading
- Offering to give back the client's money even though you've just spent an hour and a half with them working your hardest
- Focusing on the one or two things you didn't see, when in fact you know you saw enough to take up more than an hour of your time

Just this last week, I found myself offering to refund a client's money, even though I had already spent close to an hour with him. I realized I was working so hard to access the information that I was sweating more than I do when I physically work out! He wanted to know if a particular woman loved him, but every image that came to me clearly indicated that this woman was absolutely enraged with him. It seemed as though things could easily lead down the path of physical violence if they hadn't already. However, every time I described what I was getting, the man replied that he did not understand me, that what I was seeing could not be correct, and please could I help him. I could feel myself going too deeply into his energy field and felt my own being compromised, and so I finally just offered to end the reading and refund his money.

At this point he decided to explain what was really going on, which was that he was married and having an affair with this young woman who had indeed told him that she intended to marry someone else and that he must never contact her ever again. (Mind you, not once did he say to me, "You were right.") I asked him why he was still pursuing her, and he said he felt she didn't know what was best for her. Since she was from a "little village in a Third World country," he said she should be satisfied with occasional visits from a lover who would give her money as opposed to wanting to be married to someone willing to commit to her. All he needed to know was whether or not she loved him. I told him I'd take one last look at her. I saw an image of her spitting in his face. In the next one it looked as if she were slitting his throat. In the next image it was as if she were stomping on his heart. I described these images exactly as I saw them. His response: "All right, fine, but you still haven't answered my question. Does she love me?" Arggggh!!

Following this reading I found myself thinking about this client a lot and I came down with a headache that didn't go away until the next day, when I decided to clear him out of my head. I did this by visualizing a sticky rose entering my head and swirling around to absorb his energy, questions, demands, and whatever might be causing the pain in my head. I then visualized the rose getting bigger and bigger and took it out of my head. As I did this I felt a pinpoint of pain increase sharply for about thirty seconds, and then all pain completely vanished. This entire process took less than five minutes.

Categories of Resistance to Readings

- Those dealing with your doubts about your own clairvoyant abilities
- Feeling overly responsible for others
- Being overly concerned about others' opinions of you
- Not liking or wanting to read certain people
- Resisting your own matching pictures and issues
- Feeling the fear of others around you

Doubts about Your Own Abilities

The only way to work through your fear is to grin and bear it, and get enough readings under your belt with enough people in as many situations as possible until your confidence and certainty grow. This means you will have to have *faith*. You will have to say, "I feel afraid, but I am going to do this anyway."

It is really the same thing with any skill or ability, regardless of your natural talent. You need to encounter enough situations in order to know that you can really handle them. It means pushing past the fear. You will understand this if you do physical activities like motorcycle riding, snowboarding, surfing, or rock climbing. If you've never done these activities, you will have no idea if you can. The fear will be great. If you've tried any of these once or twice and did not fare so well, the fear will be almost unbearable. Yet if you try a few more times, particularly with the help of a supportive and skilled instructor and the right type of quality equipment, you will discover, "Wow, I can stand up on my feet at least part of the way," or "I made it out past the waves and back without drowning, and it was kind of fun!" or "Wow, I did make it up, back down, and around that cliff!"

Then after a few more attempts it becomes, "Wow, this is pretty easy!" or "I can make it down the mountain this time without having to slide down on my butt!" So little by little you advance and enjoy the activity more and more.

It is no different with clairvoyant reading. But still there are all the pitfalls, the little accidents, the growing and learning pains that torment us with messages such as, "No, I am not capable or cut out for this," particularly when we compare ourselves to others who have either been doing it a lot longer than we have or who have gained other comparable skills.

A guy (should I say *dude?*) who grew up riding skateboards and doing bike tricks, and has developed both the muscles and the experience to understand the physics of a board and how much tolerance and strength he has in a variety of situations, is going to do a lot better the first time he jumps onto a snowboard or a surfboard than someone who has had no experience with these things. In the same way, if you are a fledgling student who has never meditated or spent much time inside yourself in a disciplined and focused way (as opposed to daydreaming), it's important that you don't compare yourself to a classmate who is a master at Tai Chi or yoga and is now taking up learning clairvoyance. Your classmate is going to have a stronger advantage. This doesn't mean they will ultimately be better, however, so of course by no means should you should just give up; it's only that you may require a bit more time, practice, and definitely patience.

Don't Compare Yourself to Others!

The biggest problem I see with students is not just that they are comparing themselves to others, but that they also have an ideal in their mind about what they are supposed to be doing. Take one of my students, who, as I noted earlier in this book, has fantastic abilities and was able to see the contents of my room so clearly. I would notice during a reading that he would see something so clearly about a person, describe this characteristic, and then end his reading with statements such as, "But that's all I'm getting" or "But I'm not sure." From his language it's easy to determine that he is putting himself down for what he is not seeing as opposed to really congratulating himself for what he is seeing. Is the glass half full or half empty? Is it more important that you get one piece of vital information or that you don't see another piece of information?

I believe there are many reasons why we don't see what we want to see other than the possibility that we are just falling short as psychics. Some of these reasons include:

1. We are not meant to see the information. The readee needs to have an experience without interference.

2. We are too close; we have too many issues that are similar to the readee's issues.

3. The readee knows what we are talking about but isn't ready to let others know.

4. The readee is not yet ready to handle the information.

5. We are asking the wrong questions or are focused on the wrong thing.

6. Your own frame of reference is too limited, so you can't make sense of what you see.

7. There is no answer, or there are multiple answers.

8. You may in fact have already answered the question, but your readee doesn't realize that was the answer or doesn't want to accept it.

It is important to remember that when doing a clairvoyant or really any psychic reading or remote viewing, there are at least two if not several parts of ourselves that are resting, acting, and reacting at all times. One part is receiving, one is guiding, another part is assessing, assimilating, interpreting, judging. It is this last part that you must be wary of because this is the part that will torment and terrorize you. If you feel that this is the dominant part of you, tell it to go away and focus on the parts that get to have fun exploring new worlds.

Feeling Overly Responsible

There is a fine line between being ethical and caring, and taking responsibility for something that doesn't have anything to do with you. Many people believe they must protect others from their own emotional responses. They think they have to say or do the absolute right thing or else they are going to cause the other person harm or get a response that makes them uncomfortable. Such people are therefore either afraid to speak up at all, or they fall into manipulation tactics that include being extra nice, hiding the truth, and placing judgments on every word, image, and feeling.

Many men think that unless they have the power to do something about someone's problems, they might as well not even bother hearing about them, or they might believe that every time a woman complains about something she is asking for help. Sometimes she is, but many times she fully understands there is nothing this man can do except listen, which will make her feel better.

As a psychic, you are not responsible for what you see. In terms of what you communicate, there are some gray areas. However, I think you will be okay as long as you communicate from a place of love and respect and use your clairvoyance and other intuitive abilities to guide you with what you should or should not communicate. Except for occasions when I did unsolicited and uninvited readings (something I don't do anymore), I have always found that a certain bit of information came up precisely because the client did either want or need to know it. My errors came not from speaking up but from withholding the information. Again, I am not talking about just blurting out, "Your husband is having an affair" if you haven't been asked, or "I think you are going to die soon." (As noted elsewhere in this book, there would never, ever be a reason to say such things; instead you'd want to discuss the details of the pictures you saw that led your mind to form these conclusions.) But you might be surprised at how some students can barely mutter, "I see a dark energy cord poking out of the left side of your aura" or "I see an image of a refrigerator and it looks like you are eating a lot" or "I see some black colors around you" or "I see a spirit plugged into your heart that looks kind of sad" without following up that statement with an urgent, terrified remark such as "But it's okay, it's not a bad thing."

Your job as a psychic is not to say if something is bad or good, but rather to describe what you are observing. When I hear a student making such statements, it's a warning sign because I know they must be censoring and subsequently withholding other information that might really be quite valuable to their readee.

Being Too Concerned About What Others Think About You

My all-time favorite title for a book is *What You Think of Me Is None of My Business*, by Terry Cole-Whittaker. Being overly concerned about what others think about you is a set-up for misery, failure, and disaster. Again, this is about balance. Making a good impression is important for business, for relationships, and for your overall self-esteem. However, there is a fine line that is frequently overstepped, particularly by women, who don't just desire but have a strong need to feel as if they are accepted by everyone. The fact is that some people are going to hate you for being too beautiful, too successful, too wealthy, too famous, too talented, too psychic, even too nice or accommodating. They could hate you because you believe in them more than they believe in themselves. They could hate you simply because they want to hate you. Therefore, if you feel that you *need* (as opposed to *would like*) every one of your clients to like you or believe in you and what you do, then you are setting yourself up for failure before you even start.

Sometimes people you read will resist what you are saying, even if it is a compliment. For example, you might see that a client is much stronger than she gives herself credit for, that she is hiding, selling herself short, and that she has more power than she believes she does. If the client isn't ready to acknowledge these things in herself, if she wants to believe she is a victim who can only be helped through other people saving her, or by some miracle like winning the lottery, then she isn't going to want to hear that she is the one with the power to change her life. Ironically, your reading may be one stepping stone that ultimately brings your client closer to being ready to step into her power, but that readiness may not happen until a week, month, or decade after she has told you that you must be wrong or be talking about the wrong person. ("What, can't you see how sick I am? What kind of psychic are you?")

Not Wanting to Read Certain People

There doesn't need to be a deep-seated psychological reason for having the feeling you don't want to read someone. I don't need to tell you that some people, lots of them, are absolutely annoying! They are argumentative, stubborn, stuck, close-minded, and accusatory. They don't have any interest in taking responsibility for their life and are coming to you because they just want to hear about what is going to happen to them as opposed to how they can influence their own life.

It is no more fun to read these people than it is to speak with them. Getting any information for them psychically is like pulling teeth, or like having holes drilled in your teeth without Novocaine. Sometimes before a reading you will sense this even if you've never met or spoken to the person before. I am not saying you should want to read these people or need to. Many psychics begin reading people like this because they put themselves into places that more of the general public frequents, such as street fairs, restaurants, nightclubs, or stores. That being said, there is value in reading people you don't like. The main value is that you get to work on your own matches with them, those things in yourself you don't like, the things in yourself you are trying to avoid. If you want to adamantly argue with me on this point, it's just further proof that you may really have some similarities with this person, and that is precisely why I recommend reading them!

I need to emphasize that it's not about going head-to-head with the client in a combative stance or trying to get them to see or do things your way. It is about exploring what's up for them so you can hear yourself speaking some words of wisdom, which later on you can apply to your own life. If someone you don't like asks you to do a reading, I have no problem with you turning them down. Instead, what I am saying here is that sometimes before a reading you are going to feel nervous, a sense of dread, and it's important to understand that this may be because you are about to encounter a difficult person or reading, but the feelings don't mean you shouldn't do the reading. Only if you feel a sense of danger, a sense you are vulnerable to attack, do I suggest letting yourself be stopped.

If you are unsure whether or not you should read someone, I suggest agreeing to do only a phone session—the reading can be just as good as it would be in person, but your energy field will be less. The worst that will happen is that the client says no, they only want you in person, and you will lose a client, which in the end is probably the best thing that could have happened. That being said, one of the things I love most about readings is that sometimes I will completely misjudge or underestimate a person, and by the end of the reading, after spending an hour connecting with them on a deep level and really getting to know them beyond my first impressions, I will be in absolute awe of their strengths, talents, or all that they've overcome in their life.

Feeling Your Readee's Fears

Please don't think you are going to become psychic only once you sit down to do the reading or put up your reading screen! Many people about to receive readings are quite nervous. You may easily feel that person's unease or any of their emotions (including anger) prior to the reading, sometimes as soon as you wake up that day. Again, if you have close matching pictures and issues with that person, you will likely be more impacted by their feelings. Sometimes through running your energy and grounding yourself you can release these quite easily. At other times all it takes is a simple questioning or acknowledgement, "Are these really my feelings or am I picking them up from somewhere else?" At other times, you will just need to grin and bear it and not let it get in the way of you doing the reading. I guarantee that by the time the reading is over, you will very much understand what your prereading jitters or emotions were about, and you will feel 100 percent different.

Healing Resistance and Psychic Stage Fright

How do you get over psychic stage fright? Certainly not by avoiding the stage! Although some actors say the fear never completely subsides, they learn to use the energy of the emotion rather than let it take over. I believe it's the same for psychics, whether they are in front of an audience of five thousand on a soundstage or sitting on their bed in their pj's (my usual attire) while chatting on the phone. You've just got to push yourself! One thing I recommend if you have a really severe case of the jitters is, for a while, to read only your most supportive friends or those who are psychic themselves or have a strong interest in this area. Don't charge for your readings until you feel quite comfortable doing so.

Sometimes the resistance you are hitting is not so much related to an avoidance of reading as it is to an avoidance of your own growth.

That is not necessarily a bad thing. When it comes to growth, we need to pace ourselves. A rapid period of growth needs to be followed by assimilation and rest. If you've been doing a lot of clairvoyant or psychic readings packed into a short time, have been going through huge emotional shifts, or even life-changing events like getting married, having a baby, or enduring a major health challenge, you may just need a break from the intensity of readings and focusing on other people's issues.

What If You Really Do Have a Bad Reading?

If you do have an unpleasant reading experience, it is imperative that you perform another reading on a different person as soon as possible, even though your natural inclination will be to want to avoid ever reading again. You will understand what I am talking about as soon as you follow this advice. The only way to cancel out a bad experience is to create a good one in its place. You may do a hundred easy, fun, excellent readings that make you feel as though you are on top of the world, but when you do one that turns out badly (for example, the readee runs from the room crying, saying you are not psychic), it's human nature to get stuck on that bad experience and disregard all the others. When you bravely overcome your fears and resistance and go out to do one more (even if you swear it will be your last), you will again remember that you are a talented clairvoyant after all and be ready for your next adventures in clairvoyant reading.

Resistance to reading can come out of nowhere, even when all of your readings have been positive. It also comes in many forms, in many disguises. You may feel too tired or too busy to read. You may feel angry, like you don't want to be bothered by people's problems. You might feel afraid, as though you are not going to be able to see anything. You might feel overwhelmed or judgmental, like you don't think you are going to like the person you'll read. You may forget about scheduled readings, get the dates and times confused, show up late, get lost along the way, or fantasize about your readee not showing up. This resistance is energy that doesn't want you to perform the reading. It is either coming from you yourself (because you are going to blow some major matching pictures), from foreign energies connected to you (family or spirits that don't want you to make changes that the reading might inspire), or from energies surrounding your readee.

There is a difference between resistance to reading and your intuition or spirit advising you that it is not in your best interest to read. Telling the difference between these can be difficult and often impossible. If you have already done several readings one day and just feel you can't stomach another one, or are feeling really emotional and un-balanced, then reading may not be what you need to do.

Reading and healing does take a lot of energy. It means giving other people your time and attention, which you may need for yourself to accomplish personal goals. During the last several months that I was writing my first book, I performed very few readings because all of my personal resources needed to go to the book and to caring for my son. During the writing of this book, I have been doing a lot of private training sessions with students and readings, which is giving me mate-rial for the book, reminding me of the topics to cover, and giving me new bursts of enthusiasm for the subject. There is nothing wrong with making the decision not to read; it's just important to be aware of your reasons and not to let fear and other destructive energies get in the way of your enjoyment of reading.

CHAPTER 21

Psychics Are People, Too

If you aren't good at loving yourself, you will have a difficult time loving anyone, since you'll resent the time and energy you give another person that you aren't even giving to yourself.
—BARBARA DE ANGELIS

You Must Set Boundaries on Every Level

Due to the nature of what they do and who they are, psychics often have poorer boundaries than other people. Setting boundaries means knowing what works best for you and what feels right for you, and communicating this to your clients. Enforcing boundaries means sticking to your guns and making sure your clients' desires and needs don't encroach upon your own.

For many psychics, it's not just drawing the line and stopping others from crossing it, it's keeping yourself from leaping over it in desperation to save every man, woman, child, animal, and blade of grass that seems to be crying out for your help! Enforcing boundaries is not selfish; it's self-preservation. Many psychics fail to ever draw the line between acceptable and unacceptable behavior of their clients because they fear that if they do so they will repel or lose clients. The more in survival mode they are, the more inclined they are to sacrifice themselves.

Many of us psychics and healers are easily manipulated due to our tendency to be overly compassionate to the point that we experience others' emotions as our own, and because we have been brainwashed into believing we have to make up for the wrongs of other psychics or of society's stereotypes of psychics. Psychics carry around a collective sense of guilt, not because we personally have anything to be guilty about but because so many people don't believe we are doing what we say we are. We, particularly women, are controlled through guilt as much as through fear (if not more so), because we've been socialized to respond to feelings of guilt with actions that we believe will decrease this guilt. (Ridding oneself of guilt should never be a motivating factor for action; doing so only creates more problems in the long run.)

Too much compassion, poor boundaries, guilt, and self-doubt form the perfect cocktail of vulnerability for exploitation. Ironically, it's the handful of psychics who don't have these qualities and are acting selfishly that have been partially responsible for giving the rest of us a bad reputation. I say *partially* because the bigger problem is really that there still are so many people out there who have been brainwashed into believing ESP is nonsense or the work of the devil. If that's the case, then who are we to them, those of us who claim to be psychic?

The thing we need to remember is that it's not us who have the problem, it's them!

The Business of Spirituality Revisited

As a psychic, setting boundaries will make a huge difference in your readings in terms of accessing, processing, and communicating the information you receive, and will ultimately determine whether you are a healthy, happy person or a basket case. If you hope to do, are attempting to do, or are succeeding at doing psychic readings for a living, setting boundaries will make the difference between being a prosperous businessperson and spending your life in and out of financial crisis or worse.

In *You are Psychic* I included a chapter called "The Business of Spirituality," in order to help psychics figure out whether or not and when they are ready to shift from student or amateur reader to professional. Below I will highlight a few essential points that have helped the psychics I've been working with, whether they are brand-new students who are practicing on volunteers in Internet chat rooms or seasoned professionals who can barely peel themselves out of bed because they are so exhausted.

Rule #1: You don't have to give anyone a free reading to prove yourself!

Don't get me wrong. Doing readings for free is a great way to hone your clairvoyant skills and get practice under your belt. You really shouldn't be charging money for readings unless you feel confident enough and strongly compelled to do so. Charging for readings adds a whole new dimension of pressure to your readings. I've had one or two of my students begin charging after their first reading on their own, although most take much longer before they realize they really do have something of value to offer and need to be compensated for their time. What I *am* opposed to is offering readings or agreeing to do readings for free when you really feel you should be paid, and particularly when you are considering doing readings for free in order to prove yourself.

Once again, the twenty-four-hour psychic hotline craze that has infiltrated TV over the past decade can be blamed for people's misperceptions that asking for a free reading as proof of one's authenticity is acceptable. There are several reasons I will absolutely not do this. First of all, it is a waste of time and it never takes just a minute—not for a psychic who adequately prepares herself or himself before a reading and who does a thorough clean-out after a reading. I cannot guarantee anyone that I can get the answer to their question in exactly one or two minutes. It is often not that simple. The process just takes longer.

That's why I no longer offer readings that are less than thirty minutes in length and why unscrupulous hotlines that charge by the minute often do become very successful; the reading always takes longer than the client planned. Hotlines can afford to offer free readings for the same reason certain major department stores will accept returns without receipts or questions whereas smaller stores will not. The larger stores can afford the loss. Personally I can't afford the loss of my time, and I doubt if you can or want to either.

Furthermore, even if you are the best psychic in the world, the person "testing" you is not necessarily going to like what you have to say; they may not get it right away or ever. "No, you won't find Prince Charming or have a baby until you drop at least 150 pounds" isn't exactly going to bring back repeat business, although the person may be impressed that you were able to "see" over the phone how overweight or lethargic they really are!

In what other profession that you know of are people expected to provide their services for free? Can you imagine going to a doctor, a lawyer, an electrician, a mechanic, or a tutor, and telling them, "I don't really know if I'm going to like you, if I can trust you, or if you're what I'm looking for, so will you take time out of your busy schedule and do this for free so I can make sure first?" Can you imagine going to a restaurant and asking if you can taste any given dish before ordering because you aren't sure you're going to like it? Who is going to pay for the food you just tasted, or pay the cook who just created that meal? No one thinks of doing this because we know that whether or not we like what we are getting, these people are working. If I sit with you for an hour doing my best to receive clairvoyant messages, whether I ever receive one or not, I am working my butt off! As adults, we know that anytime we put down even a penny on an item or a service, we are taking the risk that we might not like it, that it might not meet our expectations. We know this going into every situation. If the risk doesn't seem worth it, then we have the choice not to go forward.

As a professional psychic, I can guarantee that I will do my best to use every technique I know, every skill I have, to access information with my abilities. From past experience I can say I am pretty confident that I will at least come up with some relevant, helpful, accurate information, but since I am in the position of receiving it and therefore dependent on forces outside myself to bring me this information, I can't guarantee that every time every person will walk away 100 percent satisfied. Does that mean I shouldn't be compensated for the time it takes for me to do the work I do? When you or I pay for a psychic, first and foremost we are paying for the time they are focusing on us instead of all the other things they could be doing, like playing with their kids, writing, doing the dishes, sleeping!

The public needs to be reeducated to understand that psychics and healers are professionals and individuals who are doing their best to help, but who also have families and needs of their own. I think the misperceptions and rude behavior will only change if enough of us stand firm, and politely explain why it's not acceptable to ask us to look at or solve others' problems for free, or to have to prove ourselves at any time of the day or night.

Rule #2: If you work for yourself, you set your own hours.
Certain hotlines can afford to offer readings twenty-four hours a day only because they have dozens of psychics working for them who are signed up for particular shifts. Some of these psychics or employees try to make themselves available around the clock for calls that come in at odd hours, and these are the psychics who have the most problems. It is therefore unreasonable and unhealthy for you to expect yourself to be available whenever someone is having a crisis and wants to talk to you. Some potential clients do have this expectation and, rather than you comprising your personal time and well-being to meet this unrealistic demand, it's up to you to educate them. If you lose that person as a client, you will soon attract someone else who has more respect for you and your time.

Rule #3: Understand your own motivations for working with repeat clients.

Nothing is wrong with working with the same people on a regular basis, as long as you feel that your work with them is about empowering them, as opposed to giving them readings on the same subject over and over again with the hope that you will eventually see what they are hoping you'll see. Ironically, you will inevitably see what they want if you keep readdressing the same topic, not because that is what is really going to happen, but because you will be merely reading their pictures of what they want to happen.

Have you ever answered a child in a certain way, only to have them ask you the same or similar questions ten more times? Kids do this because they know that if they can wear you down, catch you at a moment of weakness, you might just say yes. It is the same thing with clients who are seeking information in order to cope with their own emotions of fear or sadness. Sometimes you will spend an hour or even two hours with a client, and they have so many questions or areas of interest that you both feel it's appropriate to set up another session within the next week. However, more often and most of the time, you will find that the client would benefit by having more time before the next reading or healing in order to undergo the transformation that your session has initiated. It is ultimately about the client taking the steps and doing the work, not you, so giving them the time to do this is what will be most empowering. If you allow some time to pass, perhaps two or three months or longer, and then they come back and say things still haven't changed or they feel stuck, then you can look at why that is. Sometimes things will have changed so much that the client will have a whole new slew of questions for you to address.

I'd say that 80 percent of people (at least of the ones I read) who get readings will feel as if they got enough at the end of the first reading, so they don't feel a need to come back for another session until at least six months have passed.

Rule #4: Use your intuition to help you choose your clients, and exercise common sense.

Many people prefer to get a reading in person. If you work for yourself out of your home, be very cautious about whom you invite over. Phone readings work just as well as in-person readings, if not even better sometimes. Some clients don't understand that, or they will only want a reading if it's in person, but you should never compromise your safety or the safety of your family in exchange for money.

CHAPTER 22

Conclusion: The Awakening of America

We must be prepared to make the same heroic sacrifices for the cause of peace that we make ungrudgingly for the cause of war.
—ALBERT EINSTEIN

Americans are waking up, and this process has been painful. In the past decade alone we've witnessed not just the fall of our heroes and leaders from their proverbial pedestals but the desecration of the illusion that we live in a society where our votes count, or are even counted. We have begun to question whether we are truly free or more like indentured servants, shackled to dehumanizing jobs just to pay off our student loans (but you must go to college, how else will you get a job?) or credit cards (the only way to improve your credit score), or to keep our health insurance, car insurance, homeowner's or renter's insurance, product insurance, professional insurance—and if you love your kids, you'd better not forget that life insurance! (If you are concerned about health insurance, I highly recommend Michael Moore's film *Sicko*.)

Up until recently, many Americans thought of themselves as part of a sophisticated and evolved race that had overcome its primitive, predatory urges, and yet our society is filled with ever-craftier predators who continue to figure out more and more ingenious ways to separate us from our own money, resources, and sanity. These predators are not the ones lurking in drug-infested, urban alleyways, but rather they are in corporate cubicles and offices with their Bluetooth devices ringing into ears closed off from the beating of all human hearts except their own.

Many of us metaphysically oriented people are feeling rather schizophrenic these days. We understand the profound creative potential within ourselves. We know from personal experience and years of experimentation that our thoughts and emotions can create and impact reality, and we do our best to remain positive. However, many of us find ourselves teeter-tottering between feelings of hopeful optimism and disillusioned, even angry pessimism. I, like many of you, find myself wavering between these two positions as quickly as it takes me to shift from one foot to the other. On the one hand (or foot), I am sickened by what I see on the news and around me and by personal experiences that show me how corporate, capitalist greed is sucking the very life force out of our country. I am shocked by the gas prices, the housing prices, insurance laws and costs, and the fact that it's becoming more and more difficult to even rent a place or find a job unless you have a "competitive" credit score, which is more about how much you are willing to allow yourself to go into debt than it is a reflection of how financially responsible you are.

In the past decade we have witnessed countless scandals surrounding both our Democratic and Republican leaders. In the same way, we've seen the fall of the Catholic Church, with so many of its leaders convicted of the most heinous sex crimes imaginable against children. During this same period, millions of American workers have lost their jobs to outsourcing, have lost their retirement funds in corporate scandals and mismanagement, and have lost their homes to foreclosure.

Like children abandoned on bustling streets, many of us are crying, confused, ashamed, grieving, and in shock. We're somewhere between resisting, struggling with, and accepting the fact that in the end there is no guarantee that those who led us into this mess will stand by us. We possess a growing suspicion that they might even turn against us when the shit really hits the fan. Perhaps most difficult to handle is the realization that maybe those we idolized didn't really have the answers after all, that they didn't really know what was best for us—and perhaps never even cared in the way we needed to believe they did.

What does all this have to do with developing your psychic abilities? Everything! See, when you say you want to get in touch with your own intuition or with your heart, your spirit, your Higher Self, your guides with wisdom, or a perspective greater than your own, and when you say you want to heal yourself and others, what you are saying is that you want to see things for what they really are—not what you have been told, programmed, and brainwashed into believing. Many people in the New Age community increase their awareness of spirit but want to turn a blind eye to anything that is not full of love and light. Doing this constitutes outright denial of the world we live in. Problems such as global warming, racism, institutionalized extortion, insane gas prices, and pollution don't go away when we deny their existence, but it's also true that these problems won't get solved by obsessing about them every second, which only serves to diminish our quality of life.

When you develop and use your clairvoyance, you are essentially removing the veil that's been keeping you from seeing what is. That means you can't help but notice lots of unexpected things behind that veil, partition, or wall that is now crumbling to pieces before your very eyes. I am not just talking about seeing spirit guides or auras but rather the true intentions and behaviors of those spirits in physical bodies around you, including your parents and your political and religious leaders. I don't believe it's a coincidence that more and more people are opening up and becoming aware of their psychic abilities at the very same time they are waking up from the illusions of the American dream, a dream that has kept us milling around in a fog of ethnocentrism, elitism, racism, and a most insidious type of sadomasochism.

This awakening is not just beginning now; on the contrary, it really began in the 1960s with the uprising of American youth who protested everything from the oppression of their parents' puritanical values to the Vietnam War to racism against blacks to sexism against women to anything having to do with "the Establishment" and its authority figures. That this period also corresponded with an explosion of psychedelic, mind-altering drugs is certainly no accident. People needed a method by which to make huge leaps in the way they thought about the world, and drugs both facilitated this process and eased the pain that comes with any paradigm shift.

By the end of the 1970s, however, an interesting thing happened. Most of the population was lulled back to sleep, while only a much smaller sector remained aware. Why? How? Let me ask you this: What is the biggest reason you don't meditate, pray, or exercise as much as you'd like to? What's the biggest reason you don't get or give yourself enough of the sleep, rest, or relaxation that you know helps you connect to yourself? What's the biggest obstacle standing in your way of doing that which makes your spirit soar, whether it be writing, doing your art, traveling the world, even developing your psychic abilities? Most of us will have the same answer: *money*—either the lack of it, the need for it, the quest for it, or the fear of losing it.

Ironically, when we put first in our lives our creative projects and the people and things we love, the money often flows even more abundantly. At a time when money is going to become scarcer and more difficult to come by for millions of Americans (largely because a small group of individuals owning massive conglomerate corporations and supported by our government have figured out how to charge the rest of us more and more while offering less and less), it's vital that you take the time you need to go inward. It is imperative that you put your creative projects, your spiritual goals, and the overall health of your body at the top of your list. It is essential that you join forces with other like-minded individuals pursuing their own path of consciousness, and that you wholeheartedly believe that you can still have abundance and love and happiness in the face of everything else.

Most of us sit in our living rooms watching the news, which is doing more to traumatize us than inform us, as we are force-fed an unhealthy diet of homicide, despair, and violence. However, while we sit there wondering why we are sitting there, in that moment we really are okay. We really are warm, well-fed, and safe. If we do nothing else to protect ourselves, when we feel overwhelmed we've got to remember to bring ourselves into the present moment and remind ourselves—no matter how bad things seem, how awful we are told they are—that most of us really are just fine and dandy in this moment, and in the next moment and in the next.

These little conversations with ourselves are the only things that are going to get us through the next several years without going bonkers. I am not saying to focus only on your inner work instead of going to the job that helps you pay your bills. I am saying you can do both if you see one as being equally as essential as the other. The crazier things get on the outside, the more time you will need to revitalize yourself on the inside and connect with a solid support system of like-minded people.

A part of me believes that there are evil forces behind the corporate takeover of America. I don't know if this is exactly the case, but I do know without a doubt that what evil wants is for us to get stuck in our fearful emotions and self-defeating thoughts, because those are really the only places evil can reach us. We need to be informed, but listening to endless hours of talk radio or depressing and violent TV broadcasts mostly filled with propaganda is as unhealthy for us as adults as it is for our children. It is easy to get addicted to newscasts and talk shows because they infuse our sometimes monotonous lives with a quick fix of adrenaline, and they serve to make us feel that we are not alone in our frustration. They help us to feel connected. But what are we connecting to?

There are many people who believe we are going to ascend in the year 2012, which is the end of the Mayan calendar. There are many who think World War III is about to start and we have already entered the beginning of Armageddon. I find when I am excited about my life and the money is flowing, I am inclined to believe in the first version of the future. When I am feeling bored, ignored, or defeated in my own life, I lean toward the latter, pessimistic view. I know I am not alone in my projections.

So what to do? First, we need to replace our negativity with humor and inspiration so that we can raise our vibrations and manifest the things that truly make us happy. Utilizing the psychic's tools in the first part of this book and practicing your clairvoyant readings and healings will most certainly help with this. Do whatever you have to do to secure peace in your personal life, and at the same time do whatever you can, in whatever way comes naturally to you and excites you the most, to help out as many people as you can without draining yourself. We can let ourselves sink down into hopelessness or bring ourselves to a vibration where the evil can't reach us. Remember: when you are happy, your happiness brings more happiness to others. Happy people are less likely to go around fighting, raping, and killing each other or attract others who engage in these behaviors. To a great extent, you can make yourself happy by thinking happy thoughts.

The expenses and stressors in our lives are not going to decrease any time soon, but there are ways we can cope and rise above them. Stop giving the credit-card companies your power. If you are at the top of the credit-card game and understand how to work the system, then more power to you. But if you are already losing, then just opt out. Do your best to pay off any debt you've accrued but forgive yourself and let yourself off the hook. Those people calling you every day are earning about ten dollars an hour and are drowning in as much shame and debt as you are. Save your cash and pay for things with cash. Buy only what you love or really need, and then appreciate those items for being available to you—even if it's just a roll of toilet paper!

When someone calls you demanding money you don't have, don't argue with them, bless them! Tell them you love them. They really won't know how to respond! Regardless of the state of your credit score or bank account, let go of the shame. It is vital to understand that just about everyone else around you is struggling in the same way. Most Americans are one or two paychecks away from poverty. Start a dialogue about this. Admit what you are going through.

Have you ever noticed that finances are the one topic we are still not supposed to talk about? It's okay to share the most intimate details of a sexual encounter with someone you hardly know, but telling someone what you earn, how much money you have in your bank account, or—gasp!—what your credit score really is, is just not done. Why? I'm not sure. I know my parents told me that money is a very private matter. People won't respect you if they think you don't have it. If you do have it, people will try to take it from you. Well, I have news for you. Abuse can only happen in secrecy and in isolation. This is true on an individual level and on a national one.

Most important, remind yourself that the status quo doesn't matter. Even if your credit score is zero, you can simply imagine that you are going to find the best place to live, that you will manifest cash for a home you wish to buy, or that you will find a landlord who could not care less about credit (maybe they're aware of the game and have dropped out, too) and who will love you at first sight. Delight in the fact that you obtained these so easily and effortlessly before you even go about trying to obtain them. Do this at least a few times a day until you manifest that which now seems quite unreachable.

The clearer you are about what you want and whether or not you deserve it, the easier it will be to draw these things to you on the physical level. I am utterly convinced that it's getting easier and faster to manifest with our thoughts. This is why everything seems so intense right now. Use this to your advantage rather than to your detriment.

In Search of a New Freedom

Most Americans have been taught that democracy is the most important tenet of our country. We've been taught that democracy is what gives us our freedom, what sets us apart as leaders and heroes in the world. The most essential component of American democracy is our right to vote, to choose our own representatives. If we believe we have exercised this right, then we're taught that this means that no matter how ignorant or unethical our leaders are, we must bear the cross that it's us who have chosen them and therefore accept the consequences. This is, of course, a pretty silly idea, and it's one that I believe has led to us allowing our leaders to degrade the integrity and reputation of America. Our voting system is severely outdated and has very little to do with the interest and voice of the people anymore (particularly when we can't trust the results of our own elections or when our choice of leaders is between the not-so-bad and the worse).

Depressing? Well, yes, of course it is depressing on one level. But on another level, I find these revelations quite exhilarating. Why? Because once we get past the stages of whining, anger, and grief, we can really get to the good stuff. Once we've cut through the illusions, we get to experience the pulse of life authentically and fully. We can begin to update and introduce a new version of democracy that better encompasses the needs of people today, in the present time.

New ideas and new ways of being start with visionaries who create the future first in their mind's eyes and then are courageous enough to share these revolutionary ideas with others. That's where you come in, as an extraordinary psychic. Whether you are American or from Saudi Arabia, whether you speak English, Polish, or Bengali, you have the power to start making changes by simply turning inward and imagining a new world with new solutions where *you* are the heroes and heroines, leading to the light those who can only see the bleakness.

On a national or global scale, I cannot guarantee things are going to get better anytime soon. They may, very possibly, get worse. But regardless of the outer conditions, if you practice the techniques in this book, whether on a constant basis or when you find yourself slipping back into the muck, you will always have a way to pull yourself up and out.

You have been given gifts that keep on giving. Whether you gain the whole world or lose it all, you will always be okay, because with the information in this book, you now have all you need to create what you need when you need it.

Security is ultimately not found in a retirement fund; it's found in the skills, including your innate psychic gifts, that can never be taken from you once you are aware of them. When all else is gone, you will still have *you*. That is the true freedom.

Bibliography

Of all that is written, I love only what a person has written with his own blood.

—FRIEDRICH NIETZSCHE

Brinkley, Dannion. *Saved By the Light*. New York: HarperTorch, 1995.

Brown, Courtney. *Remote Viewing: The Science and Theory of Nonphysical Perception*. Atlanta: Farsight Press, 2005.

Buchanan, Lyn. *The Seventh Sense: The Secrets of Remote Viewing as Told by a "Psychic Spy" for the U.S. Military*. New York: Paraview Pocket Books, 2003.

Cole-Whittaker, Terry. *What You Think of Me Is None of My Business*. New York: Jove, 1988.

Cumming, Heather, and Karen Leffler, *John of God: The Brazilian Healer Who's Touched the Lives of Millions*. New York: Atria Books/Beyond Words, 2007.

Dourif, Joni. *The Matrix Newsletter*. PSI TECH, 2007. Online at http://www.remoteviewing.com/remote-viewing-news-articles/the-matrix-newsletter/index.html.

Hicks, Esther, and Jerry Hicks. *Ask and It Is Given: Learning to Manifest Your Desires.* Carlsbad, CA: Hay House, 2004.

Karma-glin-pa, and W. Y. Evans-Wentz. *The Tibetan Book of the Dead.* Oxford: Oxford University Press, 2000.

Katz, Debra Lynne. *You Are Psychic: The Art of Clairvoyant Reading and Healing.* St. Paul, MN: Llewellyn, 2004.

Knight, J. Z. *Ramtha: The White Book.* Yelm, WA: JZK Publishing, 2005.

Kolodiejchuk, Brian, and Mother Teresa, *Come Be My Light.* New York: Doubleday, 2007.

Licauco, Jaime T. *The Magicians of God: The Amazing Stories of Philippine Faith Healers.* Manila, Philippines: National Book Store, Inc., 1980.

———. *Jun Labo: A Philippine Healing Phenomenon.* Manila, Philippines: self-published, 1984.

McMoneagle, Joseph. *Memoirs of a Psychic Spy.* Charlottesville, VA: Hampton Roads, 2006.

———. *Remote Viewing Secrets: A Handbook.* Charlottesville, VA: Hampton Roads, 2000.

McMoneagle, Joseph, and Charles T. Tart. *Mind Trek: Exploring Consciousness, Time, and Space Through Remote Viewing.* Charlottesville, VA: Hampton Roads, 1997.

McTaggart, Lynne. *The Field: The Quest for the Secret Force of the Universe.* New York: Harper, 2003.

———. *The Intention Experiment: Using Your Thoughts to Change Your Life and the World.* New York: Free Press, 2007.

Morehouse, David. *Psychic Warrior: The True Story of America's Foremost Psychic Spy and the Cover-Up of the CIA's Top-Secret Stargate Program.* New York: St. Martin's, 1998.

Myss, Caroline. *Anatomy of the Spirit: The Seven Stages of Power and Healing.* New York: Three Rivers Press, 1997.

———. *Three Levels of Power and How To Use Them.* Louisville, CO: Sounds True Publishing, compact disc.

———. *Why People Don't Heal and How They Can.* New York: Three Rivers Press, 1998.

Radin, Dean. *Entangled Minds: Extrasensory Experiences in a Quantum Reality.* New York: Paraview Pocket Books, 2006.

———. *The Conscious Universe: The Scientific Truth of Psychic Phenomena.* New York: HarperOne, 1997.

Roberts, Jane. *The Nature of Personal Reality: Specific, Practical Techniques for Solving Everyday Problems and Enriching the Life You Know.* San Rafael, CA: Amber-Allen Publishing, New World Library, 1994.

———. *Seth Speaks: The Eternal Validity of the Soul.* San Rafael, CA: Amber-Allen Publishing, 1972.

Swann, Ingo. *Everybody's Guide to Natural ESP: Unlocking the Extrasensory Power of Your Mind.* New York: Tarcher, 1991.

———. *Penetration: The Question of Extraterrestrial and Human Telepathy.* Rapid City, SD: Ingo Swann Books, 1998.

———. *To Kiss the Earth Good-Bye: Adventures and Discoveries in the Nonmaterial, Recounted by the Man Who Has Astounded Physicists and Parapsychologists throughout the World.* New York: Hawthorn, 1975.

———. *Your Nostradamus Factor: Accessing Your Innate Ability to See Into the Future.* New York: Fireside, 1993.

Tamura, Michael J. *You Are the Answer: Discovering and Fulfilling Your Soul's Purpose.* Woodbury, MN: Llewellyn, 2007.

Targ, Russell. *Limitless Mind: A Guide to Remote Viewing and Transformation of Consciousness.* Novato, CA: New World Library, 2004.

Targ, Russell, and Harold E. Puthoff. *Mind-Reach: Scientists Look at Psychic Abilities,* new edition. Charlottesville, VA: Hampton Roads, 2005.

Wallace, Amy, and Bill Henkin. *The Psychic Healing Book.* New York: Delacorte, 1978.

Glossary

The true poem rests between the words.
—VANNA BONTA

ANALYTIC OVERLAY: A common term used in remote viewing, it refers to the analytical response of the viewer's mind to make sense of information it receives. Often, the interpretation is wrong although it tends to be based on data that is valid. There is no formal word for this in clairvoyant training, although the tendency of psychics, particularly new students, to provide inaccurate interpretations of the data is common.

ASTRAL PROJECTION OR ASTRAL TRAVEL: The ability of one's spirit to leave one's body and travel on the astral plane, in other dimensions, and to remote locations.

ATHEISM: A lack of belief in the spiritual, including God, psychic phenomena, or the human soul.

ATTENTION: A focus on something without intent. Intention is focus with a desired outcome.

AURA: The energetic field surrounding every living organism, which contains information about the organism and energies affecting it.

The aura can be thought of as the organism's spirit extending outward from the body.

BLIND: Term used in psychological research and among remote viewers to describe the lack of awareness of the person participating in the experiment regarding the purpose, target, or other elements that otherwise might influence the experiment's perceptions, observations, and results.

BOSTWICK, LEWIS: Father of clairvoyant training in the United States and founder of the Berkeley Psychic Institute.

CHAKRAS: Sanskrit word for "spinning wheels," chakras are energy centers that correspond to certain parts of the human body and that regulate the body's overall functioning.

CHANNELING: A psychic ability in which a person receives and communicates information coming directly from a source outside themselves.

CLAIRAUDIENCE: A specific psychic ability in which information inaudible to human ears is heard inside one's mind.

CLAIRSENTIENCE: A specific psychic ability in which information is received through touch or on a physical body level.

CLAIRVOYANCE: A specific psychic ability located within one's sixth chakra, or third eye, that involves accessing information in the form of images, visions, and pictures.

CLAIRVOYANT HEALING: An act in which visualization is utilized to alleviate or transmute emotional or physical pain or negative energies and restore one to a healthier state.

CLAIRVOYANT READING: An act in which information in the form of mental images, visions, and pictures is accessed.

CLAIRVOYANT TRAINING SCHOOL: A school that offers a course in clairvoyant development. The first of these included the Berkeley Psychic Institute, founded by Lewis Bostwick. Several of his original students have gone on to establish their own training programs, including the Aesclepion Healing Center, Intuitive Way, and Psychic Horizons.

CODEPENDENT RELATIONSHIP: An unbalanced relationship in which one person sacrifices their own ideals or ignores their own inner voice in order to maintain the relationship or get other needs met within the relationship.

CONSCIOUSNESS: Perceiving, apprehending, or noticing with a degree of controlled thought. It involves rational power, perception, and awareness. The "conscious" part of the human being is that portion of the human consciousness that is linked most closely to and limited by the material world.

CONTROL: A person who assists a clairvoyant during a reading by providing analytical support through the process of posing questions or structure for the clairvoyant to focus on. The control may also help the clairvoyant prepare for and debrief from the session. Controls are used in many long-term clairvoyant training programs for beginning students, and often are students themselves who are learning to work with their crown chakras.

CONTROL FREAK OR CONTROLLING PERSON: A person who needs to understand or determine every element in life and interferes with the natural course of things, and who expends energy trying to control that which is out of their control. One who intends to circumvent God's will.

COORDINATE REMOTE VIEWING (CRV): The process of remote viewing using geographic coordinates for cueing or prompting.

CORE MEI PICTURES: An MEI picture that is developed early in life and that over time attracts similar clusters of thoughts and emotions that influence our perception and behavior. Personal transformation occurs when these pictures are destroyed or deenergized.

COSMIC ENERGY: Energy that originates from the air, sun, atmosphere, the spiritual realm, or God.

COUPLE'S READING: A clairvoyant reading in which the psychic reads the relationship or joint goals between two or more readees who are physically present.

DESTROY: To eliminate or alter a creation.

DISEMBODIED SPIRIT: A spirit that no longer belongs to a physical body.

EARTH ENERGY: Energy that originates from within the earth.

ENERGY: Life force; the essence of all things physical and nonphysical. Matter, atoms, thoughts, emotions, and pain consist of energy.

ENLIGHTENMENT: A state in which a person has become actualized, has accumulated a certain level of wisdom; when a person's body, mind, and spirit are fully integrated and their being holds more lightness than darkness.

ETHICAL DILEMMA: A conflict in which one must choose between two seemingly opposing values.

ETHICS: The study of rules of right and wrong in human conduct.

EXPECTATION: Having a predetermined set of ideas of how an event will unfold.

EXTENDED REMOTE VIEWING (ERV): A hybrid method of remote viewing that incorporates relaxation and meditation with the scientific protocols of Coordinate Remote Viewing.

EXTRASENSORY PERCEPTION: Perceiving information through means other than the five physical senses.

FAITH: Belief or trust in an outcome before the outcome occurs.

GROUNDING CORD: An energetic connection securing an object or person to the earth. Others energies can be released through this cord through conscious intent and visualization.

GROWTH PERIOD: An intense period of personal transformation during which one's beliefs, thoughts, perceptions and self-image are altered. This can result in a temporary period of emotional or cognitive turbulence, corresponding with a paradigm shift.

IMAGINATION: The act or power of creating pictures or ideas in the mind.

INCARNATION: A lifetime in a particular body.

INTENTION: Focus with a desired outcome.

KARMA: Spiritual award system that can include both desirable and undesirable consequences for one's prior conduct either in the present life or in prior incarnations.

KIRLIAN PHOTOGRAPHY: Heat-sensitive photography that can record information not ordinarily registered by the physical eye.

KNOWINGNESS: A psychic ability located in the crown chakra, or seventh chakra, in which a person instantaneously knows information in the form of a thought, without having to go through logical steps to gain that information.

LIBRARY OF SYMBOLS: A collection of symbolic images.

LITERAL IMAGE: An image that is what it appears to be.

MEDICAL INTUITIVE: A psychic who focuses primarily on the physical body and its ailments, in order to determine the cause, cure, and connection between an illness or disorder of the body and the mind and spirit of that being. Some psychics specialize as medical intuitives while others will act as medical intuitives in addition to focusing on other areas of a person's life as well.

MEDITATION: Turning inward and focusing within oneself or an outside object for the purpose of clearing one's mind and/or achieving a certain state of mind, which often includes relaxation and acceptance. Meditation is a technique for improving your life, healing yourself, and getting through difficult situations.

MEI PICTURE: Mental Emotional Image picture. This is an emotionally charged thoughtform that influences one's perceptions and behavior and is located within one's body, mind, and energetic field.

MONITOR: A person who oversees and assists a remote viewer during a remote-viewing session by providing analytical support to the viewer. The monitor provides the target and records relevant session information, providing feedback when appropriate.

MULTIPLE PERSONALITY DISORDER: A psychological dissociative disorder in which aspects of a person have split off from the person's awareness and behave and respond independently of other aspects.

NAVIGATING: The science of figuring out where one is heading. Charting a course, a path, or a plan that will lead to an intended goal.

NEUTRALITY: Being neutral; maintaining a state of emotional and cognitive balance that is not invested in a particular outcome.

NONATTACHMENT: Having no emotional investment in an object or in the outcome of a situation.

OMNIPRESENT: Being everywhere all at once.

OMNISCIENT: All-knowing. A quality of God.

PRAYER: The act of talking to God or to a higher power.

PRECOGNITION: Knowing that something is going to happen before it happens.

PROGRAMMING: Beliefs, thoughts, ethics, information, feelings, or perceptions that are passed from one person to another that may or may not be in harmony with the recipient's own information or way of being.

PROJECTION: Seeing one's own qualities in someone else, often unconsciously; assigning particular attributes to another that really belong to oneself.

PSYCHIC EXPERIENCE: A supernatural experience in which information is sent or received through means other than the five senses.

PSYCHIC TOOLS: Visualization techniques that affect and influence energy that can be utilized for psychic reading and healing and to enhance the quality of one's life.

RELATIONSHIP READING: A psychic reading that focuses on issues regarding the relationship between two or more individuals.

REMOTE VIEWER: A person who employs their mental faculties to perceive and obtain information to which they would have no other access and about which they have no previous knowledge. This information can concern people, places, events, or objects separated from the remote viewer by distance, time, or other obstacles.

REMOTE VIEWING: The act of accessing information through one's psychic abilities about a distant location, object, or person.

SELF-ENERGIZATION: Calling one's life force to oneself.

SEPARATION OBJECT: A mental image or visualization that defines boundaries and serves as protection.

SKEPTICISM: A closed state of mind in which one doubts or questions things, sometimes to the point that these doubts obscure the truth.

SPIRIT: The essence of a person.

SPIRITUAL PATH: A course that one's spirit is destined to follow in order to gain certain life experiences while in the physical body.

STANFORD RESEARCH INSTITUTE (SRI): A research laboratory in California that spearheaded the research and formulated protocols that were utilized in clandestine remote-viewing programs in the United States.

STAR GATE, SUN STREAK, GRILL FLAME, CENTER LANE, INSCOM, AND SCANATE: Some of the names of remote-viewing programs financed and administered from the 1970s until at least the 1990s by the Defense Intelligence Agency and the Central Intelligence Agency of the United States government. (There may still be programs that we are unaware of!)

SUBCONSCIOUS: Existing in the mind but not immediately available to consciousness; affecting thought, feeling, and behavior without entering awareness. The mental activities just below the threshold of consciousness.

SUPERNATURAL: Beyond the physical sense; beyond the natural.

SYMBOL: An object or sign that represents another object, idea, person, or quality.

SYMBOLIC IMAGE: An image that is representative of something other than itself.

TARGET: A subject that remote viewers have been assigned to observe.

TARGET NUMBERS: Randomly selected numbers assigned to a target used in a remote-viewing session. These numbers enable viewers to remain "blind" or unaware of the item about which they are attempting to access information, in order to keep their own logical assumptions from tainting the information. The numbers have no significance in themselves.

TELEKINESIS: A psychic ability in which one can move or alter objects with the power of thought, emotion, or other energy, through non-physical means.

TELEPATHY: Transferring information from one mind to another without the use of the physical senses.

THIRD EYE: The center of one's clairvoyance. The third eye corresponds with the sixth chakra and is located inside the forehead, slightly above and between the physical eyes.

TRANSFORMATION: Effecting change.

TRANSMEDIUMSHIP: A spiritual ability in which a person's spirit leaves the body and accepts a foreign spirit or energy into their own. This happens both consciously and without awareness.

VALIDATION: Confirming one's value.

VISUALIZATION: The act of calling forth images, visions, pictures, and colors in one's mind through conscious intent.